Exile and Nomadism in French and Hispanic Women's Writing

LEGENDA

LEGENDA, founded in 1995 by the European Humanities Research Centre of the University of Oxford, is now a joint imprint of the Modern Humanities Research Association and Maney Publishing. Titles range from medieval texts to contemporary cinema and form a widely comparative view of the modern humanities, including works on Arabic, Catalan, English, French, German, Greek, Italian, Portuguese, Russian, Spanish, and Yiddish literature. An Editorial Board of distinguished academic specialists works in collaboration with leading scholarly bodies such as the Society for French Studies, the British Comparative Literature Association and the Association of Hispanists of Great Britain & Ireland.

MHRA

The Modern Humanities Research Association (MHRA) encourages and promotes advanced study and research in the field of the modern humanities, especially modern European languages and literature, including English, and also cinema. It also aims to break down the barriers between scholars working in different disciplines and to maintain the unity of humanistic scholarship in the face of increasing specialization. The Association fulfils this purpose primarily through the publication of journals, bibliographies, monographs and other aids to research.

Maney Publishing is one of the few remaining independent British academic publishers. Founded in 1900 the company has offices both in the UK, in Leeds and London, and in North America, in Philadelphia. Since 1945 Maney Publishing has worked closely with learned societies, their editors, authors, and members, in publishing academic books and journals to the highest traditional standards of materials and production.

EDITORIAL BOARD

Chairman
Professor Colin Davis, Royal Holloway, University of London

Professor Malcolm Cook, University of Exeter (French)
Professor Robin Fiddian, Wadham College, Oxford (Spanish)
Professor Anne Fuchs, University of Warwick (German)
Professor Paul Garner, University of Leeds (Spanish)
Professor Marian Hobson Jeanneret,
Queen Mary University of London (French)
Professor Catriona Kelly, New College, Oxford (Russian)
Professor Martin McLaughlin, Magdalen College, Oxford (Italian)
Professor Martin Maiden, Trinity College, Oxford (Linguistics)
Professor Peter Matthews, St John's College, Cambridge (Linguistics)
Dr Stephen Parkinson, Linacre College, Oxford (Portuguese)
Professor Ritchie Robertson, The Queen's College, Oxford (German)
Professor Lesley Sharpe, University of Exeter (German)
Professor David Shepherd, University of Sheffield (Russian)
Professor Michael Sheringham, All Soul's College, Oxford (French)
Professor Alison Sinclair, Clare College, Cambridge (Spanish)
Professor David Treece, King's College London (Portuguese)

Managing Editor
Dr Graham Nelson
41 Wellington Square, Oxford OX1 2JF, UK

www.legendabooks.com

STUDIES IN COMPARATIVE LITERATURE

Editorial Committee
Professor Stephen Bann, University of Bristol (Chairman)
Professor Duncan Large, University of Swansea
Dr Elinor Shaffer, School of Advanced Study, London

Studies in Comparative Literature are produced in close collaboration with the British Comparative Literature Association, and range widely across comparative and theoretical topics in literary and translation studies, accommodating research at the interface between different artistic media and between the humanities and the sciences.

PUBLISHED IN THIS SERIES

1. *Breeches and Metaphysics: Thackeray's German Discourse*, by S. S. Prawer
2. *Hölderlin and the Dynamics of Translation*, by Charlie Louth
3. *Aeneas Takes the Metro*, by Fiona Cox
4. *Metaphor and Materiality: German Literature and the World-View of Science*, by Peter D. Smith
5. *Marguerite Yourcenar: Reading the Visual*, by Nigel Saint
6. *Treny: The Laments of Kochanowski*, translated by Adam Czerniawski
7. *Neither a Borrower: Forging Traditions in French, Chinese and Arabic Poetry*, by Richard Serrano
8. *The Anatomy of Laughter*, edited by Toby Garfitt, Edith McMorran and Jane Taylor
9. *Dilettantism and its Values: From Weimar Classicism to the fin de siècle*, by Richard Hibbitt
10. *The Fantastic in France and Russia in the Nineteenth Century*, by Claire Whitehead
11. *Singing Poets: Literature and Popular Music in France and Greece*, by Dimitris Papanikolaou
12. *Wanderers Across Language: Exile in Irish and Polish Literature*, by Kinga Olszewska
13. *Moving Scenes: The Aesthetics of German Travel Writing on England*, by Alison E. Martin
14. *Henry James and the Second Empire*, by Angus Wrenn
15. *Platonic Coleridge*, by James Vigus
16. *Imagining Jewish Art*, by Aaron Rosen
17. *Alienation and Theatricality: Diderot after Brecht*, by Phoebe von Held
18. *Turning into Sterne: Viktor Shklovskii and Literary Reception*, by Emily Finer
19. *Yeats and Pessoa: Parallel Poetic Styles*, by Patricia Silva McNeill
20. *Aestheticism and the Philosophy of Death: Walter Pater and Post-Hegelianism*, by Giles Whiteley
21. *Blake, Lavater and Physiognomy*, by Sibylle Erle
22. *Rethinking the Concept of the Grotesque: Crashaw, Baudelaire, Magritte*, by Shun-Liang Chao
23. *The Art of Comparison: How Novels and Critics Compare*, by Catherine Brown
24. *Borges and Joyce: An Infinite Conversation*, by Patricia Novillo-Corvalán
25. *Prometheus in the Nineteenth Century: From Myth to Symbol*, by Caroline Corbeau-Parsons
26. *Architecture, Travellers and Writers: Constructing Histories of Perception*, by Anne Hultzsch
27. *Comparative Literature in Britain: National Identities, Transnational Dynamics 1800-2000*, by Joep Leerssen with Elinor Shaffer
28. *The Realist Author and Sympathetic Imagination*, by Sotirios Paraschas
29. *Iris Murdoch and Elias Canetti: Intellectual Allies*, by Elaine Morley
30. *Likenesses: Translation, Illustration, Interpretation*, by Matthew Reynolds

Exile and Nomadism in French and Hispanic Women's Writing

Kate Averis

LEGENDA

Studies in Comparative Literature 31
Modern Humanities Research Association and Maney Publishing
2014

Published by the
Modern Humanities Research Association and Maney Publishing
1 Carlton House Terrace
London SW1Y 5AF
United Kingdom

LEGENDA is an imprint of the
Modern Humanities Research Association and Maney Publishing

Maney Publishing is the trading name of W. S. Maney & Son Ltd,
whose registered office is at Suite 1C, Joseph's Well, Hanover Walk, Leeds LS3 1AB

ISBN 978-1-907975-94-3

First published 2014

All rights reserved. No part of this publication may be reproduced or disseminated or transmitted in any form or by any means, electronic, mechanical, photocopying, recording or otherwise, or stored in any retrieval system, or otherwise used in any manner whatsoever without the express permission of the copyright owner

© Modern Humanities Research Association and W. S. Maney & Son Ltd 2014

Printed in Great Britain

Cover: 875 Design

Copy-Editor: Rebecca du Plessis

CONTENTS

	Acknowledgements	ix
	Note on Translations	x
	List of Abbreviations	xi
	Introduction	1
	PART I: NOMADIC CONSCIOUSNESS, NOMADIC NARRATIVES	
1	Exile, Identity, Nomadism: Key Terms and Concepts	9
2	Writing (in) Exile: Six Contemporary Women Writers	38
	PART II: OVERSTEPPING THE BOUNDARIES: WOMEN'S NARRATIVES OF EXILE	
3	Vicissitudes of Language: Nancy Huston's *L'Empreinte de l'ange* and Cristina Siscar's *La sombra del jardín*	67
4	Writing Home: Malika Mokeddem's *L'Interdite* and Laura Restrepo's *Dulce compañía*	98
5	Alternative Femininities: Linda Lê's *In memoriam* and Cristina Peri Rossi's *Solitario de amor*	130
	Conclusion	163
	Bibliography	168
	Index	177

In memory of Nellie Nichol

ACKNOWLEDGEMENTS

I wish to warmly acknowledge the people who have played a role in the development of this book. I am especially grateful to my doctoral supervisors, Catherine Boyle and Siobhán McIlvanney, whose unfaltering support and guidance was not limited to academic expertise, meticulous reading and criticism of my research at every stage, constant encouragement and generosity with their time. I wish to thank Diana Holmes and Claire Lindsay for their time and effort in offering invaluable support and guidance in the process of development from thesis to book. Others to whom I also owe sincere thanks for widespread academic and administrative support at all stages of this project in the form of reading chapters, providing feedback, recommending sources, asking fruitful questions, and providing practical advice include: Johanna Malt, Nicholas Harrison, Patrick ffrench, Sanja Perovic, Anna Kemp, Hector Kolias, and Alicia Kent. For creating opportunities to rehearse the ideas explored and expressed here, for being perceptive readers and interlocutors, and for providing guidance and mentorship, from its incipient through to its very final stages, thanks to Gill Rye, Shirley Jordan, Claire Taylor, Anna-Louise Milne, and Isabel Hollis. Portions of this book appeared in earlier versions in the journals *Women in French*, *Francosphères*, and *Essays in French Literature and Culture*. For permission to republish this material in revised and expanded version, I thank the editors of these journals. My thanks to Graham Nelson at Legenda, who offered invaluable editorial guidance, and I am also grateful for the support I have received from the British Comparative Literature Association and from the University of London Institute in Paris. All my appreciation and affection goes, as always, to Tato, whose longstanding and unfailing support plays no small role in the realisation of this book.

K.A., Paris, May 2014

NOTE ON TRANSLATIONS

Where possible, I have used commercially available English translations, for which full bibliographic references are given in the bibliography; all other unattested translations are my own.

LIST OF ABBREVIATIONS

DC   Restrepo, Laura, *Dulce compañía*, 2nd edn (Bogotá: Alfaguara, 2005) [first edition: 1995].
EA   Huston, Nancy, *L'Empreinte de l'ange* (Arles: Actes Sud; Montreal: Leméac, 1998).
I   Mokeddem, Malika, *L'Interdite* (Paris: Grasset, 1993).
IM   Lê, Linda, *In memoriam* (Paris: Christian Bourgois, 2007).
SA   Peri Rossi, Cristina, *Solitario de amor*, 2nd edn (Barcelona: Lumen, 1998) [first edition: 1988].
SJ   Cristina Siscar, *La sombra del jardín* (Buenos Aires: Simurg, 1999).

INTRODUCTION

This study explores the ways in which contemporary women writers have engaged with the negotiation and representation of identity following the rupture with the established sense of self in the homeland that is brought about by exile. This negotiation is necessarily a forced one insofar as the originary markers of identity are destabilised, and the exile *must* relocate herself in the new surroundings in order to reassert a sense of self. The lost homeland does not necessarily represent a place of secure locatedness for women but a site in which identity was often already problematic, as indicated by the disaffected ties to the homeland to which displaced women frequently testify even before exile. As such, the negotiation of women's identity in displacement belies the notion of identarian destabilisation as a primarily negative event, and exile can be seen as a privileged site for the expression of women's identity. The analysis undertaken here builds on current critical thought in which the notions of home and homeland as given places of comfort, safety, nurture, and belonging are increasingly contested, and lasting familial, national, sexual, and gender identities are consequently questioned. Exiled women's writing substantiates such doubts about the fixity of determining factors of identity and reveals the different sets of realities that are opened up to women upon distantiation from the ties of family, society, and nation that shape identity from birth. The texts here analysed indicate that the otherwise traumatic experience of exile nevertheless provides propitious circumstances for the renegotiation of women's identity in that it interrupts the hold of the limited available roles for women in the homeland, broadens the space and scope for self-realisation, and offers the freedom of a sense of belonging that is located between, and beyond, fixed sites.

Examining the novels of women writers from a range of cultural backgrounds, this book contests the idea that current theoretical discourses of exile adequately account for women's exile, and sets up ways of thinking that offer a more inclusive vision of exile. This does not aim to be a sociological study of the impact of exile on women's social, economic, or political roles, but rather it investigates women's negotiation of identity following the experience of exile through an examination of the literary expression of the inhabitation of the space of exile. As well as literary criticism, this study draws on and enters into dialogue with a range of theoretical discourses, including history, philosophy, psychology, sociology, ethnology, and feminism in the analysis of key works by six contemporary women authors.

Exile, as both a feature of personal experience and a literary theme, appears with frequency in the lives and works of a great number of women writers from postcolonial nations that have retained the colonial legacy of the French and Spanish languages, and particularly those of South American countries that suffered the brutal military dictatorships of the 1970s and 1980s, and North African countries devastated by the fallout from the dismantling of colonial structures in the latter half of the twentieth century. Temporally proximate but geographically diverse, the authors that form the focus of this study — Linda Lê, Nancy Huston, Malika Mokeddem, Laura Restrepo, Cristina Peri Rossi, and Cristina Siscar — are from Vietnam, Canada, Algeria, Colombia, Uruguay, and Argentina respectively, and share the experience of having been exiled from their birth countries, and having relocated to the metropolitan centres of France, Spain, and Mexico. These authors have been included for the diversity of their experiences of exile, and the novels analysed here have been selected for their range of contributions to the consideration of women's identity in exile. The works of Luisa Valenzuela, Alicia Partnoy, Albalucía Angel, Tununa Mercado, Marta Traba, or Zoé Valdés in Spanish might equally have been considered in the present study, as might the works of Assia Djebar, Leïla Marouane, Anna Moï, Gisèle Pineau, or Leïla Sebbar in French, many of whom have already received a great deal of critical attention. An interest in combining established figures of exiled women's writing (such as Cristina Peri Rossi and Linda Lê) with less prominent writers (such as Cristina Siscar) as well as writers who have received less critical attention than might be expected (such as Laura Restrepo) also guided the selection of the primary corpus of study.

Insofar as the writers whose works form the focus of this study experienced exile for vastly different reasons, and their geographical trajectories of exile are varied, they can be considered a representative community of exiled women. Equally, their demonstration of a certain nonconformity to the designated roles that were available in the home country, and their intellectual engagement with the particular difficulties and privileges of exile for women, constitute further grounds on which they can be considered a representative sample of exiled women. These traits — diversity, nonconformity, and engagement — result in hybrid texts which illustrate the current trend of nomadism in exiled women's writing that this book identifies and explores. Neither 'at home' in the place left behind, nor in the new place of residence, these exiled women writers are seen to turn to the interstitial space of displacement which they affirmatively cultivate as a site of creativity and cultural production. The radical diversity of their backgrounds and individual circumstances of displacement only better demonstrates the common shared trends in the way in which they have experienced and engaged with exile, as illustrated by the overlapping concerns and narrative strategies of their texts, which provide a rich diversity of material for a selective, comparative discussion.

The analysis of recent novels (with one exception, the principal novels analysed here were published in the two decades spanning 1990–2010) by these women writers raises a number of considerations concerning a particularly feminine experience of exile, such as how (thematically and formally) these authors negotiate their displacement through literary discourse; in what ways these texts can be said to deal with a specifically feminine experience of exile; and how the loss of a fixed (albeit problematic) site of identity impacts on notions of belonging and identity for women in the process of their negotiation. My reading of these authors' works repeatedly comes across the declaration of a sense of alienation in the birth country even before departure into exile. This alienation is attributed to vastly different factors, including cultural isolation, political dissonance, non-hegemonic sexuality, and non-conforming gender roles, suggesting that the experience of exile for many women heightens an already marginal sense of identity which is nevertheless experienced as a positive distantiation from the restrictions of home, and which offers a new space of agency. Two key concerns investigated here are how this already existing sense of alienation affects, firstly, the decision to go into exile, and secondly, the way in which the marginalisation of exile is inhabited, negotiated, and resolved.

Divided into two parts, this book firstly outlines the theoretical underpinnings and methodological approach of my investigation of exiled women's writing in the two chapters of Part I, 'Nomadic Consciousness, Nomadic Narratives'. Chapter 1, 'Exile, Identity, Nomadism: Key Terms and Concepts', complicates some of the current theoretical notions at stake in the discussion of exile, and establishes my use of the key terms and concepts associated with women's exile, and women's writing of and in exile. It reconsiders exile as viewed as a primarily masculine phenomenon which has overlooked feminine experience, and argues the necessity of rethinking and recalibrating the existing lexicon and discrete categories of exile to provide a more effective framework for the discussion of women's experiences of exile. Addressing some of the anxieties surrounding the currency of the terms 'exile', 'displacement', 'home', 'nation', and 'nomadism' in current discourses of exile, this chapter highlights the importance of historicising and conceptualising experiences of displacement. Beginning with a discussion of the problematic dichotomy of 'true' and 'false' exile, displacement is rethought, not in terms of 'enforced' and 'voluntary' exile, but in terms of 'political', 'cultural', 'economic', or other types of exile. Such designations are shown to better account for women's exile, and the notion of 'forced choice' is proposed to convey the degree to which displacement is experienced through both force *and* choice. The first chapter concludes that a consideration of women's exile in relation to recent theoretical discourses points to a nomadic configuration of identity that is located in mobility and transition, between fixed sites, and that is posited as an ongoing process of becoming rather than a static state of being.

Following the discussion of the application of theoretical discourses of exile to women's experience, Chapter 2, 'Writing (in) Exile: Six Contemporary Women Writers', identifies a literary nomadism in exiled women's texts that is commensurate with and reflects their nomadic subjectivity as developed in exile. Through an exploration of the linguistic and generic hybridity characteristic of exiled women's writing, this chapter demonstrates the nomadic hybridity of exiled women's writing, which combines historical with literary discourses, and subjective with objective voices. The stakes of language as a definitive marker of identity, and the linguistic shift that exile frequently incurs are also discussed in terms of the fundamental impact of linguistic plurality on the renegotiation and expression of identity in exile. Such considerations lead to a discussion of the role of writing for women in exile, for whom biography and text become inextricably linked, and writing *in* and *of* exile merge together. Biographical information on each of the six authors is also given in Chapter 2, in accordance with the methodological approach of contextualisation adopted in my feminist readings of exiled women's texts: in order to fully apprehend the identarian concerns at stake for their authors, it is vital to read texts in light of their historical, cultural, and political contexts.

Each of the three chapters of Part II, 'Overstepping the Boundaries: Women's Narratives of Exile', subsequently considers the negotiation of women's identity in exile through the comparative analyses of a key work by each author, focusing on two authors and novels in each chapter, whilst taking into account each writer's wider corpus of works, permitting both the consideration of a broad range of texts, as well as the proximity of close reading and comparative textual analysis, and allowing like texts to be grouped together in such a way as to develop the similarities and characteristics of exiled women's writing. The first two of the six key texts analysed are paired together for the manner in which they explicitly manifest the experience of exile, focusing on the representation of the disorientation and trauma of arrival in exile. The other four novels analysed demonstrate more implicit strategies of representation of exiled women's negotiation of identity in exile. The second pair of texts focus their representation not on the country of exile, but on the abandoned homeland, adopting a common denunciatory, testimonial tone, and are thus grouped together for the similar politicisation with which the texts are infused. The final pair of texts are those which present the reader with the least explicit representations of exile, and are compared for the way in which paradigms of gender can be seen to have both affected the passage into exile, and undergone profound reconfiguration subsequent to the experience by two authors who, after spending the greater part of their lives in exile, can be seen as representative of many of the concerns of exiled women writers more generally.

Chapter 3, 'Vicissitudes of Language: Nancy Huston's *L'Empreinte de l'ange* and Cristina Siscar's *La sombra del jardín*', begins the analysis of contemporary exiled women's writing by looking specifically at two exile narratives which represent the silence and vulnerability women must overcome in the highly charged period of arrival of exile. It compares two novels by Huston (Canada, 1953) and Siscar (Argentina, 1947) which explicitly recount the initial stage of exile immediately after their protagonists' arrival in the new country. This moment is depicted as one of intense spatial, temporal, and linguistic disorientation in which the present is all but uninhabitable due to its infiltration by the past and to the constant deferral to the future. Chapter 3 examines the textual strategies of fragmentation and multiplicity that these authors employ to express the instability and vulnerability of their female protagonists upon arrival in exile, and introduces the particularity of the notion of 'resolution' of the fragmentation of identity in displacement as it applies to the feminine experience of exile. Initially clarifying the points that unite the two women (migration to Paris in the 1970s, a linguistic shift to French, and the ways in which residing in the French capital has been experienced as positive), it then underlines those which distance them (the vastly different circumstances of displacement, the different ways in which they arrived at the French language, and their contrasting relationships to French). After contextualising each woman's particular positioning in exile, it analyses the treatment of exile in the two texts, thus illustrating the overarching comparative aim of the study, which is to examine how women writers, whose experiences of exile may differ dramatically, use common narrative strategies to articulate similar existential concerns following the experience of exile. This chapter is primarily concerned with the ways in which women exiles manage to overcome silence, invisibility, and vulnerability in exile and in the acquired language, and as such it examines how language is used by these two writers as both a literary theme and a narrative strategy to reflect the fragmentation of the experience. This chapter establishes the literal and metaphoric nomadism of the early stage of exile, and posits the notion of exiled women's identity as defined by the liminality of the outside and by the in-between: the tendency of exiled women to define themselves by who or what they are *not*, rather than by who or what they *are*, is then furthered explored in the two subsequent chapters.

Chapter 4, 'Writing Home: Malika Mokeddem's *L'Interdite* and Laura Restrepo's *Dulce compañía*', examines the identarian concerns of exile after return becomes possible and which pose the problem of the exiled women writer's sense of critical, representative, and political responsibility towards the home culture. Examining two works by Restrepo (Colombia, 1950) and Mokeddem (Algeria, 1949) in which their authors turn their gaze away from the country of exile, and back towards the birth country to denounce the shortcomings of the countries from which they were exiled, this chapter examines women's exile writing which is motivated by political, documentary, and testimonial drives. Building on the wide-ranging comparative approach of this book, a comparison is drawn between the Colombian and the Algerian author who were both exiled as a direct result of violence in their home countries, and considers the important role that violent displacement has played in the entry to writing for both women, and the ongoing impact of exile in their most recent works. With the notion of the re-encounter with the home society central to both authors' concerns, this chapter considers to what degree their adopted critical and testimonial positions are problematised by their fragmented identities, as 'estranged outsiders' to the societies they criticise, and whose contemporary histories they are concerned with representing from a marginal — feminine and external — viewpoint. Whilst extremely critical of the structures of power and authority in their home countries, they express a desired sense of solidarity with the disempowered, silenced women of their home countries, and the analysis extends to a consideration of the tensions between the individuality of the position of the returned exile and the desired sense of collectivity that is articulated in their novels. This chapter concludes with an examination of the problematic nature of the project for mimetic as well as political representation that Mokeddem and Restrepo implicitly set out for themselves in these novels by discussing their investment in a belief in the potential of literature to bring about social and political changes in the lives of those it seeks to represent. The political imperatives present in testimonial, denunciatory works are shown to be frequently viewed by women exiles as a responsibility to other women in the homeland.

Chapter 5, 'Alternative Femininities: Linda Lê's *In memoriam* and Cristina Peri Rossi's *Solitario de amor*', focuses on two texts which posit the ongoing location of women's identity in the 'in-between' of exile and propose alternative paradigms of femininity which echo the productive alterity of the state of exile. In the two novels analysed in this chapter, by Peri Rossi (Uruguay, 1941) and Lê (Vietnam, 1963), the negotiation of women's identity which defines itself against the norms of an alienating society is expressed in the depiction of female protagonists who disrupt and overturn received gender roles. Examining the representation of exile as as much a corporeal as a spatial phenomenon, this chapter demonstrates how these two authors also highlight the representation of the female body in the altered space of displacement as a means through which to deconstruct frequently alienating historical representations of women, and posit new paradigms of femininity. Through envisaging new modes of inhabitation of gender and expression of gendered identity, Peri Rossi and Lê foreground the way in which the exiled woman intellectual's gender is at stake in exile and suggest new ways of configuring gendered identity that attempt to extricate women's identity from restrictive, alienating roles. The two authors are shown to affirmatively appropriate the alienation of the position of exile as a positive marker of identity, rather than consider it a state to be 'resolved' or 'overcome'. The final chapter draws out a defining feature of contemporary exiled women's writing that is explicitly manifested in the works of Lê and Peri Rossi: the centrality of the act of writing. Writing is shown to constitute a site of belonging for exiled women writers, and can be seen as a way not of resolving, but of inhabiting the state of exile.

This study does not seek to find comfortable resolutions to the negotiation of identity in exiled women's writing, but to draw out its characteristics, consider its mechanisms, reveal its strategies, and accept its contradictions and inconsistencies. The theoretical considerations of the next two chapters, and the textual analyses of Part II, examine the works of contemporary women writers who have experienced exile from a position of nomadic subjectivity, revealing a writing that is nomadic, decentred, and hybrid, where writing itself is the unsettling new site of belonging that trades fixity for mobility, and restoration for creation.

PART I

Nomadic Consciousness, Nomadic Narratives

CHAPTER 1

Exile, Identity, Nomadism: Key Terms and Concepts

Despite increased academic interest in recent decades in the multiple, interstitial subjectivities produced in and by transnational displacement, there is still much anxiety surrounding its key terms and concepts. Scholars argue the need to elucidate the terms and tropes used, and to consider the ways in which these politicise research practices. The ongoing debate regarding the naming and categorisation of experiences testifies to a continuing need to critically examine, and rethink, the way in which displacement is named, classified, and theorised.

Euro-American discourses of displacement have been criticised for glossing over differences and creating ahistorical amalgams. Caren Kaplan cautions against assembling universalised tropes of displacement which have the adverse effect of conflating experiences and overlooking historical specificity.[1] Clearly, the issues at stake differ greatly for individuals who have experienced radically different circumstances of displacement. How can the experiences of Latin Americans who fled military dictatorships in the 1970s and 1980s in fear of their lives be constructively compared to the struggles of those from economically and politically stable countries who departed in pursuit of cultural affinity and intellectual freedom? The negotiation of a sense of self within the space of displacement differs for those who have left the homeland for reasons which can range from political persecution, economic need, cultural disaffinity, intellectual dissonance, or for more personal reasons. Conditions such as gender, the age at which an individual leaves the birth country, whether he or she leaves alone or accompanied, whether a future return is possible or even desired, and the perception of the homeland in the new country of residence also have profound effects on the experience of displacement, as well as on the strategies that are employed to negotiate the new identity that displacement necessitates.

Kaplan counters her warning against universalised tropes of displacement by suggesting, on the other hand, that overemphasising the differences between types of displacement through a rigid allocation of terminology can bring about a counterproductive moralising evaluation of experiences and behaviours. Looking, for example, at the mechanisms and strategies that disparate groups of displaced peoples do in fact share elucidates the inevitable processes of renegotiation of identity incurred by the removal of the familial, social, and linguistic bonds through which identity is produced and sustained. Despite obvious differences between different groups, such as, for example, those displaced by the threat of violence at home, or a privileged international elite able to relocate for more personal reasons, they do, in fact, prove to undergo common processes of identity re-adjustment in displacement that reinforce the primacy of shared experience over differentiating factors.

James Clifford advocates a thoughtful and sensitive approach in his appeal for an inclusive theoretical and discursive framework which allows for difference without homogenising experiences.[2] In his examination of the discourse of diaspora, Clifford states that while it is useful to define terms, we must be wary of classification by recourse to an 'ideal type' where experiences become more or less exemplary according to the frequency with which they display defining features. To use Clifford's terms, an inclusive theoretical framework would allow the 'tracking', rather than the 'policing' of experiences, and avoids the kind of moral evaluation of experiences against which Kaplan warns. Winifred Woodhull builds on such efforts to avoid the conflation of experiences, and to seek out historical specificity by highlighting that it is essential to differentiate not only *between* but also *within* groups of 'cultural others' living in displacement.[3] The terminology and paradigms circulating in current discourses of subjectivities produced in and by displacement offer a useful framework when these are permeable and subject to questioning, rather than exclusive and hierarchical.

This introductory chapter considers the ideological associations of the terms and concepts used in current theoretical discourses of displacement in order to establish a conceptual framework for the analysis of displaced women's identity as explored and expressed in the recent fictional works analysed in the Chapters 3, 4, and 5. Terms such as 'exile', 'displacement', 'home', 'nation', and 'nomadism' are the cornerstones of discourses of displacement, and ones which require clarification in order to draw out the ideas and assumptions that they evoke. Their frequent use as metaphors expands their meanings so that these can signify quite differently in different situations. Kaplan describes how research practices can be politicised through questioning how these metaphors work, and opting to use them in specific ways rather than merely assuming their value and currency.[4] That these are contested and fluid terms is further reinforced by the changes these concepts undergo with translation. The currency of the English term 'exile' is certainly far removed from the resonance the Spanish 'exilio' holds, particularly in the context of Latin American Spanish. Broadly speaking, and for diverse cultural, economic, and political reasons, English-speaking cultures in recent history can be said to have been societies of reception of exiles, while Spanish-speaking cultures have sent large numbers of their populations into exile. This pattern has had a distinctive effect on each linguistic community's literary canon: the canon of modern English literature has absorbed practitioners born beyond its shores and comprises a significant number of exiled writers,[5] whereas Latin American literature has been, and continues to be produced in great geographical diversity, and writers such as Uruguayan Juan Carlos Onetti, who remained in his native country throughout his life, have become the exception rather than the rule. The English term 'home' provides another example: the absence of terms in both French and Spanish that combine the domestic and the affective meanings of 'home' with the notion of a place that is also a site of origins and belonging underlines how these meanings are located differently in different languages as well as how terms signify differently within the same language. Whilst the French *foyer* and the Spanish *hogar* adequately, albeit in different measure, convey the domestic meaning of 'home', as well as its association with shelter and refuge, these terms lack the association of origins and belonging present in 'home', as well as the term's spatial elasticity which can expand to include a hometown, a community, and/or a nation. Additionally, the English term's more frequent use in both discourse and in the cultural imaginary differentiates it from both its French and Spanish counterparts, thus highlighting the fluidity and shifting nature of the location of affect and meaning both within and between languages.

Enforced and Voluntary Exile: A False Dichotomy

The complexity of the arguments surrounding the terms used in the discussion of displacement is demonstrated by Amy K. Kaminsky's criticism of what she refers to as the 'evacuation of meaning of the term "exile"'.[6] Kaminsky's very specific use of the term defines a particular experience of displacement resulting from enforced removal, or banishment from the homeland for reasons of political persecution. For Kaminsky, 'voluntary exile' is a misnomer which, at best, suggests ignorance of, and at worst, indifference to the resonance of the term in the context of the military dictatorships in Latin America that murdered, disappeared, and displaced tens if not hundreds of thousands of people in the 1970s and 1980s. By insisting on a narrow definition of the term, Kaminsky raises the problem of using exile as a metaphor to describe various types of displacement and alienation from an originary culture which differ from the conventional definition of violent political exile. Whilst the indiscriminate overuse of the term can clearly have a detrimental effect on understanding the impact of the singularly traumatic experience of violent ousting from one's country of origin, the term 'exile' nevertheless has a valuable purchase not present in other terms. The scope of the term includes a resonance that is not present in the more neutral 'displacement', and which is key to understanding the psychological processes of displaced individuals across the wide range of situations of displacement. While 'displacement' has sufficient flexibility to express a variety of historical constructs of movement, its advantageous neutrality consequently dilutes the nuance of trauma present in the term 'exile'.

The cautious and contiguous use of both terms affords benefits to the discussion of the processes of identification in alienation where specificity is recognised, and perhaps more importantly, where unexpected commonalities are identified. One of the main aims of this study is to identify common processes of identification of exiled women writers, whilst drawing distinctions within and between the variously exiled writers at hand. What is at stake here is the way in which different modes of displacement generate cultural practices, and in particular, how exiled women formulate and express their identity through literary discourse. Greater importance will thus be given to elucidating the ways in which exiled women negotiate and define their identity in displacement, than to the task of hierarchising types of displacement according to a hypothetical scale of trauma. In this, I follow the example set by Marina Franco in her study of Argentine exiles in France during and following Argentina's most recent military dictatorship (1976–1983) where she distinguishes between the self-designation of exiles as such, and researchers' designation of exiles.[7] Sophia McClennen also identifies the problem of the non-coincidence of the designation of exile by its actors, on the one hand, and its theorists on the other, in *The Dialectics of Exile: Nation, Time, Language and Space in Hispanic Literatures*, a work 'dedicated to reconciling the exile of theoretical discourse with concrete cases of exile'.[8] That there exists a need to reconcile theoretical discourse with actual cases of exile implies theory's tendency to disregard exiles' own agency in the analysis of their own displacement. The recognition of subjects' self-designation in displacement allows for the heterogeneous nature of displacement to surface, and perhaps most importantly, works to avoid the kind of neocolonialist gesture that critics risk when they fail to recognise the agency of their subjects of study, which this book likewise aims to avoid. Here, particular attention is paid to each writer's own designation of their position in displacement, in addition to their explicit or implicit literary self-representation.

The six women writers who form the focus of study here come from diverse backgrounds, and represent different permutations of exile. Cristina Peri Rossi, Cristina Siscar, and Laura Restrepo, from Uruguay, Argentina, and Colombia respectively, most closely adhere to a conventional notion of political exile. Nephrologist Malika Mokeddem's professional migration from Algeria to France was instigated by political violence in her native country, as was Linda Lê's family migration from Vietnam to France in childhood. Nancy Huston is alone in having emigrated to France from her native Canada for cultural reasons and in the absence of the threat of violence. The patterns of displacement manifested in these women's lives can be traced back to the different trajectories of each of their birth country's colonial legacy. The wars in Vietnam and Algeria in the mid-twentieth century can be directly attributed to French colonialism, only dismantled in the last century and whose history has played out very differently from Spanish colonial history. The political instability that engulfed Vietnam and Algeria in recent history, and that also characterised Latin America for most of the twentieth century, can be said to have similarly arisen from conflicting notions of nationhood and national identity that has been one, and certainly not the only, unfortunate legacy of colonial rule. Likewise, I would argue that Canada's relatively peaceful postcolonial history, as a colonised nation that, like Australia and New Zealand, exterminated the vast majority of its indigenous population, has a role to play in Huston's decision to emigrate to Europe by virtue of her location in the white, cultural elite of a country that enjoys political stability and economic prosperity precisely because of its violent colonial past. As an exile and an intellectual, Huston has scrutinised this problematic position in her literary output which repeatedly addresses such issues.

While differentiating between the various types of political, cultural, and intellectual exile, common and overlapping processes as well as problems arise and become evident. The displaced individual's struggle to accommodate apparently conflicting psychological, cultural, and linguistic aspects of subjectivity into a coherent identity in the new environment throws up a number of similar strategies despite vastly different displacements. While distinction between individual circumstances of displacement is necessary to establish the divergent difficulties that varying situations of displacement pose — and certainly, not even displaced individuals within the same 'type' of exile can be said to suffer similar difficulties — the aim here is to avoid making the (contrived) distinction between 'true' and 'false' exile, or establishing a moral order or hierarchy of different experiences. The rather forced polar distinction between 'true' and 'false' exile stems from assumptions about the relation of exile to the exercise of will, and as such, exile has commonly been qualified as either 'enforced' or 'voluntary'. Yet even scholars working within the field of what conventional wisdom refers to as 'enforced exile' problematise this distinction as difficult to pin down. Franco, for example, questions the validity of such a binary distinction:

> suele superponerse que la migración política o exilio define la situación de quienes salieron de su país por una decisión voluntaria o no, pero en cualquier caso no deseada, forzada por las circunstancias políticas que los afectaron como miembros de una comunidad. ¿Pero cómo se determina el carácter forzado de esas circunstancias? ¿A partir de qué elementos se puede hablar de motivos políticos? ¿el miedo lo es? ¿Cuál es la diferencia entre un exiliado político y un exiliado económico cuando ambos son víctimas de un régimen cuyas políticas de gobierno son expulsivas?[9]
>
> [it is usually assumed that political migration or exile refers to the situation of those who left the country, voluntarily or not, but in any case against their wishes, forced by political circumstances which affected them as members of a certain community. But how can the forced nature of those circumstances be defined? is fear a defining characteristic? What is the difference between a political exile and an economic exile when both are the victims of expulsive regimes?]

Franco eventually settles for 'relativamente electivo' [relatively elective] to qualify the Argentine experience of exile in the wake of the country's most recent dictatorship, thus definitively granting even 'enforced' exile a degree of choice.[10]

While Franco picks up on the difficult distinction between the varying degrees of will exercised by political and economic exiles, Huston, self-designated voluntary or self-imposed exile, considers the implications of the question of will for cultural or intellectual exiles. According to the received notion, 'forced' (political or economic) exile constitutes a 'true' exile, as distinct from 'voluntary' (cultural or intellectual) exile deemed somehow arbitrary, as though a kind of self-immolation rendered meaningless because wilfully induced. Huston describes her exile to France as an arbitrary choice generated by her biographical circumstances, nevertheless she couches this choice in terms of the need to escape from what she perceives as the historical and cultural vacuum that is Canada: 'Pourquoi la France, pourquoi le français? En fait, ce fut plus ou moins l'effet du hasard. La nécessité, c'était de me sauver' [Why France, why French? In fact, it was more or less out of chance, and the need to save myself].[11] In an epistolary meditation on exile with Leïla Sebbar, published as *Lettres parisiennes*, she reiterates the necessity of relocating herself in a different cultural environment, '*j'ai besoin d'histoire*, précisément à cause de la modernité irréductible de mon passé' [*I need history*, precisely because of the intractable modernity of my past], implying both 'I need history' and 'I need *a* history'.[12] There is a constant anxiety in Huston's non-fictional works (which are largely autobiographical and many of which reflect upon the process of her arrival in France and insertion into French culture) to calibrate her own intensely felt exclusion and isolation against others' experiences, as is clear when she states:

> j'envie aussi les 'vrais' exilés, ceux qui disent aimer passionnément leur pays d'origine, sans pouvoir pour des raisons politiques ou économiques y vivre; dans ces moments, mon exil à moi me semble superficiel, capricieux, individualiste [...], mais il n'en est pas moins réel, et de plus en plus réel à mesure que le temps passe.[13]
>
> [I also envy 'real' exiles, those who say they fervently love their country of origin, but for political or economic reasons cannot live there. At such times, my own exile seems superficial, fickle, individualist [...], but no less real because of that, and more and more real as time goes by.]

In making the distinction between herself and 'real' exiles, Huston acknowledges the unspoken hierarchy of exiles that largely corresponds to the hypothetical scale of trauma against which both Kaplan and Clifford advise. Despite the apparently self-deprecatory gesture of classing herself a 'second-class' exile, Huston only more forcefully asserts her self-identification as an exile: the absence of political or economic motivations does not lead Huston to consider her exile to be any less 'real'. Despite insisting on her status as an exile, the willed nature of Huston's exile is extremely problematic for her own self-designation in terms of the authenticity of that status, and she constantly demonstrates a need to defend her self-representation as such.

The idea of 'will' as being that which distinguishes between 'exile' and other types of displacement is indeed a nebulous notion, and raises the question of another of exile's related issues: that of guilt. A persistent sense of guilt is commonly expressed by displaced individuals from across the spectrum of experiences of displacement — guilt at having abandoned a cause, a people, or a nation — and ongoing guilt regarding the failure to return once return becomes possible, where this is the case. The two notions of will and guilt clearly intersect: guilt is not — in theory — provoked by misfortunes of destiny or other external catalysts but by the actions and decisions one perceives as having chosen. Yet even those banished from their home countries by violent political regimes, and whose exercise of will can be said to be greatly limited, often express an intense sense of guilt, suggesting a perceived degree of will even in 'enforced' exile.

Our understanding of the relation of guilt to will is complicated by unjustified feelings of guilt, or guilt that is imposed by others, as described by Cristina Siscar, exiled from Argentina from 1979 to 1986 as a result of the military dictatorship: 'No, *yo no sentía culpa* porque yo sabía muy bien lo que había vivido, yo tenía muy claro eso, *yo no sentía culpa*, nunca sentí culpa. Me culpabilizaban, que era otra cosa, pero *yo no sentía culpa*' [No, *I didn't feel any guilt* because I knew very well what I had been through, that was very clear to me, *I didn't feel any guilt*, I never felt any guilt. I was blamed, which is different, but *I didn't feel any guilt*].[14] Siscar adamantly denies harbouring any feelings of guilt with an insistence that suggests an oft-repeated response to others' projections of guilt over the many years since her return from exile. Opponents of the dictatorship unable or unwilling to leave Argentina during the period of repression were often intensely critical of those who 'abandoned' the nation and the struggle against the military juntas. The myth of the *exilio dorado* [golden exile] was mobilised by both the military to condemn the 'subversives' living abroad, as well as by militants and dissenters to tar exiles as 'traitors'. Siscar describes 'un ambiente que no era favorable para los que se habían exiliado' [an atmosphere that was not favourable for those who had gone into exile] in the years following her return to Buenos Aires, and recalls that her survival was charged with being at the cost of others' lives: in the words of her critics, 'vos te salvaste porque otros están muertos' [you survived because others died].[15] Siscar's forceful denial of bearing any sense of guilt for her exile constitutes a defiant refusal of the guilt that her critics have attempted to impose on her, and testifies to her limited set of choices in the extremely threatening circumstances in which she found herself leading up to the decision to leave. I refer to Siscar's 'decision' to leave in order to illustrate the opaque overlap between choice and lack of choice, between will and guilt. Despite the overwhelming and pressing danger with which she was faced, and the limited options to escape this, it could be argued that her critics have succeeded to some degree in instilling a sense of guilt over the personal impact of her exile, such as 'leaving behind' her five-year-old son, and failing in her later efforts to be reunited with him in France.

It thus appears of limited usefulness to police the boundaries of 'enforced' and 'voluntary' exile, or to make conjectures about what the presence or absence of guilt reveals. Can political exile be considered devoid of any scope for the exercise of agency in the fact of displacement? Or do feelings of guilt provide evidence of a degree of choice for political exiles who were, at most, able to decide the moment and the manner in which they left? Can displacement be said to be strictly voluntary for the individual who feels culturally isolated and stifled in his or her home country? For such individuals, being prevented from fulfilling their intellectual, creative or professional potential, while not life-threatening, can be extremely crippling, and may or may not lead to future feelings of guilt for past decisions. Discrete categories of displacement prove to be difficult to delimit, and indeed tend to blur their own borders.

As Kaminsky uses the term, exile is always coerced, nevertheless she emphasises that her concern lies less with testing for 'real' exiles than with representations of the processes of exile. Simplistic qualifications of what does or does not constitute exile shift the focus away from the processes and experiences of displacement and reduces the conditions of exile to binary oppositions: forced/voluntary, possible/impossible return, suffering/liberation. Jean Déjeux's discussion of exile in the context of Maghrebi women writers suggests that the ability to return to the homeland is sufficient to disqualify the denomination of exile, reducing the possibility of return to a juridical decision and overlooking the real conditions that return would hold for Maghrebi women:

> En fait, aucune n'a été bannie de sa patrie ou de sa terre natale. Chacune parmi celles qui habitent l'étranger peut reprendre l'avion et aller résider en Algérie, Maroc ou Tunisie. On peut aimer le soleil et se dire 'exilé' du soleil, mais en réalité, les femmes-écrivaines du Maghreb qui habitent l'étranger sont bien contentes d'y vivre, pour diverses raisons d'ailleurs. Il y a souvent des façons incongrues de faire des variations verbales et littéraires sur le terme 'exil', alors qu'on n'en souffre pas ou qu'on a aménagé pour le mieux cette vie 'ailleurs'.[16]
>
> [In fact, none of them has been banished from her homeland or country of birth. Each of them who live abroad could take a plane and go and live in Algeria, Morocco, or Tunisia. It's possible to like the sun and to call oneself 'exiled' from the sun, but in reality women writers from the Maghreb who live abroad are more than happy to be there, for many reasons. There are many ways of creating incongruous verbal and literary variations on the term 'exile', when in fact one doesn't suffer from, or has managed to make the most of this life 'elsewhere'.]

Such clear-cut distinctions are eroded by actual discourses of exile and displacement which describe a far more heterogeneous experience whereby aspects of the same binary opposition may (and often do) reside in individual experiences of exile.

My analysis relies on the observation of the characteristics of different types of exile such as Gonzalo Aguilar's distinction between 'exilio político' [political exile] and 'exilio cultural' [cultural exile] in the case of exiled intellectuals:

> En el letrado, entiende que — básicamente — hay dos tipos de exilio que denominaré 'exilio político' y 'exilio cultural'. El primero es un exilio forzoso y su núcleo es la creencia en el cambio. La tierra que se debe dejar es una tierra prometida (hay un deseo de volver). [...] El otro, el exilio cultural, es un exilio relativamente voluntario. El núcleo de este exilio es el escepticismo, la renuncia. La patria es una tierra abandonada (no hay deseo de volver sino deseo de huir).[17]
>
> [For the writer, there are — basically — two types of exile that I will call 'political exile' and 'cultural exile'. The first is a forced exile and its essence lies in the belief in change. The land left behind is a promised land (there is a desire to return). [...] The other, cultural exile, is relatively voluntary. The essence of this exile is scepticism and resignation. The nation is an abandoned land (there is no desire to return, but rather to flee).]

In rethinking types of exile, not in terms of 'enforced' and 'voluntary' exile, but in terms of 'political' and 'cultural' exile, Aguilar redirects the focus away from the conventional distinction between 'genuine' and 'false' exile, whereby the latter is considered a mendacious usurpation of the signifying weight of 'genuine' exile and thus an illegitimate use of the term. While he describes political exile as 'un exilio forzoso', its essence lies elsewhere, notably in the desire to return to the homeland, and the belief in the eventual possibility of return, rather than in its forced nature. In describing cultural exile as only 'relativamente voluntario', like Franco, he too problematises any clear-cut role of will in the classification of displacement.

The impossibility of unproblematically attributing Huston's exile to a choice, or Siscar's exile to the total absence of choice points to a false dichotomy between the binary positions of choice/no choice, will/no will, or guilt/no guilt. If concrete cases of exile cannot coherently be narrowed down to either choice or imposition, but prove to incorporate varying degrees of both, the aporia that remains suggests a kind of 'forced choice'. The notion of 'forced choice' allows us to account for the possibility — in fact, the necessity — of speaking of the 'choice' exercised by the political exile from an authoritarian regime, where we refer to a limited, yet nevertheless existing set of choices, as well as of the 'need' for flight from a home environment perceived as culturally inhibiting or disabling in the case of intellectual dissonance at home. Understanding exiled subjectivity as situated along a spectrum of free will in even the most constraining circumstances corresponds to an understanding of subjectivity constituted of both a Sartrean, existentialist notion of subjectivity governed by free will and responsibility, and a structuralist, deterministic account of subjectivity, and allows us to reconcile the apparently contradictory presence of both choice and imposition in each individual case of exile. Thinking of exiled subjectivity in terms of the aporia of 'forced choice' allows us to better account for the irreconcilability of the extent to which displacement is undergone by force or by choice, and to better understand the similar strategies that are shared by variously exiled subjects in disparate circumstances, such as as those of Huston and Siscar.

If classifying the nature of an individual's exile is contentious, along with its comparison to others' experiences, so is the notion of its longevity and the persistence of its psychological effects after the period of exile is over or after return becomes possible. Raising a polemic similar to that surrounding other 'post-'s, the notion of the 'post-exile' implies a discrete period of time which we call 'exile', presumably demarcated by the moment when return becomes possible, beyond which the exile is no longer 'in exile'. However, exiled individuals indicate that the displaced subject frequently continues to consider him or herself 'in exile' when he or she remains in his or her adopted place of residence after return becomes juridically and practically possible, and 'in exile' of a different kind if they do return to their native country. Mario Benedetti coined the term *desexilio* to refer to the experience of 'reverse displacement' of the passage from exile to repatriation in the context of the end of military rule in the Southern Cone states, highlighting the new process of adaptation, and the ongoing state of marginality for those who returned 'home'.[18]

As criticism overwhelmingly concurs, exile is irretrievably tied to the notion of return, in which home is granted a definitive role. As indicated by Laura Restrepo, exiled from Colombia in the mid-1980s, the all-consuming focus on return in the early stage of exile underscores the definitive role of home, where 'return' can be a projected ideal of return as much as the actual voyage 'home':

> El primer año de mi exilio en México fue un tiempo de aislamiento y de añoranzas, de soñar a todas horas con el momento en que me fuera dada la posibilidad de regresar a Colombia, de andar pendiente de cualquier noticia o periódico viejo que llegara de mi tierra y de mi gente, de andar rodeada de otros exiliados con quienes compartía destino común.[19]
>
> [The first year of my exile in Mexico was a time of isolation and longing, of dreaming at every moment of the day it would be possible to return to

Colombia, of looking out for any piece of news or old newspaper from my country or my people, of being surrounded by other exiles with whom I shared a common destiny.]

Restrepo's remark additionally accentuates an understanding of exile as process as well as physical displacement. That she retrospectively refers to her first year in exile in Mexico as a period spent consumed by the desire for return correlatively implies a later stage in the process of exile where this was not the case. More than merely geographical and spatial displacement, the experience of exile is also a process of movement and change over time, thus exile is both a spatial *and* a chronological phenomenon. Just as no two displacements are the same, individual displacements evolve and are subject to change over time, as discussed further in Chapter 3.

Thus the subject produced in and by exile will retain a consciousness of displacement whether they remain in exile, or eventually make the return to the homeland. In addition, the processes of exile are irreversible, in that the subject can no longer return to the pre-exile self or even to the same geographical place they left behind upon departure into exile, as the exile will experience him or herself *and* his or her place of origin as irrevocably changed. As Malika Mokeddem, in permanent exile in France, makes clear, return home may not necessarily be actual, but symbolic: 'j'étais revenue vers l'Algérie par l'écriture' [I came back to Algeria through writing].[20] Even when return is idealised rather than actual, the notion nevertheless plays a defining role in the subject's experience of exile.

Leaving Home

Concurrently present in the idea of return is the notion of 'home' (where this means an originary site of familiarity and belonging and a place where one feels 'at home', as well as what the *Oxford English Dictionary* refers to as 'the fixed residence of a family or household; the seat of domestic life and interests; one's own house; the dwelling in which one habitually lives, or which one regards as one's proper abode'). Kaminsky discusses the stakes of the notion of home for exiled women writers in relation to the conventional masculine gendering of the exile in the Western imaginary.[21] In the conventional masculine configuration that she describes, exile is characterised by movement and dynamism, space is feminised, and the feminine position is posited as one of stasis and stability. The country to which the male exile arrives is a space to be conquered, and home a place to which the masculine-gendered exile can, when he is able, return. The 'infantile desire' to return home is sustained by a notion of a maternal homeland. This gendering of exile and place is disrupted by the female exile who overturns conventional notions of female immobility and receptivity and who, according to Kaminsky, tends not to confuse the maternal body with the lost homeland. This is particularly clear in the cases of Nancy Huston, Linda Lê, and Malika Mokeddem. For Huston the maternal association with the homeland is disrupted by her own mother's departure from the family home and country of origin when Huston was six years old, and her father's subsequent marriage to a German woman. The maternal, for Huston, is therefore associated with travel, mobility, and the exotic rather than with the homeland.[22] In the cases of both Lê and Mokeddem, the father comes to represent the homeland, as indicated by the nostalgic haunting of Lê's texts by the figure of the father in Vietnam,[23] and by the dénouement of Mokeddem's autobiographical novel, *La Transe des insoumis*, which recounts her return to her home village and her parents after a twenty-four-year absence, and features a reconciliation with the father (to whom the novel is dedicated).[24]

Departure from home, and the homeland, plays out differently for women due to the discontinuation of the association of women with the home. As Kaminsky states: 'Women leave home too.'[25] If home is the locus of long-standing familial and social ties, the break from home also brings about a rupture with the expectations and roles embedded in these relations. By leaving home, women both symbolically and literally deterritorialise and relocate women's positioning. As Janet Wolff suggests, the radical revision of female subjectivity characteristic of women's experience of exile can perhaps be attributed to the fact of leaving home rather than to the inhabitation of the status of outsider in the new country: 'perhaps the point is the not-being-at-home, and not the foreign residence'.[26]

The separation from home and its associated roles, and the immersion in an unfamiliar environment where an individual is marked by their difference from the norm, inevitably leads to both reflection upon, and examination of one's sense of self. Separated from the constraints of home and family, women exiles are led to reconsider and question roles which may have seemed 'natural' in the home environment. The literal and symbolic displacement that exile incurs dispenses with the determining function of the originary home, and leaves the way open for the construction of the self in the present. While the same could be said for men's experience of exile, women exiles experience the rupture with the ties of home quite differently, as these ties are frequently shaped by alienation and disempowerment, and women are thus often reluctant to replicate the constraints that limited their roles previous to exile. In the case of Tzvetan Todorov, a self-declared 'exilé "circonstanciel", ni politique, ni économique' ['circumstantial' exile, neither political nor economic], who arrived in France from Bulgaria in 1963, 'à la fin de mes études supérieures, pour y passer une année à "parfaire mon education"' [at the end of my tertiary studies, to 'round off my education'], a quite different discourse of departure from the country of birth and arrival in the country of adoption can be observed from that of the writers we will examine in the following chapters, and indeed from the vast majority of women in exile.[27] In describing his departure from Bulgaria and arrival in France he attests not to a desire or need to break away from limitations at home and to break new ground abroad, but rather refers to the ease with which he was able to recover the sense of belonging left behind:

> Je peux évoquer la facilité que j'ai eue à m'assimiler en France, dans un premier temps, sans craindre de paraître immodeste, car elle n'implique aucun mérite personnel: elle était due, d'une part, à mon milieu familial, qui m'avait amené à faire des études supérieures et à apprendre des langues étrangères; et, d'autre part, au régime politique qui régnait sur mon pays natal et qui a incité tant de mes anciens compatriotes à le fuir.[28]
>
> [I can cite the ease with which I assimilated in France, firstly, without sounding immodest as this implies no personal merit on my part, due to my family

> circumstances which had led me to pursue higher education and to learn
> foreign languages. And secondly, due to the political regime in my country of
> birth which had caused so many of my compatriots to flee.]

Indeed, the home environment is characterised as nurturing and supportive, and any dissonance is attributed to the totalitarian regime in power at the time, and thus an alteration of the standard state of the nation, and not to any inherent sense of alienation from the available ethnic, national, and gender roles available. Where for Todorov displacement was experienced as 'un passage imperceptible de la position de l'*outsider* à celle de l'*insider*' [an imperceptible passage from the position of *outsider* to that of *insider*], indicating a process of recovery of the sense of belonging he had enjoyed prior to displacement, the in-between space of exile is frequently experienced as a liberating locus for women in large part due to the disruption of the association of women with the home and its limitations, and the cultivation of the space of the outsider.[29]

Kaminsky has described exile as a condition that is not unfamiliar to women, and has remarked on the overlap between femininity and exile: 'although both positions are considered deviant, exile and femininity both occur with striking frequency, often in the same place.'[30] The notion of women's alienation from society (even before exile) is indicated by the frequent use of exile as a metaphor for depicting women's relation to the dominant culture. In such a model, androcentric society has historically placed women on the periphery and, as such, alienation has been the inherent quality of women's experience in society. For displaced women, the alienation of exile thus redoubles an already present marginalisation which Ana Vásquez and Ana María Araujo have described as the dual nature of the woman exile's alienation: 'Être femme et exilée politique comporte un double exil, une double lutte, une double recherche de nos identités, une double affirmation de nos différences' [Being a woman and a political exile entails a double exile, a double struggle, a double search for our identity, a double affirmation of our differences].[31] This 'double exile' places women at a greater distance from the centres of power, in an autonomous site of alterity in which historical schemas and conventions can be bypassed or dismantled.

The way in which one positions or accommodates oneself within the interstitial space of exile, between sites of belonging, where the old structures of home are rejected, in turn proves challenging to define and exiled women frequently define themselves in the negative, against who or what they are *not*. Not only does this suggest a radical freedom from existing paradigms and parameters of identity, but also testifies to the basic human compulsion to define identity by differentiation from others. As Roy F. Baumeister explains, the desire to set oneself apart from others and establish one's identity as unique and therefore special is the first of the two main criteria of identity formation, the second being continuity (the unity of the self over time).[32] Despite having suffered many of the experiences of traditional political exile — being threatened by violence, prevented from practising her profession, and facing insurmountable obstacles in her day-to-day life — Mokeddem rejects identification as an exile: 'Je ne me sens pas une exilée; je suis une expatriée!' [I don't feel that I'm an exile, I'm an expatriate!].[33] She thus emphasises her differentiation from others, placing herself outside of the already marginal group of exile, and locates her displaced subjectivity beyond an imposed position commonly used by others to refer to her. These strategies of differentiation and occupation of the margins are also replicated by Huston when she describes herself as 'une fausse Française, une fausse Canadienne, une fausse écrivaine, une fausse professeur d'anglais' [a fake French woman, a fake Canadian (woman), a fake writer, a fake English teacher].[34] Huston emphatically places herself in the in-between when she declares: 'Je ne *subis* pas l'écart, je le *cherche*' [I don't *suffer* the margin, I *seek it out*].[35] She repeatedly defines her identity in terms of what she feels she is not, as each aspect of her identity — French, Canadian, writer, and exile — infringes and encroaches upon the other, preventing her from fully inhabiting any. Huston instead defines herself within a fluid, in-between space; between countries, between languages, and between her public and private roles.

Leaving the Homeland

Place is central to the negotiation of identity, and thus of particular significance for exiles, who are largely defined by their relation to place: both by the separation from the one left behind, and the unfamiliarity with the one in which they arrive. Central to the exile's relation to place is the notion of nation as well as that of home. As a place of belonging from which the exile has been removed and views from a distance, the nation, as much as home, plays a crucial role in the exile's new sense of belonging and the way in which they define their identity in the present. Offering an alternative yet complementary perspective to that of Baumeister on the mechanisms of identification, David C. Gordon demonstrates how an individual *must* identify in some way with those around him or her, and he states accordingly that 'an individual may choose to migrate and adopt a new identity, but still needs a community to sustain a sense of identity'.[36] This notion is particularly pertinent to the exile, who experiences an abrupt change in the community around him or her before and after exile. Given that identity, dependent on differentiation from and identification with others, only exists in society, and that living in society conversely necessitates the development of identity, the exile's case is particularly pronounced as he or she is forced to consider his or her identity and relation to the community at a point where the sense of self may be severely debilitated and destabilised.[37]

For Kaminsky, 'The experience of living within any modern nation state is informed by gender, [and] so is the experience of being cast out of a nation state.'[38] Kaminsky approaches the question of the gendered nature of the exile's relation to the nation by insisting on the need to question women's investment in the notion of a national identity. Claire Lindsay correspondingly highlights the central paradox in women's identification with a national identity: that despite being the ones who reproduce nations biologically, culturally, and symbolically, women have been excluded from fully occupying the national space and comprehensively embodying a national identity.[39] The ways in which women express their identification with a national identity, and whether in fact they should or should not do so given that, historically, they have not enjoyed full access to national citizenship, most certainly differentiates men's and women's experiences of exile, insofar as ideals of national identity have been, and arguably still are, embodied by men.

For women exiles, a sense of national identity may be the first marker of identity to be shed, replaced, or disrupted upon exile. If the women writers of this study do not overtly renounce any sense of national identity in the manner of Peri Rossi,[40] they certainly problematise it in many ways, as has already been seen in the case of Huston, who sees herself as 'une fausse Canadienne'. Siscar's identification with Argentina is, in turn, extremely complex and relies on the re-assignation of the criteria of national identity in order to distinguish between 'Argentines' and 'non-Argentines' — much, in fact, as did the military dictatorship. Siscar describes Argentina, and more particularly Buenos Aires, as 'una extensión de mí misma, un espejo en el que me reconocía y, en cierta forma, el ombligo del mundo' [an extension of myself, a mirror in which I recognised myself, and in a way, the centre of the world], demonstrating a strong sense of identification with the nation.[41] The physiological imagery of her connection to Argentina as an extension of her own body casts the severance of this connection by the military junta as an act of bodily maiming, reflecting dissidents' perception of the military violence as an attack on the national body. The military dictatorship, in turn, used the same logic to expel its undesirables from the nation, as the naming of 'subversives' suggests, characterising them as harmful to an ideal of national identity.[42] In the conflict, each side considered its own image of 'Argentineness' as the true, authentic image, and constituted the other's as a corruption of national identity. This differentiation between a 'true' nation and national identity, and a corrupted idea of nation and national identity enforced by an illegitimate authority, is perhaps the only way that exiles such as Siscar, who were violently cast out of the nation, can reconcile rejection by the nation with a desire to return and re-integrate into the national identity.

Mokeddem's understanding of exile offers a further permutation of the role of the nation in defining exile: 'L'exil, je le définis par rapport à une famille, une tribu, pas par rapport à un térritoire' [I define exile in relation to a family, to a tribe, not in relation to a territory].[43] Mokeddem rejects identification with the nation as the defining characteristic of exile, and redesignates separation from the familial and tribal space as the prime factors, thus overriding the nation and national identification with the personal and familial in the configuration of her displaced identity. Lê, resident in France since her departure from Vietnam at fourteen years of age, also circumvents the nation in her account of her exiled identity, claiming literature as her sole recognised homeland, thus entirely replacing geographical and national identification with identitification in a cultural and intellectual space,[44] much in the same way that Peri Rossi too relocates her site of belonging in writing, as indicated by the title of her recent publication, *Mi casa es la escritura* [My home is writing].[45]

Femininity and Exile

Often overlooked in literary studies due to the 'relentless engendering of expatriation as a masculine phenomenon',[46] the particularities of the processes of female identification as it is negotiated within the space of exile deserve special attention for their divergence from men's experience. Modern literary studies have reserved attention almost exclusively for the masculine position of the subject in exile that celebrates the qualities of solitude, self-sufficiency, and resilience that are associated with breaking away from the familiar, maternal space of origin. Julio C. Raffo's remark that 'El exilio es siempre para un hombre verdaderamente fuerte no una disminución, sino un aumento de sus fuerzas' [For a man who is truly strong, exile is always an increase, not a decrease in his strength], exemplifies the historical blind spots of much critical attention towards the subject in exile.[47] Feminist criticism tends to agree that there exists a particularity to women's experiences of exile which diverges from masculine experiences, as illustrated above by the discussion of women's ties to home and nation. For women exiles, displacement less frequently represents banishment from a place of belonging and securely located identity, of the kind observed above in the case of Todorov. The existence of such a place of originary belonging is less certain for many women exiles, as seen in the disaffected relation of women to the home and nation. The lost home and homeland do not necessarily represent loci of secure locatedness, but sites in which identity was already problematic.

Following wider long-standing androcentric conventions, the model of the solitary exile of Euro-American discourse has generally been presented as male, thus overlooking the ways in which men and women experience exile differently, or else the experience of exile has been thought of in terms of a generic experience based on a masculine model. If it is important to distinguish between different types of exile — political, economic, cultural, intellectual, or other — the same could be said for the distinction between the different ways that exile is experienced by men and women. Just as the conflation of different types of exile obscures the understanding of the psychological and identarian processes at work following experiences of displacement, so too does assuming that men's representations of exile suitably express and account for women's experiences. Janet Wolff points out that all of the writers mentioned in Terry Eagleton's seminal book, *Exiles and Emigrés*, are men, and she highlights one of the ways in which women's displacement differs fundamentally from men's:

> Like the *flâneur*, the [implicitly male] stranger and the wanderer may be able to pass in anonymity; women, however, cannot go into unfamiliar spaces without drawing attention to themselves or without mobilizing those apparently necessary strategies of categorization through which they can be neutralized and rendered harmless. Such strategies range from finding the man to whom they are attached [...] to stigmatizing them as eccentric or non-respectable (because they are unattached and out of place).[48]

Not only must women's experiences be included in discourses of displacement, but they must be examined in their own light, and not under the umbrella of an androcentric model of exiled consciousness that would universally account for experiences of exile. Euro-American literary criticism's heightened interest in discourses of exile is perhaps due to a widespread desire to understand the processes of negotiating the anguishing experience of separation from the familiar and beloved that is inherent to exile and experienced by few, yet which strikes a chord with all. Yet despite widespread interest in the way that exile marks individuals in irreversible ways and draws attention to the ways in which identity is (trans)formed by the experience, criticism has tended to foster a narrow, monolithic view of exiled subjectivity largely defined by the archetypal solitary, male exile.

For, of course, displacement may be a collective experience, particularly when it is the result of political upheaval in the homeland, yet it is often expressed in individualistic terms. Euro-American criticism certainly posits exile as a psychological and aesthetic experience which triggers self-reflection and self-discovery in a predominantly solitary, male subject. This critical tradition conceptualises exile as a profitable experience, where the subject may take advantage of isolation and detachment to see the world and themselves in a new light, providing access to new patterns of thought. Literary criticism's interest in the discursive representation of the processes of exile may be explained by the fact that the production of literature is a singularly individualistic activity, the individual nature of writing fueling a fantasy of the tortured, solitary writer. Whilst this may ring true for some exiled women writers — and Lê and Peri Rossi might certainly be seen as conforming in a number of ways to the masculine stereotype of the tortured, solitary writer, as discussed in Chapter 5 — women exiles frequently foreground collective practices in their writing. This is particularly the case for writers whose texts are politically or didactically driven, as is the case with Restrepo and Mokeddem. These two writers in particular illustrate what Andrew Gurr refers to as 'home-based' identity, where the exiled writer turns their focus to depictions of the home country from which the exile remains separated, or to which he or she has returned, in contrast with those writers whose focus is on the individual's processes of negotiation in the place of exile.[49] Both Restrepo and Mokeddem's novels address the depiction of the injustices and violence of their home countries which sent them into exile, and foreground the potential for change through collective female political mobilisation, as explored in Chapter 4. Where women exiles do represent exile as an individual experience, this is often in terms of the embodied, and thus individual nature of exile which complements exiled women's interest in their relation to the collective social body.

Where, in the androcentric tradition, exile has primarily been regarded as a psychological and aesthetic phenomenon, it has been at the expense of the embodied nature of exile. As an event which is primarily a spatial phenomenon that is experienced through the body and mediated by language, the embodied nature of the experience can hardly be overstated. Few studies have examined exile as a bodily experience which gives rise to the psychic dislocation at the heart of the material processes of exile.[50] Elia Geoffrey Kantaris is one of the few scholars to have looked in depth at the role embodied gender has played in women's experiences of exile. Working in the context of Latin America, Kantaris develops the idea of the relation between the Latin American military dictatorships which sent an unprecedented number of women into exile, and the 'desire to reimpose "traditional" strong Catholic patriarchal values by projecting a system of social organization predicated on naturalized gender stereotypes'.[51] In such a system, Kantaris declares, the Catholic rhetoric of the idealisation of a certain notion of womanhood relied on the covert violation of women's bodies, and as such, women were a, if not the, prime target of the enforcement of the 'traditional' strong patriarchal Catholic values of the military ideology.

The military authority's ideological project reinforced an extreme version of an existing patriarchal social structure, and thus in many ways replicated and augmented an already present strict encoding of gender through the threat of bodily violence on those bodies that did not adhere to these gender ideals. Peri Rossi's early texts illustrate the pre-existing and implicit conservative encoding of gender that was taken up by the military and enforced through the routine violation of non-conforming bodies.[52] In these early texts, women's identity is portrayed as restricted to the traditions of marriage and maternity, and Parizad Tamara Dejbord describes how they portray the body as central to the constraints placed on women:

> En estos textos se subraya el modo en que el cuerpo de la mujer deviene *locus* de su dominación. Vale decir que se señala la manera en que, tradicionalmente, el eje de su dominación, por parte de la sociedad patriarcal, ha sido su cuerpo, el control de su sexualidad y el control de sus funciones de reproducción.[53]
>
> [These texts highlight the way in which a woman's body becomes the site of her domination. They show the way in which, traditionally, the axis of her domination in patriarchal society has been her body, the control of her sexuality and the control of her reproductive functions.]

In later texts such as *Solitario de amor* (analysed in Chapter 5), Peri Rossi furthers her defiance of the strict encoding of gender of her early texts by profoundly disrupting notions of the masculine and the feminine, and positing gender as pluridimensional.[54] Exile is inextricably linked to the encoding of the gendered body for Peri Rossi, both as one of its causes and its effects, and she has consistently reconfigured the conservative gendering that was one of the causes of her exile into the notion of radical gender pluralism that she has developed in the space of exile.

Where Peri Rossi opts for gender pluralism in the embodied expression of exile, Mokeddem posits the hybridity of displacement through the metaphoric imagery of bodily grafting. In Mokeddem's autobiographically referential novel, *L'Interdite* (analysed in Chapter 4), the main character, a nephrologist, treats a (French, male) kidney-transplant patient (recipient of a kidney from an Algerian woman) whom she encounters on her return home to her native Algeria.[55] Through the metaphor of grafting, or transplanting, medical science metonymically performs a transcultural, integrative operation on the metaphorical social body via the physiological individual body.[56] Organ transplants, of course, are a matter of life and death, an implication that is not lost on the author's use of the metaphor of the transplant. In creating a racially and sexually hybrid body through the device of grafting part of a body onto another body, Mokeddem explicitly illustrates the incorporation of the other by both the exile and the receiving country that must necessarily occur in the process of transculturation. In doing so, Mokeddem also re-allocates women's positioning from a socially and bodily marginal space, to a central and vital place in society.

The alienation which women exiles attempt to redress by bringing the exiled female body to the centre of discourse is a remarkably salient aspect of their lives before exile as well as becoming a site for the negotiation of alterity and the reconfiguration of identity in exile. My reading of the six contemporary authors at hand repeatedly comes across the declaration of a sense of alienation in the native country even before departure into exile. These authors attribute this distantiation to vastly different factors, including cultural isolation, political dissidence, non-hegemonic sexuality and gender restrictions. Marina Franco raises the subject of women's expected and actual roles before the departure into exile as having a profound impact on the way in which women react to their new circumstances and relocate themselves afterwards in the unfamiliar location. For Franco, the fact that women, 'culturalmente más obligadas a resolver problemas cotidianos en relación con los hijos, [y] el cuidado de la casa' [culturally, bearing more of the responsibility for resolving day-to-day problems in relation to the children [and] the upkeep of the home], and their tendency to more readily verbalise the difficulties of displacement, are therefore more likely to experience exile in profoundly different ways from men.[57]

Whilst Dejbord and Franco's observations are made in the context of Latin American women, it can equally be said that the conventional social and familial roles assigned to women across a wider geographical and cultural spectrum play an important part in the differing exilic experiences of men and women. Confronted with different moral and social codes, a new language, and with reception in the new country as a 'cultural other', many women have made of displacement an opportunity to adopt new behaviours and roles, that of undertaking writing being a prime example of this.

In experiencing alienation from societies which already cast them into marginality, exiled women are granted access to a new space outside and beyond the symbolic framework which marginalises them. More than simply breaking free of traditional constraints, exiled women are afforded the freedom to create new frameworks, with new meanings and possibilities: by leaving places where roles are allocated and ingrained, women exiles move into spaces where structures are yet to be mapped out, and identity models are open to negotiation. These new meanings and possibilities are, however, not always self-evident, and the space of exile is not a utopian one free of problems or challenges. Vásquez and Araujo describe the experience of Southern Cone women exiled in France who had been active in left-wing militant organisations and political struggle in their home countries.[58] Whilst the sole feat of participating in active political struggle meant breaking the constraints traditionally imposed on women in patriarchal Southern Cone societies, they discovered in exile that the chauvinism at the heart of those societies was reproduced within the revolutionary left-wing organisations in which they were involved. In effect, the struggle of the militant organisations only addressed the domination of one class over another. In order to avoid replicating their own oppression, militant exiled women were forced to rethink their roles in relation to their participation in left-wing militant activity, and distance themselves from the inherent chauvinism of the military organisations with which they were associated. In an interview with Psiche Hughes (published in its English translation), Peri Rossi describes a similar overshadowing of feminism in Latin American by other political struggles:

> Feminism has been problematic in Latin American countries [because of] the priority writers have given to the political struggle, justified by political tyrannies and by the economic crisis which the continent has suffered and is still suffering. This has pushed other struggles, equally justified, in [sic] the background.[59]

The discord between left-wing and feminist activism has not been limited to struggles in Latin America, as Algerian women discovered during and after the war of independence from France: 'Pendant la guerre de libération les femmes croyaient avoir acquis la liberté en prenant les armes. L'indépendance a éveillé un formidable espoir qui s'est rapidement transformé en amère désillusion' [During the war of liberation women believed they had achieved freedom in taking up weapons. Independence awoke in them a great hope which quickly turned into bitter disillusion].[60] Michèle Amzallag's observation testifies to the constant shifting between exclusion and inclusion that women frequently undergo in their social and cultural identities which cautions against the oversimplification of the freedoms and new choices that the space of displacement offers.

Exiled women's writing demonstrates how displacement from fixed places of belonging to the mobile, interstitial space of exile provides women the scope to radically alter their social and cultural identities, whilst giving voice to the problems and obstacles that arise along the way. Separation from long-held family, social, and political roles of the home environment, and integration into re-evaluated roles in the dislocated, disconnected space of exile can be said to have vastly radicalised women's roles. The key questions addressed in this study of exiled women's identity are how this already existing sense of marginalisation affects, firstly, the decision to go into exile, and secondly, the way in which exiled women writers inhabit and live out the experience of exile, as represented discursively in their texts written in exile.

Nomadic Consciousness

A productive approach to these questions is to consider them in light of the paradigm of a nomadic configuration of identity. The heightened alienation of exiled women who already experienced marginalisation from the social order in the home country leads them to seek out and define their identity in new ways that resist previous structures of identity and avoid replicating the original constraints of the society of origin. We can think of women's restructuring of identity and relocation in the power structures that govern social interaction through the lens of the Deleuzian notions of 'deterritorialisation' and 'reterritorialisation'. As Deleuze and Guattari utilise these terms, 'deterritorialisation' is 'the movement by which "one" leaves the territory. It is the operation of the line of flight.' Deterritorialisation 'may be overlaid by a compensatory reterritorialisation obstructing the line of flight', and 'Anything can serve as a reterritorialisation, in other words, "stand for" the lost territory; one can reterritorialise on a being, an object, a book, an apparatus or a system.'[61] Deterritorialised from the birth society, and reterritorialised in a place of alterity in the country of arrival, exiled women are located between polarities in a fluid, interstitial space favourable to the rethinking of women's identity.

Rosi Braidotti offers a useful theoretical model of subjectivity for examining the processes of negotiation of identity at work in exiled women's writing in her notion of 'nomadic consciousness', that turns lack of stability into fluidity, rootlessness into freedom from constraint, and a sense of 'unbelonging' into a belonging of a new order.[62] Braidotti borrows from Deleuze and Guattari's antihierarchical structures, and their criticism of static, binary logic to rethink women's identities and their location in hierarchical power structures. Deleuze and Guattari take the metaphor of fungal 'rhizomes', or thread roots, that can send up new growth anywhere along their length and that are not subject to a centralised control or structure in order to unseat the primacy of static logic that has dominated what has come to be known as 'Western' thinking. According to the characteristics that Deleuze and Guattari enumerate, the rhizome is antihierarchical by virtue of the principles of connection and heterogeneity: any point along the rhizome can (and must) be connected to any other.[63] The rhizome is also organised on the principle of multiplicity: there is no point of centrality or unity in the rhizome, but only multiple lines of connection and movement. The rhizome encourages rupture in its segmentary lines in the form of 'lines of flight' which cut across and flee from the rhizome's own structure: 'There is a rupture in the rhizome whenever segmentary lines explode into a line of flight, but the line of flight is part of the rhizome. These lines always tie back to one another.'[64] A further characteristic, and perhaps the most pertinent one to a configuration of women's identity in the transient, interstitial space of exile, is the rhizome's engagement with the principles of cartography and decalcomania: 'a rhizome is not amenable to any structural or generative model[, i]t is a stranger to any idea of genetic axis or deep structure', where genetic axis and deep structure are associated with the reproducible possibilities of tracings. By suggesting map-making as an alternative to tracing, Deleuze and Guattari offer a way in which the fundamental structures of knowledge can be unseated by modifying the unconscious: 'What distinguishes the map from the tracing is that it is entirely oriented toward an experimentation in contact with the real. The map does not reproduce an unconscious closed in upon itself; it constructs the unconscious.'[65] The map, 'which has to do with performance', brings about the consciousness it maps, rather than replicating existing consciousness as does tracing.[66] Thus Deleuze and Guattari's model of the rhizome as a lateral, non-hierarchical structure rallies against the static, vertical structure of the traditional 'Western' arborescent symbol of knowledge:

> A rhizome has no beginning or end; it is always in the middle, between things, interbeing, *intermezzo*. The tree is filiation, but the rhizome is alliance, uniquely alliance. The tree imposes the verb 'to be', but the fabric of the rhizome is the

conjunction, 'and... and... and...' This conjunction carries enough force to shake and uproot the verb 'to be'.[67]

By operations that follow segmentary 'lines of flight' that depart from pre-existing forms and structures, new ways of thinking can be brought into being, a mechanism which is of particular interest for theorising women's identity in exile.

Braidotti extends the metaphor of the notion of 'rhizomatic thinking', which is lateral, fluid, and dynamic, by highlighting, above all, the mobility inherent to the rhizome which celebrates dynamism and process rather than points of arrival along a line of movement. Deleuze and Guattari's 'interbeing' expresses an idea of a performative and continuous *becoming*, contrary to thinking of identity in terms of *being*, which communicates a sense of arrival at a fixed point of identity. For Braidotti, nomadic consciousness is about locating and maintaining identity in movement, between fixed identities, and between static paradigms of behaviour, thus the significance of the model for exiled women who have distanced themselves not only from the homeland, but from the roles and behaviours assigned to them in the homeland. As Emily Jeremiah points out, while mobility is key, nomadism does not denote actual movement or travel but is a style of thought that resists socially coded modes of thought and behaviour, or as she puts it: 'You don't have to be nomadic to think nomadically, but it helps.'[68] As 'nomads' who no longer occupy their former place in the home society, and who are located in the marginality inherent to the exiled subject, exiled women are in a prime position to relocate and reconfigure their identity within the fluid space of displacement.

It is worthwhile pausing to consider the historical associations of the term 'nomad' to avoid the dilution of meaning or the oversight of historical embeddedness that the use of the nomadic model risks committing. In her essay on exile referred to earlier, Winifred Woodhull draws attention to the need to distinguish between the significance of the term 'nomad' 'in the lives of literal nomads, such as migrant workers, from its meanings in the life and work of expatriate writers on the one hand, and in the work of theorists on the other'.[69] To this I would add the additional need to be mindful of historical nomads, and the similarities and divergences of the situation of these literal nomads with the nomadism of recent exiled women writers. Whilst historical nomads have traditionally occupied sparsely populated, rural, desertic spaces, recent 'nomads' inhabit, and move between, metropolitan spaces of dense and heterogeneous populations. The two constructs of nomadism are further differentiated by the fact that historical nomads share their nomadism with the cultural birth group, whereas for recent 'nomads' this is an acquired characteristic which sets them apart from their cultural birth group. However, both historical and recent constructs of nomadism share a disruptive quality which threatens 'settled' cultures, in that nomads exist outside — both spatially and ideologically — the governing mechanisms of static cultures.[70] Above all, language and 'telling' become paramount for both groups: in the case of historical nomads, in orally perpetuating a tradition in a culture that does not erect or produce material cultural monuments, and for recent nomads, in discursively negotiating and expressing nomadic space.

If the nomad radically rethinks his or her occupation of space, the idea of home is fundamentally altered as a consequence: the nomad altogether reconfigures the notion of what 'home' is. According to John Durham Peters, nomadic consciousness, or nomadism, dispenses with the idea of a fixed home or centre.[71] Nomadism deterritorialises home, and reterritorialises it in a present locus of belonging: the nomad carries their home with them. Whilst the nomad does not entirely do away with the basic human compulsion to seek out a space of belonging, posited by David C. Gordon and referred to earlier, she or he does not seek this space either retrospectively in the original place of belonging that has been lost with displacement, or in a new fixed site that aims to replicate the lost home. Rather, the nomad creates their own new space of belonging within the fluid, mobile space of displacement.

The figure of the nomadic subject has attracted widespread attention across different strands of literary and cultural criticism. The hybrid, multiple, and fragmented subjectivity of the nomad subject has a certain appeal in the current climate of interest in transcultural literatures and identities, in that it shuns limitations imposed by identification around fixed, binary poles of identity. By remaining in constant motion, and avoiding identification along binary oppositions and dualities, the nomadic subject creates new ways in which to define and express his or her identity. Yet despite nomadism's apparent dismantling of historical power relations, it has been charged with overlooking the reality that 'the resources for self-invention are unequally distributed',[72] echoing Wolff's reminder that the 'suggestion of free and equal mobility is itself a deception, since we do not all have the same access to the road'.[73] The privileged nature of nomadic roaming and the casting-off of imposed identities certainly raises the question of who exactly is able to benefit from nomadism's radical repositioning of identity. A number of critics consider Braidotti's identarian flux too seductive, too comfortable, and have identified that the freedoms envisaged by nomadism often overlook the fact that the privilege of mobility only encompasses certain types of mobility, and that privileged mobility also entails the luxury of choosing to stay where one is. Sara Ahmed et al. have warned against, firstly, 'the privileging of movement over "staying put" which masks the potential for grounded homes to be sites of change, as well as 'the romanticization of mobility as travel, transcendence and transformation' which may lead to an overzealous celebration of mobility as detachment and freedom when, of course, it can be a symptom or a consequence of a marked lack of freedom.[74] Mobility may be foisted upon individuals, and particularly women, through conflict, sexual violence, economic dependence, or other factors, and the question of the freedoms enabled by mobility must be considered alongside that of the freedom to 'stay at home'.

Irene Gedalot points to two methodological problems in Braidotti's approach to nomadic subjectivity. Firstly, that in denouncing hierarchical structures, and describing a nonhierarchical identarian model — the nomad — Braidotti commits the crime of hierarchisation herself by privileging the nomad over other figurations of postmodern, cosmopolitan identity. If one of Braidotti's objectives in foregrounding the nomad as a productive figure of identity is in order to account for difference(s) between men and women, and between women themselves, the de-authorisation of other figurations or other subject positions can be seen to run counter to this objective. Gedalot's second objection, one that is shared by a number of critics, is that the transnational fluidity of bodies and identities occurs within spaces governed by the constraints of particular articulations of power, hierarchies, and positionings.[75] For Braidotti, gender is a primary marker of subjectivity and the principal grounds on which to negotiate a sense of self, yet foregrounding gender makes it difficult to fully engage with other markers of identity — ethnicity and nationality to name just two — which come into play to differing degrees. In Gedalot's charge of unexamined elitism, Braidotti's other differences go unnoticed: 'it is so much easier for white westerners to refuse the limits of fixed racial or national identities, when "whiteness" and "western-ness" continue to function as the invisible, unmarked norms that don't seem to fix identity at all'.[76] In failing to adequately address the question of space and the existing power structures within which the nomad has to operate, and which indeed permit or deny access to the status of Braidottian nomadic subject, Braidotti risks falling short of reconciling an individual's choice to no longer regard or define herself according to fixed or existing identity structures, and her power to impose this shift on others — and particularly on state authorities — which will be more or less limited depending on the individual's place of birth, ethnicity, religion, and economic status as well as gender.

We can consider then that Braidotti's approach is problematic in taking as a point of departure her own autobiographical experience as geographically, linguistically, and ideologically displaced, and from there extrapolating to a general theory of subjectivity, where in fact the model of subjectivity developed is rooted in a privileged ethnic, cultural, and economic background. Braidotti nevertheless acknowledges the specificity of her location and speaking position, and is aware of the difficulties nomadic ethics presents, emphasising engagement with difference and with others.[77] Nomadic ethics promotes mindful reflection of one's own situation and thoughtful encounters with others, and it advocates a challenge to fixed structures of thought and behaviour which bring out homogeneity, exclusion, or violence. While travel and physical displacement have been seen to be instrumental in facilitating the ideological freedom that nomadism seeks, material and/or cultural privilege is also key to the development of Braidotti's nomadic subject, and it is through a focus on a 'grounded' or 'situated nomadism' that the nomadic thought adopted in this study, rhizome-like, departs from Braidotti's own strictures to provide a more precise, contextualised model of nomadic subjectivity.

Huston indicates that nomadic writers themselves are not blind to the privilege of the possibility of casting off imposed identities: 'Ceci est l'énoncé d'une privilégiée. Rien de plus facile, en effet, pour une jeune femme intellectuelle que de se déclarer apatride et antipatriotique. Rien de plus tenant que de renvoyer dos à dos toutes les identifications aliénantes' [This is the statement of a privileged woman. Nothing could be easier, in fact, than for a young intellectual woman to declare herself stateless and antipatriotic. Nothing could be more seductive than to dismiss outright all alienating identifications].[78] Huston, and the other writers who form the focus of this book, if not of middle-class origins, have certainly accessed a high level of education (they have universally acceded to postgraduate-level university educations), permitting them a high degree of both social and physical mobility. The conditions that enabled this access to education range from the cultural if not material capital of their familial and social backgrounds, an already evident tendency to subvert the norms for women's behaviour in their respective cultures which limited their activity to essentialised domestic and sexual female roles, and sheer personal tenacity. Braidotti emphasises the active nature of identification through the symbolic system of nomadism that disrupts the passivity of imposed identities and roles. Once again, as for the qualification of exile, we are confronted with the question of choice. Not because women in differing circumstances are faced with different sets of choices should it be hastily assumed that certain choices are less difficult than others: while an economic exile (a permutation of exile not represented by any of these six authors) is certainly subject to a very limited set of choices, we may well ask whether the expectations and restrictions imposed on women of either inherited or acquired middle-class status can be said to be experienced as less difficult. Once again I wish to prioritise differentiation over hierarchisation. While choice is exercised to a greater or lesser extent in the fact and circumstances of displacement, and impacts on the way in which that space of displacement is occupied and identity therein configured, it is of limited usefulness to hierarchise experiences and more productive to examine them in their diversity.

In addressing questions of choice and freedom, Kaplan warns against the blind spots of the application of Deleuze and Guattari's theorisation of power relations in relation to displacement. She cautions that an emphasis on deterritorialisation over reterritorialisation in Euro-American theory means that 'nomadology both raises and suppresses the question of location'.[79] Kaplan calls for greater critical attention to be paid to the factors of location and situation of the critic in order to avoid reproducing the type of neocolonialist gesture that nomadology reacts against. This corresponds to a more historically and geographically specific theorisation of displacement, as referred to in this chapter's introduction, which aims to precisely locate subjects and subjectivities, and to avoid homogenising experiences. By way of resolution, Kaplan echoes Kaminsky's injunction, referred to earlier, that critics 'leave home too': 'First world feminist criticism is struggling to avoid repeating the same imperializing moves that we claim to protest. We must leave home, as it were, since our homes are often sites of racism, sexism, and other damaging social practices.'[80]

With this suggestion, Kaplan anticipates Wolff's flagging-up of another problem associated with nomadism's postmodern deconstruction of grand narratives: 'The problem with an over-enthusiastic embrace of the postmodern is that the same critique undermines the very basis of feminism, itself necessarily a particular narrative.'[81] By dismantling grand narratives, are we not merely formulating new grand narratives to take their place? Kantaris highlights the paradox of defining new spaces for identification that attempt to redress historical exclusion and alienation:

> What has not clearly emerged is how it is possible to define a space whose limits are *not* exclusion and alienation: how is it possible, while partaking inevitably of the symbolic order, to avoid the hierarchies of dominance and possession upon which it relies?[82]

This paradox reinforces the urgency of maintaining an attentiveness to location and positionality in line with Kaplan's historical and geographical specificity, and of emulating McClennen's sensitivity to the relation between actual, individual cases of exile and theoretical discourses of exile.

How then can texts be said to express a nomadic consciousness, and to what purpose? Valérie Orlando offers the suggestion that 'the nomadic novel posits identity in a third space of negotiation' beyond polar identity components, a space which promotes decentred, fragmented subjectivities shaped by their trajectories through spaces.[83] Orlando promotes this as a particularly effective identarian strategy for North African Francophone women writers who inhabit various, often incompatible, spheres of identity. Orlando quite clearly champions nomadic subjectivity as a liberating strategy that leads to new modes of existence for women who have experienced difficulty, if not downright danger, in their inhabitation of traditional spaces of identity. Christopher L. Miller, on the other hand, has criticised theorists for adopting nomadology as an ideology rather than using it as a tool for analysis. In particular, he criticises Françoise Lionnet's rhetoric in her reading of a number of nomadic authors. Charging her with reinforcing the binary logic and dialectical thought that nomadology aims to disrupt through advocating it as a strategy for women's configuration of identity, he states: 'The task of the critic is to maintain inasmuch as it is possible a visible distinction between description and prescription, and therefore to describe what one has read without projecting desiderata into it.'[84]

Miller's critique of the way in which nomadology has been applied as a critical tool raises questions of the critic's supposed objectivity, and the importance of situating the theorist in relation to their object of study, as Kaplan emphasises. Given the fact that many of the theorists of nomadism are themselves displaced women, the question is raised of whether objectivity is either possible or desirable. Vásquez and Araujo address the question of authority and voice in their research on Latin American exiles in France, declaring their positioning on both sides of the critical divide (as both theorists and Latin American women exiles in France) as key to their understanding and analysis of their subject. Presenting both the advantages and disadvantages of their insider/outsider status, they vouch for their privileged position from which to understand and investigate the processes of identity for Latin American women living in exile in France. In accord with recent feminist theory, Wolff argues that 'the separation of the academic and the personal is not only artificial, but also damaging', and gives the experience of Alice Kaplan as an example of the merging of academic with personal experience to illustrate the difficult dissociation of academic, intellectual concerns from personal, subjective ones.[85]

If we are to analyse texts of displacement whilst bearing in mind our own positionality in relation to the texts at hand, such supposed critical anonymity, in the name of objectivity, poses more problems that it seeks to resolve. In this regard, reconnecting, or at least recognising the link between the theoretical and the subjective is in itself a feminist approach in tune with nomadism. In accordance, Braidotti describes 'the mixture of speaking voices or modes' as a related feature of the nomadic style and indeed her own writing, and declares this a deliberate tactic to 'mix the theoretical with the poetic or lyrical mode',[86] and urges that it is 'important for feminists to break away from the patterns of masculine identification that high theory demands, to step out of the paralyzing structures of an exclusive academic style'.[87] Braidotti's claim to 'fictionalize [her] theories, theorize [her] fictions' resonates in profound ways with the texts of the six writers who form the focus of this book, and anticipates the way in which their texts exhibit a literary nomadism of their own, as explored in the next chapter.[88]

This study posits the notion of nomadic consciousness as prevalent in contemporary women's exile writing from across a spectrum of different national, cultural, and social backgrounds. In demonstrating a nomadic reading of these texts to be a fruitful approach, it also confronts the problems that I have referred to concerning the adoption of nomadism as a paradigm for exiled female subjectivity: the problematic intellectual elitism of nomadic consciousness for which Braidotti is often criticised; the neocolonialism of nomadology; and nomadism's emphasis on deterritorialisation at the expense of attention to reterritorialisation. Mindful of the questions of who is speaking when nomadology is promoted, and who is the object of nomadism's discourse, the textual analyses undertaken here demonstrate that reading women's narratives of exile through the paradigm of nomadic consciousness provides valuable insight into the processes of negotiation of women's subjectivity in exile.

Notes to Chapter 1

1. Caren Kaplan, 'Questions of Travel: An Introduction', in *Questions of Travel: Postmodern Discourses of Displacement* (Durham, NC, and London: Duke University Press, 1996), pp. 1–26.
2. James Clifford, 'Diasporas', in *The Ethnicity Reader*, ed. by Montserrat Guibernau and John Rex (Cambridge: Polity, 1997), pp. 283–90.
3. Winifred Woodhull, 'Exile', in *Transfigurations of the Maghreb: Feminism, Decolonization, and Literatures* (Minneapolis and London: University of Minnesota Press, 1993), pp. 88–133.
4. Kaplan, *Questions of Travel*, p. 26.
5. See Terry Eagleton, *Exile and Emigrés: Studies in Modern Literature* (London: Chatto and Windus, 1970).
6. Amy K. Kaminsky, *After Exile: Writing the Latin American Diaspora* (Minneapolis and London: University of Minnesota Press, 1999), p. xi.
7. See the Introduction to Marina Franco, *El exilio: Argentinos en Francia durante la dictadura* (Buenos Aires: Siglo Ventiuno, 2008), pp. 17–32.
8. Sophia McClennen, *The Dialectics of Exile: Nation, Time, Language and Space in Hispanic Literatures* (West Lafayette, IN: Purdue University Press, 2004), p. 1.
9. Franco, pp. 19–20.
10. Franco, p. 290.
11. Nancy Huston, 'En français dans le texte', in *Désirs et réalités: Textes choisis 1978–1994* (Paris: Babel, 1995), pp. 263–69 (p. 264).
12. Nancy Huston and Leïla Sebbar, *Lettres parisiennes: Histoires d'exil* (Paris: J'ai lu, 1999), p. 90 (original italics). Originally published as *Lettres parisiennes: Autopsie de l'exil* (Paris: Barrault, 1986), the change in the subtitle suggests a subjective shift from the uncertainty and questioning of the investigative 'autopsy', to the more assured, narrative tone of 'stories'. All citations and references to *Lettres parisiennes* throughout refer to the 1999 edition.
13. Huston, *Lettres parisiennes*, p. 22.
14. In a conversation with Siscar conducted in Buenos Aires (March 2009), NB Siscar's emphatic repetition of 'yo no sentía culpa' (my italics).

15. In an interview with Kate Averis, 'La casa de la escritura: Entrevista con Cristina Siscar' (Buenos Aires, March 2009), <http://www.igrs.sas.ac.uk/centre-study-contemporary-womens-writing/languages/catalan-galician-spanish/cristina-siscar> [accessed 23 January 2014].
16. Jean Déjeux, *La Littérature féminine de langue française au Maghreb* (Paris: Karthala, 1994), p. 211.
17. Gonzalo Aguilar, 'Prólogo para un ensayo sobre el exilio', in *Travesías de la escritura en la literatura latinoamericana: Actas de las X Jornadas de Investigación* (Buenos Aires: Instituto de Literatura Hispanoamericana, 1995), pp. 179–89 (p. 187).
18. Mario Benedetti, *El desexilio y otras conjeturas* (Madrid: El País, 1984).
19. In an interview with Jaime Manrique, 'Entrevista con Laura Restrepo', in *El universo literario de Laura Restrepo*, ed. by Elvira Sánchez-Blake and Julie Lirot (Bogotá: Alfaguara, 2007), pp. 353–67 (pp. 360–61).
20. In an interview with Yolande Aline Helm, 'Entretien avec Malika Mokeddem', in *Malika Mokeddem: Envers et contre tout*, ed. by Yolande Aline Helm (Paris: L'Harmattan, 2000), pp. 39–51 (p. 50).
21. See Kaminsky, 'After Exile', in *After Exile*, pp. 1–21.
22. Huston's mother's departure to the USA, then Spain, and then England is recounted in Huston, *Lettres parisiennes*, p. 55, and in Huston, 'En français dans le texte', in *Désirs et réalités*, pp. 263–69.
23. See Linda Lê, *Les Trois parques* (Paris: Christian Bourgois, 1997); *Voix: une crise* (Paris: Christian Bourgois, 1998); and *Lettre morte* (Paris: Christian Bourgois, 1999).
24. Malika Mokeddem, *La Transe des insoumis* (Paris: Grasset, 2003).
25. Amy K. Kaminsky, *Reading the Body Politic: Feminist Criticism and Latin American Women Writers* (Minneapolis and London: University of Minnesota Press, 1993), p. 29.
26. Janet Wolff, *Resident Alien: Feminist Cultural Criticism* (New Haven: Yale University Press; Cambridge: Polity, 1995), p. 2.
27. Tzvetan Todorov, *L'Homme dépaysé* (Paris: Seuil, 1996), p. 13.
28. Todorov, p. 24.
29. Todorov, p. 14.
30. Kaminsky, *Reading*, p. 29.
31. Ana Vásquez and Ana María Araujo, *Exils latino-américains: La malédiction d'Ulysse* (Paris: L'Harmattan, 1988), p. 129.
32. See Roy F. Baumeister, 'Basic Conceptual Issues', in *Identity: Cultural Change and the Struggle for Self* (Oxford: Oxford University Press, 1986), pp. 11–28.
33. Christiane Chaulet-Achour and Lalia Kerfa, 'Portrait de Malika Mokeddem', in *Malika Mokeddem: Envers et contre tout*, ed. by Yolande Aline Helm (Paris: L'Harmattan, 2000), pp. 21–34 (p. 32).
34. Huston, *Lettres parisiennes*, p. 101.
35. Huston, *Lettres parisiennes*, p. 210 (original italics).
36. David C. Gordon, *The French Language and National Identity (1930–1975)* (The Hague: Mouton, 1978), p. 13.
37. For further information on the way in which identity is defined and organised by society, see Baumeister, 'Introduction', in *Identity*, pp. 3–10.
38. Amy K. Kaminsky, 'Gender and Exile in Cristina Peri Rossi', in *Continental, Latin American and Francophone Writers: Selected Papers from the Wichita State University Conference on Foreign Literature 1984–1985*, ed. by Eunice Myers and Ginette Adamson (Lanham, MD: University Press of America, 1987), pp. 149–59 (p. 150).
39. Claire Lindsay, see the 'Introduction' to *Locating Latin American Women Writers* (New York: Peter Lang, 2003), pp. 1–18.
40. See Lindsay, *Locating*, p. 29.
41. In an interview with Jorge Boccanera, 'Entrevista con Cristina Siscar: "Yo conocí los dos exilios"', in *Tierra que anda: Los escritores en el exilio* (Buenos Aires: Ameghino, 1999), pp. 51–61 (p. 59).
42. For an insightful discussion of the way in which Argentina's military dictatorship was essentially a staging of conflicting visions of national identity see Diana Taylor, 'Military Males, "Bad" Women, and a Dirty, Dirty War', in *Disappearing Acts: Spectacles of Gender and Nationalism in Argentina's 'Dirty War'* (Durham, NC, and London: Duke University Press, 1997), pp. 59–89.

43. Chaulet-Achour and Kerfa, p. 32.
44. Catherine Argand, 'Entretien avec Linda Lê', in *Lire* (April 1999), <http://www.lexpress.fr/culture/livre/linda-le_803102.html> [accessed 23 January 2014].
45. Cristina Peri Rossi, *Mi casa es la escritura: antología poética* (Montevideo: Linardi y Risso, 2006).
46. Kaplan, *Questions of Travel*, p. 45.
47. Julio C. Raffo, *Meditación del exilio* (Buenos Aires: Nueva América, 1985), pp. 2–3.
48. Wolff, p. 8.
49. Andrew Gurr, *Writers in Exile: The Identity of Home in Modern Literature* (Brighton: Harvester, 1981), p. 9.
50. Such as Kaminsky, *Reading*, and Elia Geoffrey Kantaris, *The Subversive Psyche: Contemporary Women's Narrative from Argentina and Uruguay* (Oxford: Clarendon, 1995).
51. Kantaris, *Subversive Psyche*, p. 19.
52. See Cristina Peri Rossi, *Los museos abandonados* (Montevideo: Arca, 1969); *El libro de mis primos* (Montevideo: Biblioteca de Marcha, 1969); *Indicios pánicos* (Montevideo: Nuestra América, 1970); *La tarde del dinosaurio* (Barcelona: Planeta, 1976); *La rebelión de los niños* (Barcelona: Seix Barral, 1980).
53. Parizad Tamara Dejbord, *Cristina Peri Rossi: Escritora del exilio* (Buenos Aires: Galerna, 1998), p. 112.
54. Cristina Peri Rossi, *Solitario de amor*, 2nd edn (Barcelona: Lumen, 1998) [first edition: 1986]. See also the more recent short stories anthologised in *Cuentos reunidos* (Barcelona: Lumen, 2007): 'Fetichistas S.A.' (pp. 603–14); 'Una consulta delicada' (pp. 658–70); 'Extrañas circunstancias' (pp. 671–81); and 'Entrevista con el Angel', (pp. 690–97).
55. Malika Mokeddem, *L'Interdite* (Paris: Grasset, 1993).
56. I use the term 'transcultural' in the sense established in 1940 by the Cuban anthropologist Fernando Ortiz in *Cuban Counterpoint: Tobacco and Sugar*, trans. by Harriet de Onís (Durham, NC: Duke University Press, 1995 [1947]) and taken up by Mary Louise Pratt in her *Imperial Eyes: Travel Writing and Transculturation* (London: Routledge, 1992). Ortiz described the cultural encounter between the Spanish and the indigenous Americans during the colonisation of central and south America as a process of 'transculturation', whereby both the invading, as well as the invaded culture absorbs and normalises aspects of the other culture, transforming both, and resulting in a new homogenised culture.
57. Franco, p. 64.
58. See Vásquez and Araujo, pp. 142–43.
59. Psiche Hughes, 'Interview with Cristina Peri Rossi', in *Unheard Words: Women and Literature in Africa, the Arab World, Asia, the Caribbean and Latin America*, ed. by Mineke Schipper, trans. by Barbara Potter Fasting (London: Allison and Busby, 1985), pp. 255–74 (p. 260).
60. Michèle Amzallag, quoted in Chaulet-Achour and Kerfa, p. 25. This observation is echoed in conclusions reached by Danièle Djamila Amrane-Minne in 'Women and Politics in Algeria from the War of Independence to Our Day', in *Research in African Literatures*, 30.3, Special Edition: 'Dissident Algeria' (1999), 62–77.
61. Gilles Deleuze and Félix Guattari, *A Thousand Plateaus: Capitalism and Schizophrenia*, trans. by Brian Massumi (New York: Continuum, 1987) [first edition: 1980], pp. 559–60.
62. Rosi Braidotti, *Nomadic Subjects: Embodiment and Sexual Difference in Contemporary Feminist Theory* (New York: Columbia University Press, 1994)
63. Deleuze and Guattari, see 'Introduction: Rhizome', in *A Thousand Plateaus*, pp. 3–28.
64. Deleuze and Guattari, *A Thousand Plateaus*, p. 10.
65. Deleuze and Guattari, *A Thousand Plateaus*, p. 13.
66. Deleuze and Guattari, *A Thousand Plateaus*, p. 14.
67. Deleuze and Guattari, *A Thousand Plateaus*, p. 27 (original italics).
68. Emily Jeremiah, *Nomadic Ethics in Contemporary Women's Writing in German: Strange Subjects* (Rochester, NY: Camden House, 2012), p. 3.
69. Woodhull, p. 89.
70. For a detailed discussion of the way in which the nomad, 'the Deterritorialized par excellence' according to Deleuze and Guattari (*A Thousand Plateaus*, p. 421), circumvents and threatens the authority of the State by reterritorialising on/in deterritorialisation itself, see Deleuze and

Guattari, '1227: Treatise on Nomadology — The War Machine', in *A Thousand Plateaus*, pp. 387–467.
71. John Durham Peters, 'Exile, Nomadism and Diaspora: The Stakes of Mobility in the Western Canon', in *Home, Exile, Homeland: Film, Media, and the Politics of Place*, ed. by Hamid Naficy (London and New York: Routledge, 1999), pp. 17–41.
72. Peters, p. 34.
73. Wolff, p. 128.
74. Sara Ahmed, Claudia Castañeda, Anne-Marie Fortier and Mimi Sheller, *Uprootings/Regroundings: Questions of Home and Migration* (Oxford and New York: Berg, 2003), p. 1.
75. See also Elizabeth Boa and Rachel Paltreyman, *Heimat — A German Dream: Regional Loyalties and National Identity in German Culture 1890–1990* (Oxford: Oxford University Press, 2000), pp. 204–05; Gisela Brinker-Gabler, 'Exile, Immigrant, Re/Unified: Writing (East) Postunification Identity in Germany', in *Writing New Identities: Gender, Nation and Immigration in Contemporary Europe*, ed. by Gisela Brinker-Gabler and Sidonie Smith (Minneapolis and London: University of Minnesota Press, 1997), pp. 264–92.
76. Irene Gedalot, 'Can Nomads Learn to Count to Four? Rosi Braidotti and the Space for Difference in Feminist Theory', *Women: A Cultural Review*, 7.2 (Autumn 1996), 189–201 (p. 193).
77. Braidotti, p. 32.
78. Huston, *Désirs et réalités*, p. 201.
79. Caren Kaplan, 'Deterritorializations: The Rewriting of Home and Exile in Western Feminist Discourse', in *Cultural Critique*, 6 (1987), 187–98 (p. 91).
80. Kaplan, 'Deterritorializations', p. 194.
81. Wolff, p. 128.
82. Elia Geoffrey Kantaris, 'The Politics of Desire: Alienation and Identity in the Work of Marta Traba and Cristina Peri Rossi', in *Forum for Modern Language Studies*, 25 (1989), 248–64 (p. 260).
83. Valérie Orlando, 'To Be Singularly Nomadic or a Territorialized National: At the Crossroads of Francophone Women's Writing of the Maghreb', in *Meridians: Feminism, Race, Transnationalism*, 6.2 (2006), 33–53 (p. 34).
84. Christopher L. Miller, *Nationalists and Nomads: Essays on Francophone African Literature and Culture* (Chicago and London: University of Chicago Press, 1998), p. 7.
85. Wolff, p. 15.
86. Braidotti, p. 37.
87. Braidotti, p. 29.
88. Braidotti, p. 37.

CHAPTER 2

Writing (in) Exile: Six Contemporary Women Writers

This chapter develops the discussion of the negotiation of women's subjectivity in exile by exploring the role of language and the significance of the act of writing for exiled women writers in order to demonstrate both the nomadism of exiled women's discursive configuration of identity, and the literary nomadism of exiled women's generically hybrid texts, as well as giving biographical information on each of the authors. Insofar as the texts that constitute the object of analysis here are read in terms of their authors' nomadic consciousness, which stems from their experience of exile, contextual information of each author's circumstances of exile is considered key to the identarian concerns at stake for three principal reasons: firstly, in order to contextualise their experiences within a wider cultural and historical context; secondly, to identify how their texts are inflected by their own biographical experiences; and thirdly, in order to situate each of the six writers' experiences in relation to one other.

Critical consensus agrees on a preference for contextualisation over the freestanding text as a feminist reading strategy as Amy K. Kaminsky contends when she states that 'as a feminist reader for whom the text is always contextual, it is vital to be able to place the author'.[1] Valérie Orlando outlines a similar methodological approach in her study of exiled Francophone Maghrebi women authors, highlighting the loss of meaning that occurs in the absence of historical, cultural, and political context, when she declares her 'wish to offer a cogent historico-cultural background as well as a critical analysis of each literary work studied. These novels cannot be considered without also situating historic, cultural, and political parameters of the author's space.'[2] Following the examples of Kaminsky and Orlando, I too adopt a contextual methodology of reading the texts of these six exiled women in order to draw out the specificity of each case and the differences between them. My reading of these texts is made more meaningful by an awareness of their authors' biographies: neither individuals nor texts are located in a cultural vacuum, and it is an understanding of the contextual grounding of these texts which allows the reader to examine the ways in which they are informed by the key transformative event at stake in this investigation: that of the experience of exile. To speak of 'exiled women's writing', or of an 'exiled woman writer', with the extratextual knowledge of an author's experience of exile is to approach a text's themes (such as displacement, mobility, language, and marginality) and forms (such as hybridity, autoreferentiality, testimony, and denunciation) in view of their cultural and historical specificity. The generic nomadism of exiled women's writing (explored in detail below), which is characterised by generic hybridity and is highly conscious of itself as a discursive construct, is key to the way in which exiled women express their own nomadic subjectivity. This merging is reflected in the notion of the inter-relatedness of writing in, and of, exile as expressed in this chapter's title. For these six contemporary women writers, text and biography are inextricably linked, as to 'write in exile' is to 'write exile', although these events may or may not occur contemporaneously as indicated by the observation, further developed in the next chapter, that Siscar wrote her two key exile texts during, and more than a decade after her return from exile.

Reading texts in light of the authors' personal experiences of displacement therefore necessitates enquiring into their biographies, and the motivations and circumstances of their movement from the birth culture to a new one. This is not so as to seek out autobiographical traces in their texts (although these often become apparent and certainly lead to valuable insights) but in order to consider the author's actual story of displacement alongside reading the fictional works which present the challenges and difficulties of the experience in literary form. My approach here is to analyse the *texts* in light of the concept of exile rather than analysing *the lives of the authors themselves*, in what could be articulated in terms of a distinction between a biographical, and an autobiographical reading of texts. Where an autobiographical reading may seek to find links, and draw out connections between an author's lived experience and his or her fictional accounts, a biographical reading, such as I undertake here, places the authors' experience of exile as the prime condition for analysis without superimposing their biographies onto the actions of their protagonists. What is at stake, then, is the analysis of the particular ways in which women's experience of displacement sheds light on textual content and discursive strategies, and the processes of women's identity configuration during and following the experience.

Writers may, however, encourage an autobiographical reading of their fiction in a variety of ways: Mokeddem creates fictional protagonists who overwhelmingly, yet not entirely, resemble the author herself; Lê entices the reader with recurring fictional themes and motifs drawn from her own past; and Huston's non-fictional writing complements and provides a commentary on her fictional works. Typically hybrid, Huston's writing project is entirely tied up with her displacement, and her texts themselves confound boundaries between fiction and non-fiction, between fictional 'subjectivity' and non-fictional 'objectivity':

> dans tous mes essais [...] loin d'adopter un ton universitaire aux visées sévèrement scientifiques, j'essaie de parler de façon personnelle [...] Il y a nettement plus d'autobiographie dans mes essais que dans mes romans! [...] Le *je* que j'employais dans mes essais [est] totalement nu et intime, sans protection aucune.[3]

> [in all my essays [...] far from adopting an academic tone with strictly scientific ambitions, I try to use a personal tone [...] There is far more autobiography in my essays that in my novels! [...] The *I* that I have used in my essays [is] entirely naked and intimate, without any protection.]

Huston's claim here echoes Rosi Braidotti's strategy of the merging of theory and fiction, as discussed in Chapter 1. The claimed autobiographical reliability of Huston's non-fictional essays is simultaneously an example of the conscious hybridity of exiled women's writing and a warning against any attempt to impose an autobiographical reading on her fictional works. Her injunctions on how her texts are to be read constitute, in themselves, a commentary on the supposed links between non-fiction and objectivity, and fiction and subjectivity. Huston problematises these associations through the assertion of a 'reliable I' in her essays that posits her non-fictional writing as inherently more subjective than her fiction, in that it does not wear the mask of invention, albeit positing a 'reliable I' that is more closely related to the authorial persona, than being reliable *per se*. Indeed, the instability of many of the claims made by Huston in her putatively subjective non-fiction might well be considered in light of the fact of Roland Barthes's tutelage at the École des Hautes Études en Sciences Sociales in Paris, under whose supervision she completed her Masters dissertation.[4] Huston's frequent use of highly authoritative narrators and commandeering authorial personas points to the presence in her texts of Barthes's thinking on the roles of the author and the reader in the act of reading, and the production of meaning in the text by enacting the tension between the participation of the implicit author and that of the reader in the creation of meaning in the text. The generic fusion of objectivity and subjectivity operating in and across Huston's hybrid works is replicated in the fictional works of Siscar. Siscar's texts are also haunted by an autobiographical authorial persona, despite the vastly different circumstances of writing and experiences of exile which distinguish the two authors.

In addition to generic hybridity, these two writers' works can be said to demonstrate a common linguistic hybridity as a result of the shifting between the native and the acquired language that characterises their exiles. Language and the linguistic shift are fundamental to the experience of exile, and the daily migration from one language to another is frequently a salient theme of exiled women's lives as well as their writing, and is likewise a theme which concerns all six authors of this study. Even where exiles move between places which share the same language — as is the case of Restrepo and Peri Rossi — linguistic differences nevertheless constitute a definitive marker of identity, and their writing is characterised by an extreme linguistic sensibility. Braidotti's description of language as 'the ultimate prosthesis' aptly posits language as the nomadic medium *par excellence*.[5] Insofar as language is formative and deterministic — an individual's world-view is constructed by and alongside the acquisition of language — the adoption of a new language, and the concurrent distantiation from the native language allows for a shift in that individual's world-view that I refer to here as a 'linguistic shift'. Such linguistic mobility leads Braidotti to state that, 'The polyglot is a linguistic nomad',[6] which, she cautions, is not to say that all multilingual people are automatically endowed with nomadic consciousness, but that linguistic plurality fosters the kind of awareness of an 'outside' to language and community that Edward Said evokes when he states, '[w]e take home and language for granted; they become nature, and their underlying assumptions recede into dogma and orthodoxy',[7] or as Mary

Besemeres expresses it, 'to the native speaker not confronted with another language the limits of his or her language, the ways in which it constitutes reality, remain invisible.'[8] The disruption of the myth of the 'naturality' of a single language and site of belonging by the event of both spatial and/or linguistic displacement brings about an awareness of the apparent symbiosis between location and belonging. Recognition of the myth upon the departure from home and the consequent disintegration of the exclusivity of the native language unsurprisingly coincide with the disruption of this apparent symbiosis. As Besemeres observes, 'This bond to one's native language becomes apparent to a person only when it is being replaced by another language',[9] shifting the displaced subject into multiple partial sites of belonging, with only a retrospective sense of the (real or imagined) easy coincidence of language, community, identity, and belonging.

Situations of linguistic displacement may be defined by different characteristics and features, but all have a profound effect on the lived experience of displacement. Kaminsky notes the particular implications of linguistic shift for the exile, identifying three different linguistic resonances in exile: i) where languages are completely unfamiliar; ii) where languages are familiar but still foreign; and iii) where language is the same but unfamiliar.[10] Kaminsky's theorisation of the linguistic challenges for the exile resonates strongly with the different linguistic situations of the six writers at hand and can be applied to all of their varying experiences of linguistic mobility. The schematisation of the subtle variances of linguistic shift for the exile are succinctly captured in Kaminsky's three categories, and indeed subtends my analysis of exiled women's use of language.

Nancy Huston, Cristina Siscar, and the Linguistic Shift

Nancy Huston was born in anglophone Canada in 1953. After having spent her childhood in Alberta and her adolescence in Boston, Huston went to Paris with some knowledge of French at the age of twenty as part of her programme of university studies. Arriving in Paris in 1973, after 'une enfance instable, marquée par des déménagements fréquents',[11] she soon entered into Parisian feminist, literary and cultural circles, publishing her first work, in French, in 1979.[12] Huston has since remained in France, where she has now spent the greater part of her life. Huston's encounter with the French language is accounted for by Kaminsky's second scenario, where the language encountered is familiar but still foreign: the Canadian author already had a degree of fluency in French before arriving in France, yet French was, and still remains after more than half a lifetime spent in France, a foreign language (unlike the other two Francophone authors of this study, as discussed below). Inspired by her own migration from North America to France, Huston has consistently explored the concerns associated with the experience of uprooting oneself from the birth country and constructing a new life in an adopted country and language in both her fictional and non-fictional texts. Huston still perceives the reaction of native speakers of French to her not-quite-native French as constituting a mechanism of exclusion which reinforces her 'non-belonging' to the linguistic community of French. Yet she celebrates, at the same time, the linguistic outsider status that offers her a critical distance and freedom of expression that English, as her mother tongue, does not. Another particular concern to her has been the reconciliation of what she considers to be the conflicting aspects of her identity, in particular the roles of mother and writer-creator, and what she refers to as the 'mind–body problem'.[13] Huston discursively investigates the processes of her insertion into the adopted culture, reflecting on how her cultural and linguistic identity is manifested in her writing, and how this impacts on her position within the French literary canon. As her writing has evolved, Huston has persistently revisited and revised the relations between the different aspects of her identity: as French, as Canadian, as a woman writer, and as an exile. An investigation of the development of Huston's ideological and aesthetic pronouncements throughout her prodigious corpus is illuminated by the extratextual knowledge of her personal circumstances and sheds light on the particularity of her negotiation of identity in exile.

In contrast to Huston, Siscar (born in Buenos Aires is 1947) went into exile in 1979 at the peak of the military dictatorship in Argentina which lasted from 1976 to 1983. Although from a middle-class family of modest means with little if any access to books in the family home, Siscar demonstrated a keen interest in literature as a secondary school student, and began writing poetry from an early age. After qualifying as a secondary school literature teacher, she practised her profession alongside studying for a degree in Education at the Universidad de Buenos Aires (UBA). Her university studies were, however, interrupted by political interventions at the UBA in the years immediately preceding the military coup. She nevertheless continued to write poetry, and also began to practise journalism, writing articles on books and culture for various newspapers in Buenos Aires. In the early 1970s, Siscar became politically active in militant Marxist circles that opposed the economic inequality and the increasingly oppressive atmosphere that would be exacerbated under military rule after the *coup d'état* in 1976. Under what was euphemistically referred to as the 'Proceso de Reorganización Nacional' [Process of National Reorganisation], 'The military promoted an image of the "authentic national being" and demanded that the population feel "Argentine" by identifying with their performance of national identity.'[14] In such a political and cultural climate where those who deviated from the military's national ideal were routinely eliminated from the social body, and at the peak of her activism in 1977, Siscar's husband was kidnapped and disappeared by the military, as were her sister and brother-in-law (her apartment having already been ransacked by the police in 1975 in the climate of persecution leading up to the dictatorship). Despite the clear threat of danger to Siscar herself under the regime which targeted and disappeared 'subversive' individuals through and because of their association with other 'subversives', she remained in Buenos Aires until 1979, reluctant to go into exile without her young son.[15] In 1979 she eventually went into exile (leaving her son with her parents in Buenos Aires) in a first instance to Brazil yet, driven on by the Brazilian government's complicity with the Argentine military government's persecution of its political dissidents, she sought refugee status with the UN in Brazil in order to secure her passage to Paris, where she remained in exile until

1986. In Paris Siscar continued to write, publishing her first volume of poetry there, before returning to Buenos Aires in 1986, where she has since lived and published narrative fiction, essays, and journalism.

Siscar's linguistic situation is unique among the six writers who form the object of this study, in that she arrived in France with very little knowledge of French, and while she acquired the new language during the six years spent in exile in Paris, she has only ever published works written in her native tongue. The only author of the six at hand to have experienced the necessary acquisition of an entirely unfamiliar language in exile, Siscar can be accounted for by Kaminsky's first linguistic scenario in which the language encountered was completely unknown. Kaminsky describes the psychological and physical disorientation that arises in this scenario, and that is more profound than the more obvious initial difficulties of daily interaction and integration:

> To be set down in a place where the language is unfamiliar is to be returned to a state of dependency and to be perceived as intellectually incompetent. This extreme shift in social status occurs simultaneously with the sense of physical dislocation to which it is connected.[16]

Siscar's texts make this sense of extreme disorientation apparent, and present her adherence to the mother tongue in her writing, and the recourse to the narrative device of alternative, non-verbal forms of communication as strategies through which to counter this profound linguistic unfamiliarity. For Huston, on the other hand, the acquisition of a new language was instrumental to her entry to writing, and her use of French as a non-native speaker is central to her writing project. The fact that Siscar never contemplated writing in French, as is clear when she states 'yo nunca pensé en escribir en otra lengua que no fuera la mía, ya me parecía demasiado arduo tratar de escribir en la mía, encontrar lo que yo buscaba en la mía' [I never thought of writing in a language other than my own, it already seemed terribly arduous to write in my own, and to find what I was looking for in my own] indicates that exile was, for Siscar, more a political and social phenomenon than the linguistic and cultural event that it represented for Huston.[17]

If their biographies are vastly different, so too are their bibliographies, with the extremely prolific Huston having published over forty works in as many years in Paris, in equal parts fictional and non-fictional, ranging from essays to novels, children's fiction, theatre, correspondence, and more recently, to collaborative works which combine image and text. Siscar's bibliography consists of eight published works in a range of genres, including short stories, poetry, children's fiction, essays, and a novel, in addition to which she has edited anthologies of poetry and short stories.[18] The ongoing presence of a discourse of nomadic wandering in Siscar's most recent works suggests the profound and enduring ways in which she is still marked by her exile nearly three decades after her return to Buenos Aires. Where Siscar's fiction is haunted by the violence of the past and the reasons behind her displacement, as the resurgence of memory in her texts illustrates, Huston's writing is more focused on the exile's articulation of a split subjectivity in the present, and how this is perceived by others. The theme of the identarian processes of the displaced, in-between subject is perhaps *the* principal concern of Huston's corpus of both fictional and non-fictional texts. Huston has created a multitude of geographically, culturally, and existentially displaced characters who anchor their sense of identity in the fluidity of in-between spaces. Notably, Huston is yet to write a fictional work which depicts her own displacement from Canada to France, although this has been widely documented in her non-fictional writings. The reasons for this are worth reflecting upon in light of Huston's claim for the reliability of her non-fictional 'I': such an absence in her fictional corpus implicitly suggests that, discretely and in isolation, fiction, non-fiction and the middle ground of autobiography provide insufficient scope for the exploration and expression of the exiled author's renegotiation of identity, and thus postulates a necessary recourse to generic hybridity and the complementarity of 'subjective' and 'objective' authorial voices.

Malika Mokeddem, Linda Lê, and the Status of the Non-native Writer

As a non-native user of French, Malika Mokeddem is, like Huston, accounted for by Kaminsky's second category where the language encountered is foreign yet familiar. Unlike Huston, however, she arrived in France fluent in French, which she acquired through her education in Algeria, and with a different relationship to her native language, Arabic, as this remains a spoken and not a written language for her. She therefore can be considered to occupy the position of linguistic outsider with respect to both languages in the position of mobility that she occupies between Arabic and French. Whilst Mokeddem is proficient in oral but not written Arabic, the fact of writing in French has been less a choice than a necessity for the Algerian author educated in French and for whom the French language symbolises her gradual cultural and linguistic migration from Algeria to France. This migration and its consequent ongoing linguistic nomadism are represented in her writing as symbols of the negotiation of her own mobility between Algeria and France. This is a linguistic negotiation that Mokeddem shares with many North African writers, both men and women, in exile and 'at home', for whom the French language is seen as the problematic legacy of colonisation. Writing in French has been perceived as a betrayal by some, who have represented the fact of writing in the language left behind by colonialism as a deliberate choice over Arabic, Algeria's official language since independence, rather than the result of the circumstantial factors of receiving an education in French, and the association of different languages in Algeria with different public and private spheres. Spoken Arabic, distinguishable from either its Classical or Standard written form, is often associated with the private, domestic sphere of the home and family and the sphere of everyday spoken language. It has furthermore been ideologically associated with the nationalist discourse of more recent armed struggles for the establishment of an Islamic state in Algeria.[19] Standard written Arabic has been largely inaccessible to many Maghrebi writers who, like Mokeddem, acquired French as their primary written language through the francophone schooling system. Mokeddem's relationship to French is thus marked by her education, as well as through migration and exile.

Mokeddem, however, distances herself from the anxieties of other Maghrebi Francophone writers perturbed by the colonial ties of the French language, which

Patricia Geesey points out have been particularly intensely felt in Algeria:

> The language issue in Algeria is more complex than in any other nation of the Maghreb. The recent civil crisis has exacerbated the antagonism between linguistic groups, and the Algerian government continues to manipulate ethnic and social divisions that are drawn along linguistic lines.[20]

Mokeddem portrays the influence the French language has had on her personal development as entirely positive, and has described how 'cette langue m'a structurée, elle a transformé cette véhémence qui était en moi en tenacité, en résistance, elle m'a armée; le français m'a appris à me défendre' [this language has structured me, it has transformed the vehemence in me into tenacity, into resistance, it has armed me. French has taught me to defend myself],[21] illustrating how, as Geesey also explains, the use of French has allowed Maghrebi intellectuals greater freedom to critique society and its institutions: by using a language other than Arabic they free themselves from private and public social pressures.[22]

Born in 1949 into an illiterate, formerly nomad family in the small mining village of Kénadsa on the western limits of the desert in Algeria, Mokeddem was the only girl in her village to complete secondary education. After primary school in Kénadsa, she attended a high school twenty kilometres away from the village in neighbouring Béchar, where she also occupied the post of *maîtresse d'internat* [boarding school assistant] from the age of sixteen. Significantly, employment at the school granted her an important degree of freedom in giving her a 'legitimate' reason to live away from the restrictive space of the family home. This initial distantiation from the family home can be seen as the first in a series of departures away from the place of origin: first to Béchar, then to Oran, and finally to France. Mokeddem arrived in France in 1977, initially living in Paris where she completed her medical degree, subsequently moving to the environs of Montpellier where she still lives and writes. As a medical student at university in Oran, Mokeddem's daily life in Algeria had become increasingly difficult with the advance of Islamic fundamentalism and the steadily increasing drive towards the installation of an Islamic state. The effect of rising fundamentalism intensified the already tense, restrictive atmosphere of a patriarchal society which strictly regulated and controlled gender roles for both men and women and, overwhelmed by such restrictions and prohibitions, she opted for exile in France.

As Mokeddem describes in an interview, 'franchir des frontières a été pour moi une délivrance' [crossing borders has been a liberation for me], demonstrating the sense of liberation that the gradual departure from her origins has afforded her.[23] The decision to leave Algeria to pursue opportunities for professional and, in due course, literary development in France has not been without its difficulties, and her fictional works dwell, in particular, on the obstacles she has encountered as a North African female professional and writer both in the context of her employment in the medical profession in France, and her targeting by members of the fundamentalist Front Islamique du Salut [Islamic Salvation Front] based in France. Mokeddem has published ten novels to date which are largely concerned with the mobile, transcultural identity formation of the exiled subject, and women's experiences in Algeria at the end of the twentieth century.

Similarly to Mokeddem, French was a familiar yet still foreign language for Linda Lê upon arrival in France, largely defined by its status as an adopted tongue acquired through the colonial legacy of the French education system in Vietnam, and thus also commensurate with Kaminsky's second category. Indeed, Lê attributes her feelings of alienation from her native Vietnam to the early acquisition of French language (and culture) through her francophone schooling in Vietnam, along with the use of French as the first language spoken in the family home in Vietnam even before arriving in France. If not qualifying her historically and politically as a native speaker of French, Lê's fluency in French constitutes her at least linguistically and culturally as a native speaker in France.[24] Lê's linguistic difficulties were thus other than being faced with an unfamiliar or new language upon arrival in exile. Claire Kramsch discusses the complex criteria for linguistic recognition as a native speaker in an article where she posits the notion of 'the privilege of the nonnative speaker', shedding light on Lê's (and indeed Mokeddem's and Huston's) positioning in relation to the French language.[25] Kramsch argues that the granting of native-speaker status takes into account more than mere linguistic ability and significantly relies on recognition as such by members of that linguistic community: 'it is not enough to have intuitions about grammaticality and linguistic acceptability and to communicate fluently and with full competence; one must also be recognized as a native speaker by the relevant speech community'.[26] It is the complex play between Lê's self-conscious positioning both within and outside the community of French native speakers, and her corresponding designation by the French language community as alternatively 'French' and 'francophone', which characterise her use of French.

Lê was born in 1963 and left her native Vietnam at fourteen years of age along with her mother and three sisters in 1977. The humanitarian and economic crisis which resulted from the gradual reconstruction of the war-ravaged country following the country's reunification under the Socialist regime after the Vietnam War led Lê's mother to depart with her daughters for France, where Lê has since resided. The memory of Vietnam, along with that of the father who remained behind upon the family's departure to France, occupy a central site of absence at the heart of Lê's œuvre of twenty fictional and two non-fictional works to date. The autobiographical traces in Lê's novels and short fiction depict an ongoing struggle with the anguish and alienation of displacement, the conflict of defining identity within the in-between space of exile, and an overall bleak vision of the human condition. The violence of her imagery, the extreme isolation of her protagonists, and the antagonism, even cruelty they display towards each other, suggest a virulence at the heart of Lê's œuvre which can be better understood in light of the various traumas Lê herself has experienced, including civil war, exile, and a family history of mental illness. Jack A. Yeager has observed that Lê, unlike other Vietnamese Francophone writers, never explicitly recounts Vietnam's colonial period and its legacy.[27] The absence of references to Vietnam's recent historical and political plights in Lê's fiction can perhaps be explained by her youth at the time these events took place, or by the likelihood that the political circumstances of her childhood were overshadowed by the greater personal traumas of her troubled family history and her experience of exile. The preoccupation with the alienation of exile, and the guilt at having left the home country and, moreover, the father, are played out time and again in her literary works. That depictions of her childhood in Vietnam are dominated by personal and familial scenarios in the almost complete absence of reference to the contemporary political backdrop certainly suggests that these more indelibly marked Lê as a child.

Lê's apparent lack of engagement with the political circumstances of her displacement can be seen in her unwillingness to be tied to overarching political markers of identity in favour of marking out her own personal space of identity. Her concern with laying down the personal markers of her identity is evident in her rejection of the label of Vietnamese Francophone author, and her claim to 'linguistic citizenship' within the community of French literature.[28] She paradoxically and simultaneously locates herself both at the margins as well as at the centre of the French literary canon, by claiming to belong within a tradition of writing in French and at the same time reinforcing her place on the margins of that tradition by deprecatingly referring to herself as 'une métèque écrivant en français' [a *métèque* who writes in French].[29] Lê's self-designation as both a French writer and a *métèque* stakes out a position of non-belonging (or rather, a multilocational, discursive space of belonging) that rejects imposed familial and national ties and allows her to name her own terms of identity and belonging. Warren Motte identifies the characteristic way in which Lê appropriates existing tropes and redefines them to create alternative discourses as 'a fine example of "oppositional behaviour": she takes the word *métèque* and scrutinizes it, examining the prejudice that subtends it and the xenophobic ideology that enables it, laying it bare and then reappropriating it for her own use'.[30]

Motte has also remarked on the fact that Lê's metaphoric use of the notion of exile tends to take precedence over its explicit depiction in her fiction.[31] Exile is a pivotal notion in Lê's œuvre, although it is only occasionally explicitly present in her novels, and geographical displacement is only an infrequent element of her plots. It is rather a state she deploys as a metaphor for her placement at the margins, both in terms of an existential position (as made clear when she states, 'je veux toujours savoir vivre en exil' [I want to feel myself always in exile]),[32] and an aesthetic position, as contended in the maxim, 'Écrire, c'est s'exiler' [To write is to exile oneself].[33] In this telling statement, Lê pinpoints the special role that writing occupies for exiled writers as a space for the negotiation that exile enforces — both of the processes of exile, and of the exile's own identity. As *writers*, whose tool is language and whose occupation is writing, the shift in linguistic environment, and the recourse to writing as a way of negotiating this shift, are particularly significant, as much as if not more so than the geographical and social shift. I would argue that this holds true whether exiles must learn a new language or not (or whether they write in a new language or not). As discussed below in the cases of Restrepo and Peri Rossi, even displacement to countries of the same language as that spoken in the birth country entails a linguistic shift whereby the exile is marked and identified by linguistic difference. The loss of status tied to this linguistic difference, referred to by Kaminsky above, compounds the initial loss of status that accompanies the arrival in exile, where the exile's separation from the habitual markers of identity and his or her unfamiliarity with the norms, codes, and institutions of the new country of residence mark him or her out as Other. Linguistic difference is arguably the most significant cause of 'othering' by the receiving community, as it renders the linguistic outsider different, less able to account for themselves, silent, or even invisible in the new linguistic context.

Yet, as Said and Besemeres remind us, linguistic alterity also fosters an awareness of an 'outside' to language and disrupts the illusion of the easy coincidence of language, community, identity, and belonging, and exile helps bring to light an 'outside' to the hitherto assumed 'naturality' of the home culture and its fictions. In the sudden loss of the space whose parameters had defined and sustained a sense of self, the exile is forced to reconsider his or her sense of identity outside of those defining parameters. The questioning of the exile's sense of identity is often accompanied by an exploration of the way in which they are perceived by others, which will also, inevitably, have undergone changes from the way they were perceived in the homeland. This reflection commonly manifests itself in the need to give expression to that identity, insofar as identity is linguistically constructed and in being expressed, identity is also produced. The verbalisation and communication of the processes of the negotiation of identity not only serve to express that identity to others, but to consolidate and secure a sense of identity for the exile him- or herself.

Writing, Women's Roles, and Cristina Peri Rossi

For exiled writers, the drive to express the process of negotiation of identity that inevitably takes place at a distance from the home and homeland is particularly compelling. Marked by the radical separation from the home and homeland that once determined their identity, and confronted with their difference from others and an accompanying 'acute sense of foreignness',[34] exiled writers simultaneously and symbiotically combine in their texts the reflection upon, and the assertion of, a sense of self at a moment of profound identarian destabilisation. In their texts, exiled writers prove themselves to be especially concerned with expressing the processes of a renegotiated sense of identity, and with others' perception of them. They deal with exile's identarian effects and processes in a number of different ways, whether through autobiographical writings, testimonial texts which document experiences of violence and repression, or through formally experimental writing that aims to represent the disjointed sense of self before and after exile. Very frequently it is the departure into exile itself, and the subsequent task of resituating oneself in displacement that triggers the entry into writing, to the extent that some texts might never have been written had it not been for the fact of displacement.

The departure into exile as a conduit to writing is a particularly significant passage for women exiles, for many of whom exile signifies a departure from traditional, assigned roles and the undertaking of new roles outside the familial and social spaces they formerly occupied. For Cristina Peri Rossi, liminality is already the space typically occupied by the writer, a space on the fringes of agency shared by women in patriarchal society. Thus exile, femininity, and writing converge, for Peri Rossi, in a space of liminality,[35] a position which Kaminsky corroborates when she states that 'the condition of exile and the condition of women in patriarchal culture are remarkably alike'.[36] For Kaminsky, the experience of exiles — of being invisible, of having their reality misinterpreted by the dominant group, of being marginalised, of having unwanted characteristics displaced onto them — are also familiar to women.

The departure, through exile and writing, from traditional, assigned domestic and sexual roles and the passage to new roles outside of these restricted familial and social spaces that occurs in the Latin American context from which Peri Rossi speaks is also demonstrated in other contexts, such as the North African. Valérie Orlando discusses the implications of writing for female Maghrebi writers for whom writing represents a profound change in women's roles in that it relocates women's presence from the private (the domestic, familial, and sexual), into the public space (the social, political, economic, and intellectual): 'When women breach the fine lines that have been drawn between these two spheres they are automatically overturning and displacing all preexisting social constructions.'[37] For exiled North African women writers this shift into the public space is doubled: both exile and writing move women out of the private and into the public realm. According to Orlando, exile is often an individual experience, in that the Maghrebi woman often relocates on her own, necessitating a move into the autonomous sphere of economic livelihood and social mobility that is echoed in the individual stance adopted by much Maghrebi women's writing. The adoption of a first-person narrative voice by many Maghrebi women authors in the recounting of the processes of displacement and relocation signifies a move towards individual subjectivity that disrupts a historical tradition of collective identity that is defined in relation to the community, where the use of the subjective 'I' is discouraged. For those who departed for France, as is the case with Mokeddem, the adoption of such individualising French literary techniques may be seen as a conscious or unconscious desire for integration in a country that values and rewards literary merit but which has been less than welcoming of North African citizens on its shores. The French public's willingness to adopt other 'literary outsiders' into its fold is also evident in the case of Huston. If the French public has denied Huston the cultural status of a French woman, constantly reminding her of her foreignness as testified in many of her non-fictional texts, it has, by contrast, effusively embraced her literary identification as a French writer and granted her privileged access to the French literary canon.

Yet if Orlando demonstrates how Maghrebi women reposition themselves in the public space through writing, she also shows how in moving towards a position of agency in the public space of communication, where social self-construction becomes possible and the 'hermetically sealed world that has been contrived for them by male oppression' is destroyed, Maghrebi women are also moving from one kind of marginality to another in that this is a space in which women are in a definite minority:

> Women who step into the public sphere of agency are essentially stepping into an environment of marginality and exile where their numbers are few. Once

in the sphere of agency (always public) woman gain access to the one thing that they have always been denied — the right to a voice and to negotiate their identity.[38]

From the marginality of the private space on the fringes of the seat of power, exiled women writers move into a marginality of a different kind, that of a minority at a remove from the structures which regulate power hierarchies and roles. This is a marginality that Orlando portrays as a transgressive and productive site of possibility for women: ' "overstepping boundaries" into this realm of public agency in turn frees up women's ability to reinscribe, or write, their identity'.[39] This site of marginality is trangressive insofar as it distances women from the normalised domestic and sexual roles which have historically limited their activity, and progressive in that it opens the way for women's autonomy in a new-found space of marginality not yet governed by behavioural norms and codes. The dual marginality of women's exile can be seen as exacerbating a pre-existing marginality which radically and positively repositions them in relation to hegemonic power structures.

Helena Araújo depicts the problem of women's marginality in the public space of Latin American women's writing as one of great urgency when she asks '¿Hasta cuándo será "lo femenino" una condición al margen de la historia?' [For how long will 'femininity' remain a condition on the margins of history?].[40] Like Orlando's articulation of Maghrebi women's transgression of the limits between the private and the public, Araújo too describes the condition of femininity in Latin America as limited by anonymity and the repression of female identity and desire, limits which women writers have had to breach in order to access a public identity on par with their male counterparts. Araújo describes the historical constraints and limitations on Latin American women's agency as an urgent, life-threatening prohibition, and compares Latin American women writers' struggle to Scheherazade's quest for survival:

> Scherezada sería un buen sobrenombre kitch [sic] para la escritora del continente. ¿Por qué? Porque como Scherezada, ha tenido que narrar historias e inventar ficciones en carrera desesperada contra un tiempo que conlleva la amenaza de la muerte: muerte en la pérdida de la identidad y en la pérdida del deseo. Muerte-castigo. Seguramente también, la latinoamericana ha escrito desafiando una sociedad y un sistema que imponen el anonimato. Ha escrito sintiéndose ansiosa y culpable de robarle horas al padre o al marido. Sobre todo ha escrito siendo infiel a ese papel para el cual fuera predestinada, el único, de madre. Escribir, entonces, ha sido su manera de prolongar una libertad ilusoria y posponer una condena.[41]

> [Scheherazade would be a good kitsch nickname for the woman writer from the [South American] continent. Why? Because like Scheherazade, she has had to narrate stories and invent fictions in a desperate race against time which also carries the threat of death: death in the loss of identity and in the loss of desire. Death-punishment. The Latin American woman has surely also written defying a society and a system that imposes anonymity. She has written feeling anxious and guilty of stealing hours away from her priest or husband. Writing, then, has been a way of prolonging an illusory freedom and postponing a sentence.]

Araújo compares Latin American women's traditional roles, as measured by their relationships to men and defined by the restriction to maternal, domestic, and sexual roles, to a death sentence insofar as they suppress identity and deny female desire, prohibitions which women writers defy through the very act of writing. Araújo refers to the enduring guilt of neglecting the expected, traditional role of mother which constitutes the powerful underlying essence of femininity in androcentric Latin American culture. When Araújo and Peri Rossi refer to being restricted to traditional domestic, maternal roles, they do not (just) mean being restricted to motherhood, but being restricted to this as the *only* legitimate role available to women. Indeed, for Peri Rossi, writing is in itself an act of spontaneous feminism insofar as the act of writing challenges the conventions of appropriate arenas for women's activity: 'el hecho de ser una escritora espontáneamente significa ser feminista. El acto de escribir ya es una especie de feminismo espontáneo' [the very fact of being a writer means being a feminist. The act of writing is already a kind of spontaneous feminism].[42]

It is of paramount importance to bear in mind the rebellious aspect of writing for women exiled from androcentric societies in which women's roles are stipulated and regulated by rigid religious and moral codes in order to understand writing as a important strategy for the reconfiguration of women's identity, and its contiguity with the experience of exile as a mode of flight into a public space of presence, communication, and self-assertion. Rather than constitute an incidental vehicle for the reconfiguration of identity that exile precipitates, writing for exiled women has been the very platform upon which that reconfiguration has been conducted. It has shifted the parameters of women's agency to make of women's identity something which is to be self-defined and expressed, rather than something which is externally delimited and constrained. It has, on a practical level, demonstrated paradigms of femininity which may either entirely reject historical maternal and domestic roles, or incorporate these alongside public and intellectual roles, and on an ideological level, served as a forum for the self-reflexive consideration of new paradigms for women's identity. By way of an example of the rebellious nature of writing for exiled women, we can cite Claire Lindsay's discussion of Peri Rossi's literary project as a transgressive act that has allowed her to define herself anew, outside historical gender models:

> Writing appears to have situated her as an outsider, a kind of exile... from the conventions of the domestic and social spheres [...]. Her accounts reveal, therefore, not only an inclination towards the solitude or exile of writing, but also a predilection for the sense of rebellion against traditional roles that it afforded her, in particular against the traditional female role within the family.[43]

Peri Rossi's vast literary corpus consists of novels, short stories, essays, and poetry in which the theme of geographical displacement sits alongside the wider, related themes of violently repressive state regimes, rebellion against institutional authority, and the repression of the individual unable and/or unwilling to conform to conservative social and cultural structures. Literature has also provided Peri Rossi with a site where she is able to reinforce and celebrate her marginalisation, and exile is but one of a number of the marginalising factors that outline her identity.

Like Siscar's persecution by the military regime in Argentina, Peri Rossi's failure to measure up to the ideal of national identity advocated by the military authority during the Uruguayan dictatorship also set the Uruguayan writer apart from the dominant culture and lead to her departure into exile.

In the increasingly violent political climate of 1960s and 1970s Uruguay, and in a similar strategy to that seen in Argentina's contemporary military dictatorship, left-wing sympathisers and activists were branded 'subversive' by the right-wing Uruguayan government (and subsequently, dictatorship, lasting from 1973 to 1984), and were persecuted for what were considered actions harmful to national interests and thus not recognised as legitimately embodying a national identity. Economic downturn, dating from the late 1950s, had led to the formation of urban guerrilla movements by students and workers who undertook (at times violent) protest activities. Peri Rossi's association with the Uruguayan socialist political party, Frente Amplio, and her collaboration with the distinguished Uruguayan political and cultural review, *Marcha* (closed down during the dictatorship in 1974), made her a target for state persecution and placed her personal safety at risk. Increasingly well known for her writing and her participation as a left-wing militant, Peri Rossi was forced to flee Uruguay with just twenty-four hours' notice in the knowledge of the recent disappearances of her peers involved in similar militant activities. Along with her political profile in Uruguay, Peri Rossi's homosexuality and her unwillingness to adopt traditional (maternal, domestic, and sexual) feminine roles and behaviours well and truly alienated her from the conservative patriarchal society of Uruguay at the time. Despite this sense of alienation in Uruguay, Peri Rossi's sense of identity remained firmly anchored there before exile, and her attachment to a sense of identity in Uruguay partly accounts for the decisive trauma of the departure into exile. As Peri Rossi herself states, 'Exile is always a form of tearing oneself away, a loss, a breakage. In this sense I think it is the final experience in which one's whole identity crashes', thus revealing the extent to which the experience of exile did violence to her sense of self and enforced a reevaluation of her sense of identity.[44]

Born in 1941, Peri Rossi was already an established and well-known writer of prose and poetry when she left Uruguay for Spain in 1972, having published five volumes of short stories and poetry, and won prestigious national literary awards in Uruguay. Severing her from the recognition and status as a writer, activist, and university lecturer, the 'identity crash' occasioned by her sudden departure was violent and devastating in that she was detached from the markers of both her private and public identity. Arriving in Spain in 1972, Peri Rossi found herself having to redefine an identity for herself in Barcelona in the vacuum of identity markers that is familiar to exiles in general, and more intensely felt by the exile who has enjoyed a degree of renown in the home country. Peri Rossi describes this vacuum of identity and recognition in the place of exile in terms of rebirth and reconstruction:

> Identity is to have a name in relation to others. To exist for the rest of the people, to see that their look reflects us, recognizes us. Exile is to lose this context, this look which others give us, and therefore exile sets a challenge. We

have to be reborn in a place where nobody knows us yet and can share our past. All those things which until then had been part of our identity.[45]

Unlike others, and most notably Huston, who dwell on both the positive and negative aspects of life in exile, Peri Rossi has demonstrated an apparent unwillingness to represent the more positive aspects of her exile in Spain (and these can hardly be considered insignificant, granted the marginal status of women's writing in Latin America to which Araújo refers and the deep-seated homophobia in Uruguay, and indeed more widely in Latin America, at the time of her exile). This unwillingness can perhaps be attributed to the particular conditions of her exile. Peri Rossi was effectively cast out of Uruguay by a regime which she ideologically and actively opposed, and to recognise or give expression to the positive ways in which she has experienced exile could be felt as a betrayal of her cause and seen as a desertion by her fellow militants, as well as a capitulation to the military authorities in admitting to benefiting from the banishment imposed by them. That Peri Rossi has lead a highly productive life in Spain is undeniable, given her status, alongside Julio Cortázar, Juan Carlos Onetti, and Mario Benedetti (amongst others), as one of the Southern Cone's most significant writers, and given her profile as a public figure in Spain.

In Barcelona, where she has been based since her flight into exile in 1972, writing (and initially journalism in particular) became the vehicle through which Peri Rossi was able to reconstruct a coherent sense of identity as well as being a forum for the exploration of the way in which identity is constructed. The spatial and chronological displacement experienced through exile is manifested in Peri Rossi's writing to the extent that rather than attempting to recuperate and recreate the identity that she inhabited in Uruguay, Peri Rossi has developed a sense of her identity in displacement whilst continuing to write from a position on the margins. Where her marginalisation from the dominant culture both before and after exile has consistently characterised her writing, the parameters of that marginalisation have indeed changed over time. Her early works in particular demonstrate a denunciation of the restrictive conventions of the domestic and social spheres and a rebellion against traditional female roles, whereas more recent works probe such conventions even more profoundly to question and contest the very foundations on which gender identities rely, as explored in Chapter 5. Writing has undeniably offered Peri Rossi a powerful strategy for circumventing traditional domestic and familial roles in that it both deviates from historically 'appropriate' activities for women, and provides a medium to express and manifest her nonconformity. Peri Rossi's nonconformity has also been played out through the medium of language, as a writer who is highly sensitive to the power of language as a means of constructing and of deconstructing norms, and of underpinning and exerting authority, both within and across languages. Peri Rossi's linguistic shift between Uruguayan and peninsular Spanish upon her exile from Montevideo to Barcelona can be associated with Kaminsky's third category of linguistic migration, where language is the same but unfamiliar. As Kaminsky states,

> The difference in language for the Uruguayan exile in Spain is primarily phonological, and as Cristina Peri Rossi has suggested, it is all the difference.

> This exile is known by his/her accent and what makes him/her recognisable also makes him/her 'other'.[46]

Peri Rossi's writing foregrounds the ideological contructs of language and the feelings of exclusion or pigeonholing occasioned by responses to regional differences within the same language.

Laura Restrepo, like Peri Rossi, can also be accounted for by Kaminsky's third linguistic condition of exile, of migration between different types of the same language. Displaced from one linguistic zone (Colombia) to another of the same language (Mexico), Restrepo nevertheless demonstrates a linguistic transition and a sensitivity to language in her writing which can be seen as the result of her six years spent in exile. The journalistic register of her writing before exile is still discernible in texts written during and after her exile, which move increasingly towards a hybrid literary style that incorporates the political, the testimonial, the historical, the literary, and the journalistic.

Laura Restrepo and Textual Hybridity

Restrepo was born into a middle-class family in the Colombian capital of Bogotá in 1950. After obtaining a degree in Literature and Philosophy at the Universidad de los Andes, and teaching literature at the Universidad Nacional de Colombia, she spent a number of years abroad in Spain and Argentina, working for militant left-wing organisations, including the Spanish Socialist Workers' Party in Madrid, and clandestine resistance movements opposed to the military dictatorship in Argentina.[47] Upon returning to Colombia in the early 1980s, she became involved in journalism, taking up the position of political editor at the newly established high-profile current affairs weekly, *Semana*. Restrepo has commented on the significance of her position at *Semana* in her transition from journalism to fiction, describing how her training as a journalist honed a style based on investigation and research which has carried over into her fictional writing: 'El reflejo de periodista te queda. Yo no concibo ni siquiera sentarme a escribir sin investigar antes' [The journalist's habits stay with you. I can't conceive of sitting down to write without researching beforehand].[48] In 1983 Restrepo was invited by the Colombian government to participate in peace negotiations with the guerrilla movements. This involvement had an immense impact on both her personal and professional life, resulting in her life being endangered and her consequent departure into exile in Mexico in 1985, and instigating her move from publishing in magazines and newspapers to book publishing. It was in Mexico in 1986 that she published her first book, *Historia de un entusiasmo*, which recounts the peace negotiations from the perspective of her own involvement in thirty-four chapters originally conceived as free-standing articles intended for the press.[49] They were instead compiled in one volume and printed as a book when faced with newspaper editors' refusal to print the articles due to the sensitivity of the material. *Historia de un entusiasmo* thus set a precedent for her future publications which, although increasingly moving away from journalism and closer to fiction, nevertheless consistently maintain investigation and research as the methodological basis for her writing project. Restrepo's hybrid corpus of twelve book publications to date includes novels, journalistic writing and a children's book in addition to which she had published widely in the press and in collections of essays.

Hybridity, such as that which characterises Restrepo's œuvre, can indeed be seen as a fundamental characteristic of exiled women's writing. We have already seen the generic diversity of the works of the six writers of this study, both within individual texts and across their œuvres. Literary, or generic hybridity can also be seen as a characteristic which contributes to the politicisation of exiled women's texts. Insofar as the private is political, the reflection on women's roles and their transformation during and after periods of exile provides a commentary both on women's positioning in society and on the function and status of women's writing. Whilst textual hybridity can also be an indication of drives other than the political, and exiled women's writing is certainly also motivated by less socially, and more personally defined drives (such as the psychological, redemptive, aesthetic, and poetic), exiled women's writing is nevertheless overwhelmingly political. Lê's texts of atonement for the 'abandonment' of the father, the homeland, and the native tongue, and Huston's explorations of the awkward position of 'privileged outsider' as a Canadian 'voluntary' exile in Paris are defined by very personal agendas, yet these authors and their works are nevertheless located in a context which politicises their texts. Despite Lê's apparent avoidance of a political backdrop in her novels, the shadow of French colonialism and postcolonial tensions between France and Vietnam cannot fail to haunt her texts, as does the commentary in Huston's texts on the unequal status of cultural others living in France, and the French concern with defining an established notion of French national and cultural identity.

Peri Rossi's texts offer a clear example of the way in which the personal becomes highly political, where her efforts to redefine roles for women in her writing combine her own life choices with her political agenda. For Peri Rossi, the imperative is not only that women's writing must address the historical inequality of women and restriction of women's choices, but that the very notion of what has been regarded as women's writing be challenged. She describes how the ambivalent status of women's writing in Latin America has historically been defined within very precise parameters:

> Within what is considered 'official literature' in Latin America, the attitude towards women has always been ambiguous: on the one hand it is considered proper for them to write decorative, incidental (and accidental) poetry; on the other hand we see how the very application of the word 'poetess' carries slighting connotations.[50]

Araújo identifies these parameters as defined by the domestic and religious spheres, and articulates the extreme difficulty for women to abandon such paradigms:

> En la mujer, a la culpabilidad de abandonar al padre, al esposo, o al lujo para dedicarse a la literatura, se sumaba la de abandonar a obispos o a parrocos que exigían, implacables, su colaboración en obras 'de caridad'. Tal vez por eso, cuando no componía poesía mística o amorosa, tomaba la pluma en favor del desposeído o se constituía en guardiana de la moral familiar. Fatalmente, la religión del hogar o de la iglesia, dejaba poco espacio para la imaginación.[51]

[For a woman, the guilt of abandoning her father, husband, or wealth, to dedicate herself to literature added to that of abandoning bishops or priests who relentlessly demanded collaboration in 'charity' works. Perhaps because of this, when she wasn't writing mystic or romantic poetry, she took up the pen in favour of the dispossessed, or she set herself up as the guardian of family morals. Fatally, religion in the home or the church left little space for the imagination.]

Sylvia Molloy substantiates Peri Rossi's criticism of 'official' literature's disregard for women writers and women's writing, and remarks upon the historical absence of local precursors in a regional tradition that has traditionally looked beyond its shores for inspiration: 'En nuestros países, la literatura femenina, hasta hace poco, gozaba de una recepción dudosa, sobre todo si la escribían mujeres hispanoamericanas; en la Argentina se conocía a Marguerite Duras cuando no se conocía a Elena Garro' [In our countries, women's writing until recently enjoyed a dubious reception, especially that written by Latin American women: in Argentina, Marguerite Duras was read long before Elena Garro].[52]

Against such a backdrop, it is hardly surprising that Peri Rossi qualifies women's writing as a spontaneously feminist act. As the anguished tone of Araújo's question reiterates — '¿cómo poetizar sin dejar de politizar?' [how do we poeticise without desisting from politicising?] — Latin American women writers are highly sensitive to the proximity of the literary and the political in women's writing.[53] Much as Mokeddem hypothetically contemplates writing other narratives than her characteristic critiques of oppressive social structures when she ponders 'si je devais écrire le bonheur...' [if I were to write of happiness...],[54] Araújo wonders if it is even possible for women to write anything other than contestatory, politicised texts while the conditions in which they write still prevent them from enjoying parity with their male counterparts, and while their marginal status is still at the forefront of their personal and writerly concerns. Araújo points to the inevitable politicisation of women's writing in contexts where this does not have a long-established tradition, or carry an equal status within the (implicitly masculine and 'Western') literary canon. Similar claims might be made for women writers and women's writing from the culturally (predominantly Euro-American) dominant tradition, yet the specificity of the multiple marginalisation of women writers who occupy the culturally and sexually non-hegemonic peripheries must be recognised.[55]

The similarities between the politicisation of writing by Latin American women and that of francophone women of the Maghreb are noteworthy, insofar as women from both backgrounds have had to find ways to overcome ingrained notions of 'appropriate' behaviours for women in order to take up the pen and enter the public domain of writing, and are yet to have their work considered in parity alongside works which comprise the canon. Assia Djebar declares that '[i]n reality, the feminine arena can only promote writing that is militant, journalistic, and oriented toward protest',[56] suggesting that Araújo's rhetorical question will only be resolved when the need for protest and politicisation becomes less pressing, thus also positing literature's potential to effectuate real changes in the lives of women. Orlando makes a similar claim for the perceived potential political agency of women's writing when she states: 'Francophone feminine novels are transformative and radical in the sense that the authors believe that their respective societies can change.'[57]

Restrepo's writing has been consistently political, and her representation of contemporary Colombian history consistently transgresses conventional generic boundaries between fact and fiction, both of which she treats as equally viable channels of knowledge. Based on verifiable historical fact, Restrepo's texts are the product of researched historical archives, interviews with the agents of contemporary history, and fictional embellishment. Read in light of her militant and journalistic background, they suggest that modifying the conventions of representation and authorial perspective can have a real impact on the way that history is understood and transmitted. Her writing offers a vision of a specific reality which questions who and what is deemed an appropriate object of representation, as well as redefining the conventions of the representation and recording of history. Where Restrepo's novels depict aspects of Colombian reality through the perspective of a diversity of its marginalised groups (such as victims of violence, impoverished communities on the fringes of society, prostitutes, internally displaced rural inhabitants, and the mentally ill), Mokeddem portrays a vision of Algeria largely seen through the lens of her own status as an outcast, as suggested by her apparently autobiographical protagonists. Mokeddem's novels too are overwhelmingly political in their condemnation of the violence and abuse suffered by Algerian women at the hands of fundamentalists, to the point of risking relegating literary and aesthetic concerns to a secondary role, as discussed in Chapter 4.

Nomadic Narratives

Hybridity thus characterises the textual production of exiled women writers (in that these writers typically embrace a range of genres) as well as the texts themselves. Yet this book is less concerned with identifying a genre of 'exile writing', or even 'exiled women's writing' than with examining the ways in which identity is expressed in texts by exiled women, raising the question of what it is in these texts (formally and thematically) that expresses the negotiation of a sense of identity that is inflected by the experience of exile, and what role and value writing holds for exiled women. As Orlando makes clear, exiled 'writers, intellectuals, and academics are shifting toward a nomadic philosophy that promotes the annihilation of borders and frontiers', a philosophy which belies discrete, fixed categories of identity and confounds the notion of the hold of origins in defining identity.[58] Where Orlando and others have described the nomadism apparent in exiled women's identity,[59] I would argue that it is also a characteristic of their writing: nomadism's disregard for fixity and borders is arguably a necessary condition of the merging of the private and the public, the subjective and the objective, and the personal with the literary, that is prevalent in exiled women's texts. Exiled women's narratives, like exiled women's subjectivity, can be considered in light of Rosi Braidotti's characterisation of nomadic consciousness. As the textual analyses of novels by Huston, Lê, Mokeddem, Peri Rossi, Restrepo, and Siscar in the following three chapters illustrate, exiled women's writing is also characterised by the fluidity, mobility, repetitions, and cyclical configurations by which Braidotti defines nomadic conciousness.

Orlando highlights the pertinence of looking at writing by exiled francophone women of the Maghreb through the lens of nomadism as a key to understanding both the current literary situation of these writers, and their position within Franco-Maghrebi culture, literature and identity. A consideration of the expression of feminine identity in exiled women's texts reveals how Braidottian nomadism dovetails with the Deleuzo-Guattarian theory of becoming-minority. These can be seen as intersecting ways in which women writers deconstruct and renegotiate the dialectical framework of established notions of masculine and feminine subjectivity, as Orlando states: 'By embracing their marginal position, women recontextualise feminine difference. Difference now is no longer viewed as being a subordinated, dominated, or sexually determined trait. It is rather positively considered as acentred to polar oppositions.'[60] Deleuze and Guattari's notion of becoming involves a reterritorialisation of perspectives and defining structures such that 'difference' is no longer viewed as 'subordinate', but as an elusive Other that does not adhere to established rules of the hierarchy of centre and periphery.[61] In such a philosophy of becoming, the Other (the minority) is a privileged, creative force which has special access to thinking outside the norms. Whilst the Deleuzo-Guattarian notion of becoming-minority certainly raises the problem of the homogenisation of variously marginalised groups under the single banner of 'minority', the concept nevertheless sheds light on women's dissent from the identifications and power structures upheld by the hegemonic (white, 'Western', male) majority. If the hegemonic majority at the centre of power structures has a vested interest in conserving and sustaining those power structures, it follows that those denied access to power within these structures seek to disregard and disrupt the hierarchy, and strive to define identity in breach of these norms. For writers such as Peri Rossi, writing, and more particularly writing in exile, offers a prime mode of establishing identity outside of the norms: 'I too have felt the same necessity of forcing literary forms, of utilizing a quantity of personally imaginative and creative techniques to establish my own identity outside the norm. Any kind of norm.'[62] The capacity of language and writing to offer a medium of self-invention is nowhere more deftly described than in the aphorism of the title of Araújo's article, 'Yo escribo, yo me escribo...' [I write, I write myself...].[63]

Thus the nomadic configuration of exiled women's identity addresses, and indeed reconciles, the apparently discrepant aspects of the aporia of 'forced choice' inherent in the processes of exile that were referred to in Chapter 1. As Braidotti states, 'I can say that I had the condition of migrant cast upon me, but I chose to become a nomad', to illustrate how nomadic subjectivity distinguishes between the fact and circumstances of the departure into exile, and the manner in which the state of exile is inhabited, as both a real and metaphoric state.[64] What is in question is not so much whether the woman exile 'chooses' exile or not, as how the processes of relocating identity and redefining belonging are negotiated. For it is clear that despite shifting the boundaries and markers of identity and belonging, the exile nevertheless sustains the will to belong, albeit along redefined parameters of belonging. What is, however, radically altered, is the woman exile's exercise of agency in the delimitation of the parameters of her space of belonging. Peri Rossi's fear of being perceived as a stranger where she herself does not recognise herself as such demonstrates a resistance to conforming to parameters of belonging defined by others, and a desire to designate her own space of belonging: 'My main fear, in fact, is to feel a stranger the day when I return to Montevideo, even if it is only for a visit. I prefer to feel a stranger in a country where I know I am a stranger because I know I was not born there.'[65]

As seen in Chapter 1, criticism has been levelled at Braidotti's notion of nomadism, which has been branded as elitist: critics point out that the economic and cultural resources for choosing the manner in which one inhabits displacement are not equally distributed. Yet Braidotti makes no claims for the universal applicability of what is essentially an intellectual position and methodology that accounts for mobile, transnational writers and intellectuals — such as the writers who form the subject of the present study — who have discursively reflected upon their own positioning and subjectivity in displacement and thus the privilege of the capacity to define their own home and space of belonging. Braidotti's claim that 'As an intellectual style, nomadism consists not so much in being homeless, as in being capable of recreating your home everywhere,' however, erroneously confuses 'everywhere' with 'anywhere'.[66] Nancy Huston, for example, is justified in resisting being designated a nomadic writer, where this means a writer who is 'at home' everywhere:

> Imaginer qu'un écrivain puisse être 'nomade', et se sentir 'chez lui partout où il pose le pied', cela relève ou de la dénégation ou de la naïveté [...]. L'écrivain en exil, même volontaire, loin d'être 'chez lui partout où il pose le pied', *n'est chez lui nulle part.*
>
> [To imagine that a writer can be a 'nomad' and feel 'at home wherever he or she sets foot' is either a denial or naivety [...]. The writer in exile, even voluntary exile, far from being 'at home wherever he or she sets foot', *is at home nowhere.*][67]

Rather, the exile's loss of a sense of (being at) 'home', and of having lost the originary site where belonging was a given (whether unquestioned or problematic) means that the exile is cast into the limbo of the in-between, no longer at home anywhere. It is this radical rupture with a given space of home and belonging that opens the way for the exile to exercise a degree of choice and 'set up home' *anywhere*, rather than *everywhere*. Contrary to Braidotti's claim, nomadism does not consist in an all-embracing ability to recreate home everywhere, it rather facilitates the nomadic subject's conscious recreation of home, or a sense of belonging, anywhere of his or her own choosing. That writing often provides such a site of belonging is not incidental.

The idea of 'writing as home' is not a new one: Theodor Adorno articulated the notion of writing as the only home truly available for the exile in *Minima moralia* in 1951: 'For a man who no longer has a homeland, writing becomes a place to live.'[68] The notion has been picked up and carried along in more recent criticism: Michael Seidel designates writing itself as a site of 'homecoming' in which the presence of the 'here and now' and the absence of the 'left behind' can be reunited,[69] and more recently Luis Torres has also emphasised the restorative potential of writing, and introduced the notion of writing as a *process* ('form'), as well as a *site* of dwelling:

> It can be argued that writing is in itself a form of dwelling and a way of attempting the permanence of the representation of certain experiences. It is also a perseverance to sustain a language and its cultures, and a struggle to affirm the self and the possible community in the face of the uncertainties of exile.[70]

Yet, as the absence of women from Adorno's discussion of writing as the only truly possible site of home for the exile illustrates, and as Caren Kaplan observes, the tradition of thinking of writing as 'home' appears to be far more complex than Adorno's paradigm allows for.[71]

Samir Gandesha finds Adorno's reterritorialisation of home in the space of writing an unsettling configuration: 'his writing, in the final instance, offers only cold comfort, for, as a place to live, it paradoxically takes its leave of the traditional idea of "homecoming"'.[72] At stake here is the *kind* of home that is reproduced in the in-between space of exile. Gandesha, like Seidel and Torres, refers to a restorative configuration of home in writing which attempts to retrieve a language and a culture through the permanence of representation, and to reaffirm a sense of self and community according to a 'traditional idea of "homecoming"'. Yet for exiled women writers, 'writing as home' is less about reproducing an idealised lost homeland, than about creating a new homeland that departs from traditional notions of home and homecoming, and that is truly a new site of belonging, rather than the recreation of a site of alienation and marginalisation. As Kaplan aptly prescribes, if home is a site of discrimination and alienation, we must leave home and create our homes anew. The comparative textual analyses of the following three chapters examine the new homes and sites of belonging that each of these six authors envisages for herself in nomadic narratives in which the negotiation of nomadic identity in exile is enacted.

Notes to Chapter 2

1. Kaminsky, *Reading*, p. 117.
2. Valérie Orlando, *Nomadic Voices of Exile: Feminine Identity in Francophone Literature of the Maghreb* (Athens: Ohio University Press, 1999), p. 12.
3. Nancy Huston, 'Déracinement du savoir, un parcours en six étapes', in *Âmes et corps: Textes choisis 1981–2003* (Paris: Babel, 2004), pp. 13–35 (pp. 24–25).
4. Later published as *Dire et interdire: éléments de jurologie* (Paris: Payot, 1980).
5. Braidotti, p. 44.
6. Braidotti, p. 8.
7. Edward Said, 'Reflections on Exile', in *Reflections on Exile and Other Essays* (Cambridge, MA: Harvard University Press, 2000), pp. 173–86 (p. 185).
8. Mary Besemeres, *Translating One's Self: Language and Selfhood in Cross-Cultural Autobiography* (Oxford: Peter Lang, 2002), p. 16.
9. Besemeres, p. 18.
10. Kaminsky, *After Exile*, p. 68.
11. Catherine Argand, 'Entretien avec Nancy Huston', *Lire* (March 2001), <http://www.lexpress.fr/culture/livre/nancy-huston_804287.html> [accessed 23 January 2014].
12. Nancy Huston, *Jouer au papa et à l'amant: de l'amour des petites filles* (Paris: Ramsay, 1979).

13. Huston explores the 'mind–body problem' in greatest depth in *Journal de la création* (Paris: Seuil, 1990), a book she describes as a 'Journal d'abord de ma grossesse, mais réflexion aussi sur l'autre type de création — à savoir l'art — et sur les liens possibles ou impossibles entre les deux' [Primarily a diary of my pregnancy, but also a reflection on the other type of creation — namely, art — and the possible or impossible links between them] (*Journal de la création*, p. 12).
14. Taylor, *Disappearing Acts*, p. 93.
15. Under the law of *Patria Potestad* in Argentina, a father's permission was required for a mother to take her child out of the country. In an interview with Gwendolyn Díaz, Siscar remarks that she could have declared herself her son's sole parent given the disappearance of his father, but to do so would have been to give up the search for her husband, which she was not prepared to do at the time (for further information, see Gwendolyn Díaz, 'Cristina Siscar', in *Women and Power in Argentine Literature: Stories, Interviews and Critical Essays* [Austin: University of Texas Press, 2007], pp. 257–75.)
16. Kaminsky, *After Exile*, p. 68.
17. In an interview with Kate Averis, 'La casa de la escritura'.
18. See the Bibliography for full bibliographic references to the published works of all six writers.
19. See Benjamin Stora, 'Society and Culture in Algeria (1962–1982)', in *Algeria 1830–2000: A Short History*, trans. by Jane Marie Todd (Ithaca, NY, and London: Cornell University Press, 2001), pp. 163–77.
20. Patricia Geesey, 'Commitment and Critique: Francophone Intellectuals in the Maghreb', in *North Africa in Transition: State, Society, and Economic Transformation in the 1990s*, ed. by Yahia H. Zoubier (Gainesville: University Press of Florida, 1999), pp. 143–57 (p. 155).
21. In Yolande Aline Helm, 'Entretien avec Malika Mokeddem', in *Malika Mokeddem: Envers et contre tout*, ed. by Yolande Aline Helm (Paris: L'Harmattan, 2000), pp. 39–51 (p. 42).
22. Geesey, p. 145.
23. In Chaulet-Achour and Kerfa, p. 32.
24. See Siobhán McIlvanney, '"Les mo(r)ts ne nous lâchent pas": Death and the Paternal/Amorous Body in Linda Lê's *Lettre morte*', *Romanic Review*, 100.3 (2009), 373–88 (p. 384).
25. Strikingly, the three Francophone writers of this study have all acquired and adopted French as their writing language, whereas the three Hispanophone writers have all maintained their native language as their language of literary expression. This may be attributed to a number of phenomena: the vast breadth of the Spanish-speaking world and Hispanophones' mobility within it; the status and prestige that has historically been constructed around the French language and literary tradition and its power to attract non-native writers; and the impact of the French colonial legacy whose former colonies remained culturally hybrid after decolonisation and continued to produce bilingual, bicultural subjects.
26. Claire Kramsch, 'The Privilege of the Nonnative Speaker', *PMLA*, 112.3 (1997), 359–69 (p. 363).
27. Jack A. Yeager, 'Compte rendu: Linda Lê, *Slander*', *Études francophones*, 13.1 (1998), 259–62.
28. Phrase coined by Madeleine Hage in 'Introduction to Linda Lê', at A New Generation of French Women Novelists' Colloquium, New York University, New York (3–4 November 1995), and quoted in Jack A. Yeager, 'Culture, Citizenship, Nation: The Narrative Texts of Linda Lê', in *Post-Colonial Cultures in France*, ed. by Alec G. Hargreaves and Mark McKinney (London and New York: Routledge, 1997), pp. 255–67 (p. 257).
29. Argand, 'Entretien avec Linda Lê'. Lê here reappropriates the term, *métèque*, a derogatory term for a foreigner in France, to take control of her own positioning in relation to the French identity, culture, and literary canon.
30. Warren Motte, *Fables of the Novel: French Fiction since 1990* (Normal, IL: Dalkey Archive Press, 2003), p. 62.
31. Motte, p. 59.
32. Argand, 'Entretien avec Linda Lê'.
33. Argand, 'Entretien avec Linda Lê'.
34. Braidotti, p. 24.
35. See Claire Lindsay, 'Cristina Peri Rossi: "Universality" and Exile Reconsidered', in *Locating*, pp. 19–46.
36. Kaminsky, *Reading*, p. 36.

37. Orlando, *Nomadic*, p. 10.
38. Orlando, *Nomadic*, p. 10.
39. Orlando, *Nomadic*, p. 10.
40. Helena Araújo, *La Scherezada criolla: Ensayos sobre escritura femenina latinoamericana* (Bogotá: Universidad Nacional de Colombia, 1989), p. 42.
41. Araújo, *La Scherezada criolla*, p. 33.
42. Parizad Tamara Dejbord, 'Entrevista con Cristina Peri Rossi', in *Cristina Peri Rossi*, pp. 217–47 (p. 238).
43. Lindsay, *Locating*, p. 30.
44. Psiche Hughes, 'Interview with Cristina Peri Rossi', in *Unheard Words: Women and Literature in Africa, the Arab World, Asia, the Caribbean and Latin America*, ed. by Mineke Schipper, trans. by Barbara Potter Fasting (London: Allison and Busby, 1985), pp. 255–74 (pp. 268–69).
45. Hughes, p. 269.
46. Kaminsky, *After Exile*, p. 68.
47. Although currently a centre-left Democratic Socialist party, the Spanish Socialist Workers' Party, founded in 1879, was originally inspired by the revolutionary principles of Marxism with the main goals of representing the interests of the working class and achieving socialism.
48. In Julie Lirot, 'Laura Restrepo por si misma', in *El universo literario de Laura Restrepo*, ed. by Elvira Sánchez-Blake and Julie Lirot (Bogotá: Alfaguara, 2007), pp. 341–51 (p. 344).
49. Laura Restrepo, *Historia de un entusiasmo*, 2nd edn (Bogotá: Aguilar, 1999) [first edition: 1986]. Originally published as *Historia de una traición* in 1986, the title reflected the failure of the peace negotiations which ended in 'un baño de sangre que acababa con la vida de casi todos sus protagonistas' [a blood bath which put an end to the lives of nearly all its protagonists] (*Historia de un entusiasmo*, p. 14) and suggests the government's betrayal in failing to keep the peace agreements which they signed with the guerrilla forces. Restrepo explains the change to the title of the second edition in 1999 as reflecting the shift in her recollection of the events related, from recalling the failure of the peace process to remembering the profound sense of enthusiasm at the outset of what were hailed at the time as promising negotiations and a possible end to the escalating violence that reached its peak in the mid-1980s.
50. Hughes, pp. 257–58.
51. Araújo, *La Scherezada criolla*, pp. 38–39.
52. Sylvia Molloy, 'Sentido de ausencias', *Revista Iberoamericana*, 132–33.51, Special Edition: 'Escritoras de la América Hispánica' (1985), 483–88 (p. 488).
53. Helena Araújo, 'Yo escribo, yo me escribo...', *Revista Iberoamericana*, 132–33.51, Special Edition: 'Escritoras de la América Hispánica' (1985), 457–60, (p. 460).
54. Helm, pp. 50–51.
55. I wish to draw attention here to my hesitant use of the term 'Western', a term which is frequently used in a generalising and unreflective manner, as highlighted by Claire Spencer: 'Frequent and uncritical shorthand references to the "West" [...] too often conflate U.S. policies, interests, and values with those of Europe and other developed states into a single expression of "Western values" to which "non-Western" states and regions, such as the Maghreb [amongst others], are expected to conform' ('The Maghreb in the 1990s: Approaches to an Understanding of Change', in *North Africa in Transition: State, Society, and Economic Transformation in the 1990s*, ed. by Yahia H. Zoubier [Gainesville: University Press of Florida, 1999], pp. 93–108 [p. 105]).
56. Assia Djebar in *Le Monde* (28 April 1995), quoted in Orlando, *Nomadic*, p. 12.
57. Valérie Orlando, 'To Be Singularly Nomadic or a Territorialized National: At the Crossroads of Francophone Women's Writing of the Maghreb', *Meridians: Feminism, Race, Transnationalism*, 6.2 (2006), 33–53 (p. 48).
58. Orlando, *Nomadic*, p. 58.
59. See Katharine Harrington, *Writing the Nomadic Experience in Contemporary Francophone Literature* (New York: Lexington, 2012).
60. Orlando, *Nomadic*, p. 18.
61. See Gilles Deleuze and Félix Guattari, '1730: Becoming-Intense, Becoming-Animal, Becoming-Imperceptible...', in *A Thousand Plateaus*, pp. 256–341.
62. Hughes, p. 265.

63. Araújo, 'Yo escribo'.
64. Braidotti, p. 10.
65. Hughes, p. 270.
66. Braidotti, p. 16.
67. Huston, 'Le déclin de l'"identité"', in *Âmes et corps*, pp. 57–77 (p. 71), original italics.
68. Theodor Adorno, *Minima Moralia: Reflections from Damaged Life*, trans. by E.F.N. Jephcott (London: Verso, 1978) [first edition: 1951], p. 87.
69. Michael Seidel, *Exile and the Narrative Imagination* (New Haven and London: Yale University Press, 1986).
70. Luis Torres, 'Exile and Community', in *Relocating Identities in Latin American Cultures*, ed. by Elizabeth Montes Garcés (Calgary: University of Calgary Press, 2007), pp. 55–83 (p. 67).
71. See Kaplan, *Questions of Travel*, p. 118.
72. Samir Gandesha, 'Leaving Home: On Adorno and Heidegger', in *The Cambridge Companion to Adorno*, ed. by Tom Huhn (Cambridge: Cambridge University Press, 2004), pp. 101–28 (p. 102).

PART II

Overstepping the Boundaries: Women's Narratives of Exile

CHAPTER 3

Vicissitudes of Language:
Nancy Huston's *L'Empreinte de l'ange* and Cristina Siscar's *La sombra del jardín*

Not all writing by exiled women deals explicitly with the challenges and difficulties of exile: exiled women writers who tackle the representation of exile in their works may present the particularities of the experience in more oblique ways. Chapters 4 and 5 look at works which deal with more implicit strategies of representation of exiled women's negotiation of identity in exile. This chapter begins the analysis of contemporary exiled women's writing by looking at two narratives which do explicitly manifest the concerns and experiences of exile, representing exiled protagonists in the highly charged period of arrival in exile. This chapter examines the writing of Nancy Huston and Cristina Siscar, two women who departed from their respective countries of birth, Canada and Argentina, for Paris as young women in the 1970s. As such, both experienced linguistic migration from their mother tongues (English and Spanish, respectively) into French. The dislocation from the familial and social space experienced by the two women is manifested in the subjective fragmentation that their fragmented narratives express. Characterised by multiple narrative perspectives, complex chronologies, and the potency of memory, these texts foreground the disorientation and subjective limbo of the initial stage of exile.

Criticism from across the broad spectrum of exile studies has largely converged on a tripartite understanding of the processes of exile, identifying an initial stage of arrival in exile, a period of great disorientation and uncertainty that is often characterised by trauma, mourning and guilt as the subject struggles with the loss of existing mooring points of identity, followed by a second stage of transculturation, or realignment of these mooring points of identity which are often drastically altered in the new environment, before giving way to a prolonged third stage of exile, which relates to an existential as well as a spatial positioning.[1] In this third stage, exiled women are often seen to appropriate and affirmatively inhabit the marginalisation and 'non-belonging' of the state of exile as a productive position from which to rethink and relocate parameters of identity beyond the norms which governed their pre-exile social identity. The schematisation of three such stages in the process of exile strongly resonates with exiled women's literary expression of exile, and informs and underpins my analysis here and throughout the book.

In addition to outlining the similarities of the experiences of these two writers, this chapter is also mindful of the vastly different political and historical circumstances by which their displacements were motivated, and in which they took place. Huston's cultural, or intellectual exile to Paris at the age of twenty-three bears little resemblance to Siscar's political exile, at age thirty-two, instigated by the events of the military dictatorship in Argentina. Despite Amy K. Kaminsky's claim that 'Whether forced or voluntary, exile is primarily from, and not to, a place',[2] Huston's migration from Canada to France, for reasons of cultural isolation in North America and in search of cultural and intellectual affinity in Europe, can be thought of in equal measure as an exile 'from' what she refers to as the historical and cultural vacuity of Canada and an exile 'to' Paris. As well as inflecting the outlook of the exile as either forward- (towards the place of residence in exile) or backward-looking (towards the birthplace left behind), the distinction between exile 'to' and exile 'from' is largely determined by the exile's ties with the birth country. In an epistolary exchange on exile with Leïla Sebbar, Huston reflects on her lack of affective, familial ties with her native country:

> je ne peux pas dire que ma tristesse à moi soit liée à l'exil — ou si elle l'est, c'est dans une inversion de la cause et de l'effet: je me suis exilée parce que j'étais triste, et j'étais triste (au moins est-ce ainsi que je m'explique les choses maintenant) parce que ma mère m'a 'abandonnée' quand j'avais six ans.[3]
>
> [I can't say that my sadness is the result of exile — or if it is, it's in an inversion of cause and effect — I went into exile because I was sad, and I was sad (at least that's how I explain it to myself now) because my mother 'abandoned' me when I was six years old.]

Where Huston's repeated emphasis on her greater cultural affinity with Paris — by which she accounts for the reason behind her permanent settlement there — is foregrounded in her writing, the nevertheless persistent reflection on her complex ties with Canada suggests that her displacement is as much driven by a sense of being 'out-of-place', or 'not-at-home' in Canada, as it is driven by an ideal of personal and intellectual development that Paris, in hindsight, has afforded her.

The mode of Siscar's displacement more concretely constitutes an exile 'from' Argentina, and she has tellingly described Buenos Aires before the period of political violence in the 1970s and 1980s as 'una extensión de mí misma' [an extension of myself].[4] Whilst this apparently secure sense of identification with the birthplace must be considered in light of a potential exilic nostalgia for a (real or imagined) secure sense of originary locatedness, Siscar nevertheless hereby demonstrates a strong affective tie with the birthplace. Unlike other Argentine writers who defied the military regime to lead active but vigilant literary careers in Argentina, such as the notable example of Liliana Heker who 'wrote for and edited leftist literary journals, managing a balancing act between veiled critique and oversight of the dictatorship for fear of retaliation', Siscar went into exile when the ever-present threat of violence became real with the disappearance of close family members.[5] Siscar's strong affective tie with Buenos Aires can only have been reinforced by her violent rupture from it, as argued in Chapter 1, and most certainly played a decisive if not fundamental role in both her inhabitation of the state of exile and the decision to return to Buenos Aires after six years in Paris.

It is important to bear in mind Siscar's 'privileged' status as a Latin American exile in France which, as Ana Vásquez and Ana María Araujo point out, distinguishes them from other foreigners in France: 'être exilé d'Amérique du Sud est une identité valorisée, une sorte de passeport pour se départager des autres étrangers qui ne sont pas aussi bien perçus et acceptés' [being an exile from South America is a valued identity, a kind of passport which separates one from other foreigners who are not as favourably perceived or accepted].[6] The French public was aware of, and largely sympathetic towards the plight of opponents to Argentina's military regime, to which Siscar's account of her encounter with Paris and the French testifies: 'La mayoría de los franceses que conocí estaban al tanto de la situación de nuestro país y mostraban mucho aprecio por la Argentina' [Most of the French people I met were aware of the situation in our country and showed a great deal of regard for Argentina].[7] As Siscar goes on to observe in the same interview, this was not the case for other political exiles, namely North Africans, who despite similar struggles against authoritarian regimes were not perceived in the same light. Edward Said echoes the claim for France's selective solidarity with its new arrivals when he states, 'Paris may be a capital famous for cosmopolitan exiles, but it is also a city where unknown men and women have spent years of miserable loneliness: Vietnamese, Algerians, Cambodians, Lebanese, Senegalese, Peruvians.'[8]

Huston corroborates Said's view when she too reflects upon the ambivalent status of the vastly diverse population of foreigners living in France, to which she refers alongside reflections on her own status as a North American in Paris. In identifying that she has not been the target of the xenophobia that has characterised the North African experience in France, she raises similar observations to Siscar's remark. Huston further notes that as a white, Caucasian female, she could physically 'pass' as French, yet she is 'betrayed' by her accent when speaking French. As she observes,

> Le rituel annuel de la carte de séjour est nettement plus humiliant pour eux [les 'vrais exilés'], basanés et balbutiants, que pour moi, blanche et bilingue; et quand je me promène dans leurs quartiers, ils me perçoivent très certainement comme une Française.
>
> [The annual ritual of the residency permit is far more humiliating for them ['real' exiles], dark-skinned and stammering, than for me, white and bilingual, and when I walk through their neighbourhoods they most certainly see me as a French woman.][9]

It is interesting here to note the wider network of exclusions and inclusions Huston herself creates through the designation of 'eux', or 'real exiles' (and reiterated by 'leurs quartiers'), as physically distinguishable from Europeans, and 'real exile' as, therefore, of non-European domain. Such utterances demonstrate how Huston's shifting network of inclusions and exclusions functions as part of a wider project to define her identity against what she is not (an identarian strategy noted in Chapter 1 to be common to exiled women) and to locate her primary category of identification and belonging in the liminality of the outside and the in-between. If anything, Siscar can be said to have been received more positively by the French, who reserve a particular distaste for the cliché of the North American tourist in Paris for whom Huston describes at times being mistaken. Despite participating in a long tradition of foreign writers and artists settling in the cultural and literary hub that Paris represents, Huston resents being likened to the cliché of the American tourist in Paris. Her compulsion to constantly clarify the parameters of her identity in her writing appears to stem from a fear of misidentification, and in particular, 'peur de ressembler à une "Américaine à Paris"' [fear of looking like an 'American in Paris'].[10] Neither Huston nor Siscar's characterisation of Paris is uncritically reflective, and both writers recognise and refer in their works to the complex web of inclusions and exclusions that operate in French social and cultural systems, and most notably in the dynamic between the French language and its speakers.

For Huston, the encounter with Paris is one of a cultural nature where she finds the history and culture that she finds lacking in what she refers to as Canada's cultural vacuum, yet it is perhaps most significantly her encounter with the French language which characterises Huston's encounter with the foreign city. The significance of the French language for the Canadian author who arrived in Paris with a knowledge of French that was sufficiently consolidated until it became the language in which she primarily wrote, and the Argentine writer who had to acquire French in exile albeit without adopting French as her language of literary discourse, is one of the central concerns of this chapter. As Elias Geoffrey Kantaris observes, 'The simplest and most effective form of marginalisation is to deny a person access to language and hence to any "meaning" or significance, to ignore the other person, relegate her to a "non-space".'[11] The passage from the 'non-space' of silence in a foreign language, to the construction of a social (and, for Huston, literary) space in the adopted language is a highly significant one for the exile who undergoes a linguistic as well as spatial shift in displacement. My interest in the linguistic migrations that Huston and Siscar discursively express is in examining the negotiation of the vulnerability and invisibility that silence in the foreign language induces, and to analyse how these impact on the processes of identity negotiation for the two women writers in the initial stage of exile, characterised by trauma and mourning, and by vulnerability, invisibility, and silence.

This chapter examines Huston's *L'Empreinte de l'ange* (1998)[12] [*The Mark of the Angel*] and Siscar's *La sombra del jardín* (1999)[13] [*The Shadow in the Garden*], two fictional works which recount the arrival and initial period in exile of their protagonists, and which explicitly stage the literal and metaphoric nomadism of their exiled protagonists. While the novels by Restrepo, Mokeddem, Lê, and Peri Rossi analysed in the following chapters are inspired, informed, and infused by their authors' experiences of exile they cannot strictly be described as explicit narratives of exile. By contrast, these two works by Huston and Siscar explicitly narrate the early experiences of their young, exiled women protagonists in exile. Whilst they are categorically *not* autobiographical accounts of their authors' lived experiences of exile, biographical traces are discernable in the narratives, although this is more apparent in Siscar's representation of a young Argentine woman's exile in Paris as the result of political violence at home than in Huston's account of her young

German protagonist's exile in the same city. Such autobiographical referentiality is evident in the writing of all six authors analysed here, and can be observed as a frequent characteristic of women's writing in and of exile.

The central questions that this chapter addresses are: How is language used, both as a theme and as a textual strategy of narration, in the representation of the negotiation of the fragmented identity of the exile? And how do the narrative strategies adopted contribute to this sense of fragmentation? Both protagonists are portrayed as inhibited and constrained by an imperfect knowledge of the acquired language, and each seeks alternative forms of communication, adopting other non-verbal (gestural and ritual) and creative (aesthetic and visual) modes of expression. This chapter concludes with a consideration of the role of alternative modes of communication in the negotiation of identity of the female exiled subject.

The Acquisition of (a) Language in Exile

The solitude of arrival in exile, celebrated in androcentric representations of exile as an open terrain of new-found possibilities to be tamed by a conquering, implicitly male individual, plays out quite differently for women exiles who must overcome silence, vulnerability, and disempowerment on a number of different levels, as demonstrated by the protagonists of *L'Empreinte de l'ange* and *La sombra del jardín*. Both novels emphasise the extreme disorientation and social invisibility which characterise each young woman's arrival in exile. *L'Empreinte de l'ange*, set between 1957 and 1964, tells the story of twenty-year-old Saffie from the moment of her arrival in Paris from her native Germany. Saffie immediately enters employment as a housekeeper with the celebrated French flautist, Raphaël Lepage, who hastily proposes to her, absorbing her into his comfortable middle-class life in the social and cultural epicentre of Paris's Left Bank. The third-person, unidentified, heterodiegetic narrator depicts Saffie as silent and impenetrable, and the reader initially learns little or nothing of her precipitous decision to marry Raphaël as the narration remains external to Saffie's thoughts, and characterises her as completely passive. Saffie's apparent passivity and apathy can only be attributed to the pervasive influence of her past on her present, and to her desire to distance herself from both by blocking all verbal and intellectual engagement. After the birth of their son, Emil, she enters into a passionate sexual relationship with András, an exiled Jewish-Hungarian artisan, through whom she gains access to a multinational, plurilingual underside of Paris, hermetically sealed off from the homogeneous and conservative bourgeois French milieu inhabited by Raphaël. The narration kick-starts Saffie's story *in media res* and it is her very silence and vulnerability which both suggest a traumatic past from which she seeks to escape, and spur on narrative intrigue and suspense. The gradual revelation of Saffie's past, as she partially overcomes her initial taciturnity and opens up to András, posits communication as a necessary step in the process of displacement, but its shortcomings belie its capacity to 'resolve' feelings of loss and subjective fragmentation.

The question of 'resolution' is indeed key to the portrayal of Saffie's relationship to language and communication in *L'Empreinte de l'ange*, as well as to women's discursive negotiation of the space of exile in a more general sense. In the discourse of exile, 'resolution' of displacement for the (implicitly male) exile is often commensurate with recapturing the status and authority left behind 'at home'. As women have not frequently enjoyed such status and authority in the first place, the notions of 'recapturing' that left behind, and 'resolution' mean something quite different for women exiles. According to the historical convention, 'resolution' would suggest the re-merging of the fragments of a singular, originary identity shattered by exile into an apparently cohesive albeit altered whole. In the case of exiled women writers, the 'resolution' of the troubled identity of the exile is more frequently conveyed in terms of the exploitation of the fragmentation of identity, rather than as an attempt to reunite its disparate elements. The subjective leap from a place of origin to a new space where identity is defined through displacement and difference is an irreversible one. The self in exile cannot return to the same place it left, as this is irrevocably changed by the fact of having left, nor can the self in exile be said to return to the pre-exile self for the same reason. Where this may also be the case for male exiles, women nevertheless experience this irreversibility in different ways, for the most part due to the questionable desirability of wishing to return to the pre-exile place or self. Thus the 'resolution' of the female exiled subject often manifests itself in the form of a renegotiation of a sense of self which comes to accept, and even celebrate, the fragmentation and mobility that exile provokes rather than a quest to revert the processes of fragmentation in a return to a singular, united sense of self.

The end of Saffie's relationship with András following the disclosure of her past and her unexplained disappearance from Paris at the novel's conclusion suggest the ongoing location of identity in the fragmentation and mobility of exile. *La sombra del jardín* also concludes with the unexplained departure of its young female protagonist in the closing pages. Indeed, the trope of the journey underpins Siscar's novel, which relates the experiences of its protagonist three months after her arrival in Paris, where she is haunted by the traumatic events of the military dictatorship that prompted her departure from her native Argentina. The solitary, and intensely lonely young woman (whose name remains undisclosed throughout the novel, the reader only learning her nickname, 'Miss Poupée', as she is dubbed by one of the other characters) is befriended by a multicultural and plurilingual group of itinerant performers with whom she embarks on a journey through rural France. She eventually parts company with the troupe, at which point her journey takes on the tone of a solitary quest whose goal becomes subsumed by the drive for mobility itself, eventually culminating in a new departure at the novel's conclusion.

The representation of the journey itself as a space of locatedness, in *La sombra del jardín*'s protagonist's incessant wandering, is also encountered more widely in Siscar's corpus. Imagery of train journeys and the inviting interior space of train carriages are frequently used in Siscar's fiction to represent a sense of secure locatedness within constant movement, as illustrated by Siscar's early short story, 'El andén' ['The platform']:

> Tomás anhela la región del tren. Imagina los pasillos, las butacas de cuero, las ventanillas, sobre todo las puertas abriéndose. Tomás no piensa en la estación

terminal, en ningún destino previsto. Solo piensa en subir al tren; en mirar a través de la ventanilla cómo va quedando atrás su andén, la barrera, cómo van pasando árboles, carteles, puentes, distintos paisajes. A Tomás no le preocupa adónde ir, sino ir, salir, andar, seguir.[14]

[Tomás longs for the space of the train. He imagines the aisles, the leather seats, the windows, especially the doors as they open. Tomás doesn't think about the terminus, or any intended destination. He only thinks about boarding the train, in seeing the platform, the barrier, draw away through the window, the trees, signs, bridges, different landscapes passing by. Tomás doesn't worry about where he's going, just about going, leaving, moving, pushing on.]

The sense of sheltered familiarity of the interior of the train in 'El andén' (written during Siscar's exile in Paris) is replicated in the atmospheres of the combi van, the trains, and the cars in which the protagonist travels in *La sombra del jardín*, written from the relative calm of life in Buenos Aires more than a decade after her return from Paris, with the difference that Tomás in 'El andén' is denied the mobility that the protagonist of *La sombra del jardín* enjoys.[15] The entire journey in *La sombra del jardín*, both the collective first half and the solitary second half, is represented in dreamlike imagery as a series of encounters with other characters, both imaginary and real, from both her past and her present. These characters facilitate the protagonist's passage which increasingly comes to resemble a legendary quest for the unattainable holy grail of escape from her traumatic past. Her trauma is two-fold, in that she intensely suffers the isolation which characterises her 'vida invisible y casi muda en la ciudad' [life in the city, invisible and practically mute] (*SJ*, p. 11) in Paris, where she knows no one and only partially masters the French language, as well as being haunted by the violence of the past which permeates the present through the resurgence of memory, and in the symbolic objects she carries around with her.[16]

Language, or more precisely, the acquisition of a new language, is foregrounded in both *L'Empreinte de l'ange* and *La sombra del jardín* firstly as an obstacle, and subsequently an enabling mechanism for the negotiation of the dislocated self at the moment of exile. The scope the acquired language (or rather, the acquisition of a new language) offers for the reconfigurement of the self in the dislocation of exile is a particularly powerful notion for Huston, as a writer who not only conducts her life in the acquired language, but who also writes in French and occupies a recognised position within the French literary canon. Language acquisition, and the use of a language other than the mother tongue, is staged as a prominent theme in much of Huston's fictional and non-fictional writing.[17]

L'Empreinte de l'ange is indeed no exception to this trend, and a great part of the text is dedicated to stressing the protagonist, Saffie's, encounter with and imperfect mastery of French. Whilst Saffie (like Huston herself) arrives in Paris with a basic understanding of French, she is less sensitive to its colloquialisms and figurative meanings. Her initial dialogues with Raphaël indicate her failure to grasp idiomatic expressions, demonstrate a sensitivity to the sonorities and rhythms of the new language, and underscore her fumbling for words. Raphaël's eagerness to fill the lacunæ in Saffie's speech demonstrates how her silence and her inability to express herself adequately leaves her vulnerable to manipulation by others. Raphaël's linguistic manipulation of Saffie is indicative of a wider subjective manipulation generated by the unequal power hierarchy in which she is four times disadvantaged: as a non-native French speaker, as a foreigner, as a woman, and as a domestic employee. Raphaël's precipitous marriage proposal reveals itself to be a predatory gesture which takes advantage of Saffie's disempowered state of which her linguistic deficiency is a symbol.

Misunderstandings such as those which occur between Saffie and Raphaël take on an altogether different dynamic when they occur between Saffie and András, who both use French as an acquired and imperfectly spoken language. The hierarchy which subordinates Saffie to Raphaël, both linguistically and culturally, is somewhat countered in her relationship with András. While András is politically and culturally more savvy than Saffie, she is the more proficient of the two in French and corrects his errors and his confusion with genres in French. However, the hierarchy between Saffie and András is revealed to be based on false premises, and only maintained by the concealment of his proficiency in German: 'L'allemand est une langue qu'il connaît depuis l'enfance, qu'il maîtrise à la perfection, et dont il a juré que plus un mot ne franchirait ses lèvres' [Though he's known the German language since childhood and mastered it to perfection, he has vowed that not a word of it will ever cross his lips again] (*EA*, p. 142). Their shared status as speakers of an acquired tongue sustains their relationship, as shown by their split when Saffie discovers András's knowledge of German upon the revelation to him of her past. Their relationship is revealed to be based, in part, on an imagined linguistic equal footing, disrupted when Saffie learns of his knowledge of her native tongue, and all communication between them breaks down.

Similar linguistic difficulties are seen to mark the experiences of the protagonist of *La sombra del jardín* as a recent exile in Paris. Miss Poupée (as she will be referred to throughout) is marked by an even more profound linguistic disadvantage than Saffie in that, like Siscar herself, she arrives in Paris with almost no knowledge of French. The text's narration, however, compensates for this lack by taking up her story some three months into her exile in order to explain her rudimentary knowledge of the language. Lack of French, as for Saffie, leaves Miss Poupée vulnerable to manipulation by others, and whilst the members of the theatre troupe appear to befriend her by inviting her to join them on tour, the ambivalence of the sexual relationships she enters into with two of its members suggests an altogether less altruistic intent. In contrast with Saffie, Miss Poupée demonstrates a strong desire to communicate and express herself, and she is disturbed by the distortion of meaning that occurs when others attempt to fill the gaps in her truncated speech:

> yo busco, con hambre, las palabras precisas que nadie me ha pedido [...]. A veces, alguno reacciona y se anima a completar mis frases truncas, lo que es peor, mucho peor, porque se cristaliza o distorsiona sin remedio el sentido de lo que quiero transmitir. (*SJ*, p. 22)
>
> [I search impatiently for the precise words that nobody has called for [...]. Sometimes, someone reacts and decides to complete my truncated sentences, which is worse, far worse, because it hopelessly crystallises or distorts the meaning I want to convey.]

The sexual attention of two of the members of the theatre troupe towards Miss Poupée takes on a predatory nature as they take advantage of her longing for the sense of refuge seemingly available in the shared status of non-native speakers. Yet her desire for the 'transparent' communication between native speakers of a shared native tongue is also manipulated by the male Chilean exile with whom she comes into contact. Lucio, whom she encounters upon her return to Paris at the end of her journey, responds to her vulnerability and takes her in, repeating the kind of exploitative sexual relationship experienced with the two theatre troupe members. In spite of their linguistic equality as native speakers of Spanish, her disadvantaged status as a solitary, transient women in the traumatic, guilt-ridden initial stage of exile subordinates her in relation to Lucio. In both *L'Empreinte de l'ange* and *La sombra del jardín*, the situations of the young, exiled women are thus highly gendered, as the manipulation of their vulnerability as recent exiles occurs within the framework of sexually exploitative relationships with men, who occupy a higher status in the power hierarchy. In this hierarchy, even other exiled or otherwise marginalised men prove to have and to exercise varying degrees of control over the two women. It is in this sense that the situation of the two exiled protagonists, as women, is shown to combine with and intensify the alienation of exile.

If the use of the acquired language can be considered a discursive strategy for the negotiation of women's exile, so too can silence, or the absence of language. Saffie's communication, limited to the strictly necessary, and her resounding indifference to Raphaël's projection of his desires onto her, suggest a drive to provide for her physical if not her psychological and emotional well-being in accepting marriage to Raphaël and its associated material comforts. As Marina Franco reminds us, the difficulties of exile are, in a first instance, practical before they are psychological and emotional, and language use is initially stimulated by the need to 'resolver cuestiones materiales' [resolve practical issues].[18] Yet Saffie's silence is also problematically interpreted by Raphaël as acquiescence, leading him to interpret her absent responses as indications of her conformity with the roles he projects onto her, such as her receptivity of his initial sexual advances which, in the absence of her consent, is effectively a scene of rape (*EA*, pp. 47–48). In another instance, her failure to verbalise the traumatic effect of the shrill ringing of the morning alarm clock, and Raphaël's disregard for her hysterical screaming lead him to interpret her weeping and vomiting as the emotional and physiological manifestations of her hitherto undiscovered pregnancy. Where alarm bells are figuratively and metaphorically set off for the reader, Raphaël turns a blind eye to the explicit signs of her past trauma and present instability in order to sustain her subservient relationship to him.

Silence is also textually manifested in the narration and allows for communication to take place in the absence of language. Saffie's revelation to András of her own and her mother's rape by Russian soldiers during the war, is conveyed through an absence of words: 'Ils l'ont?... –Oui. –Et toi, aussi? –Oui' ['They...? asks András. 'Yes.' 'You, too?' 'Yes'] (*EA*, p. 186). Saffie's mother's suicide by hanging is also conveyed through the gaps in language, as is the tragic accident that leads to Emil's death: 'La seconde d'après, il n'est plus là' [And the next instant, he's gone] (*EA*,

p. 317). Just as communication takes place in the gaps in language in *L'Empreinte de l'ange*, so too do loaded silences appear in *La sombra del jardín*. Rather than serving to convey information, however, silence in *La sombra del jardín* highlights the shortcoming of language to effectively articulate the trauma of the past, as illustrated by the question directed at the protagonist and left unanswered: 'Y tu amiga? —pregunta Nimis, en voz baja— Qué se sabe de ella?' ['And your friend?', Nimis asks quietly, 'is there any news of her?'] (*SJ*, p. 43). The unutterability of the disappearance by the military of Miss Poupée's friend, Lina, is shown to exceed the scope of language's communicative function.

If both novels posit the hierarchical dynamics between languages and their (native and non-native) speakers as instrumental in the negotiation of space and positionality in exile, they equally represent language as a medium in which exiles may forge and express a new sense of self. More than merely describing language's facilitating role in the renegotiation of self, Mary Besemeres goes further, highlighting language's necessary function in any displacement which involves the acquisition of a language: 'migration into a new language *requires* the person to recreate themselves in that language'.[19] Saffie's constant coming and going between the two discontinuous worlds she inhabits — of the Left Bank with Raphaël and the Marais with András — is largely accounted for in the novel by the fact that she conducts both lives in French (i.e. not her native tongue). The use of an acquired language is proffered as the device which allows her to play different roles, suggesting an inherent lack of authenticity in these roles, an intimation of inauthenticity that is also evident in Siscar's text when the narrator describes Lucio's non-native French as 'su francés impostado' [her phony French] (*SJ*, p. 131). The theme of the inauthenticity of non-native language use in *L'Empreinte de l'ange* reflects Huston's wider concern with language and authenticity.[20] When Huston's narrator states, 'la cérémonie s'est déroulée en français, et parler une langue étrangère c'est toujours, un peu, faire du théâtre' [the ceremony took place in French, and speaking a foreign language is always a little bit like play-acting] (*EA*, p. 230), he/she distinguishes between the emotional and the juridical functions of the wedding ceremony, in turn implying Saffie's mercenary opportunism in juridically, if not emotionally wedding Raphaël.

Language is thus attributed with a performative function: rather than describing an already existing entity (state, notion, identity), it in fact brings about the entity which it utters.[21] If language is performative, insofar as it has the power to bring about that which does not exist until it is uttered, for Huston this linguistic performativity is associated with inauthenticity. In *Lettres parisiennes* Huston states: 'ma fixation sur la langue française a (entre autres) pour résultat que, la plupart du temps, j'ai l'impression de vivre entre guillemets' [the result of my obsession with French is (amongst other things) that most of the time I have the impression of living in inverted commas].[22] The trope of living in inverted commas is one that Huston uses with regard both to speaking French, and to living in France, and she refers to 'le fait que j'aie l'impression non seulement de parler mais de *vivre* entre guillemets' [the fact that I have the impression not only of speaking but of *living* in inverted commas].[23]

Mary Besemeres suggests disrupting the polarity of authenticity and inauthenticity to consider the conditions in which a speaker's sense of inauthenticity arises:

> My use of 'inauthenticity' for a non-native speaker's sense of their own speech in the second language is not meant to set up a contrast with 'authenticity' [...]. It contrasts with the situation in the speaker's native language where the question of the authenticity of what is said does not arise.[24]

In interpreting what is experienced as lack of authenticity as proof, therefore, of inauthenticity, the exile confuses the self-reflection that is the by-product of the necessary recreation of the self in the acquired language with imposture. Besemeres reveals that authenticity and inauthenticity are not necessarily mutually exclusive or polar opposites, and that the scrutiny of new roles that exile provokes merely highlights the unquestioned nature of roles in the native language before displacement. Besemere's notion proves a highly fitting account of the way in which the linguistic shift is often experienced as highly traumatic for women exiles. As Huston explores in *Journal de la création*, women are often constrained to inhabit different roles which are arguably difficult to reconcile.[25] The identarian multiplicity of exile compounds other ways in which women's identity is already multiple and fragmented — divided namely between private and public roles — and exiled women undergo a subjective shift simultaneous to the linguistic shift of exile that compounds the compartmentalisation of women's identities. The perceived 'inauthentic performativity' of the inhabitation of multiple roles is intensely felt by the self in exile, in contrast with the pre-exile self where the 'native language seems to be continuous with self in a particularly strong way'.[26]

Segregating French from German, and consequently her French self from her German self, is one of the ways in which Saffie attempts to take control of her fragmented identity. Saffie's dissociation of her present (French) self from her past (German) self is manifested in her reluctance to sing to Emil in German, signalling a desire that she harbours for her son to grow up free from the 'contamination' of his maternal German heritage, characterised both by guilt, because of Germany's role in the war and her own father's participation in the Nazi regime, and trauma, due to her victimisation in Germany in the aftermath of the war. The two languages, French and German, signal the separation of past and present selves for Saffie, and the strong affective association of each language is made clear. German is associated with the violence and fear of the past, and French with the present, and with distance from both the past and past self. Such efforts to linguistically dissociate the past from the present are, however, belied by Saffie's retention of the German spelling of 'Emil', thus presaging the cohabitation of the past and present that inevitably proves necessary for the 'resolution' (in the sense qualified earlier) of displacement.

As is the case with Saffie, different languages are associated for Huston herself with different people and places, and linked to different aspects of the self. Huston has recounted in her non-fictional writing her own association of English with her mother who left the family home when Huston was six years of age — 'Donc, en matière de langue maternelle, quand j'avais six ans, elle a disparu. Ma mère. Avec sa langue dans sa bouche' [So, as far as my mother tongue is concerned, it disappeared when I was six years old. With my mother. Her tongue in her mouth][27] — and her subsequent association of German with the mother-substitute upon her father's second marriage to a German woman — 'C'était très simple. Il suffisait de changer de langue et les mots n'avaient plus le même sens. *Mutti* et *Mommy* designaient deux personnes différentes' [It was very straightforward. All you had to do was change language and the words no longer had the same meaning. *Mutti* and *Mommy* referred to two different people].[28] In turn, Huston attributes French with affording her the means for self-expression and self-determination due to its status as an (independently) acquired language: 'Pourquoi la France, pourquoi le français? [...] sans jamais me l'être consciemment dit, je devais savoir que mon salut passait par le changement de langue.' [Why France, why French? [...] without ever actually realising it, I must have known that my well-being depended on switching language].[29] The lack of any long-standing affective association that the acquired language holds for her, and its status as a language at which she arrived independently places it in the realm of freedom, of writing and, perhaps most importantly, of the creation of a new identity in the present that is distanced from her past, pre-exile identity. As we have seen, this freedom is not boundless, but accompanied by a concern for the 'authenticity' of self-determination in a new language.

The acquisition of a new language — although trying and traumatic — can thus be seen as facilitating the accommodation of a multi-faceted identity. In both *L'Empreinte de l'ange* and *La sombra del jardín*, multiple languages and the spaces with which they are affectively associated act as loci for the disparate aspects of identity, and allow for their cohabitation in the same individual. 'Resolution' of the damaged sense of self that bears the scars of past trauma is thus configured within a space of fragmentation and multiplicity, and Saffie's renegotiation of identity in exile is conclusively — and affirmatively — placed under the sign of fragmentation when the narrator states: 'Elle aime son existence comme elle est: scindée en deux. Rive droite, rive gauche. Le Hongrois, le Français. La passion, le confort' [She likes her life the way it is — divided in two. The Right Bank and the Left. The Hungarian and the Frenchman. Passion and comfort] (*EA*, p. 220). In this initial stage of exile, Saffie qualifies her fragmentation in terms of duality, as illustrated by the pairing of opposites in short, abrupt sentences. This duality is seen to give way to multiple fragmentation in the subsequent phases of exile, as developed in Chapters 4 and 5. The initial fragmentation of identity along linguistic lines, where the protagonists shift between languages without settling or becoming rooted in any single one, signals the emergence of an identarian nomadism that develops in exile over time.

The symbolic resonance of the two protagonists' encounter with the new language in Paris posits the different affective values of the native and the acquired languages for both women, and the role that these play in their respective identity negotiations in exile. Non-comprehension of the French language, referred to in *La sombra del jardín* as 'vehículo y al mismo tiempo barrera entre nosotros' [a vehicle and at the same time a barrier between us] (*SJ*, p. 67), is synonymous with exclusion in the hierarchy between members of the linguistic community of French and its outsiders. As well as being a principal thematic narrative structuring device, multiple languages are also explicitly incorporated into each text on a diegetic level, such that the narratives textually convey the multilingual communication of the other exiles and expatriates with whom each protagonist comes into contact in Paris.[30] The narrative inclusion of fragments of English, German, Hungarian, and Yiddish in *L'Empreinte de l'ange* and Italian, English, Polish, and Bulgarian in *La sombra del jardín* points to Steven G. Kellman's 'literary translingualism', which refers to 'the phenomenon of authors who write in more than one language or at least in a language other than their primary one'.[31] Despite Huston's stated preference for written over spoken French — Huston has admitted to a torturous sense of self-consciousness when speaking French and a preference for writing, where she can go back over her words, correct herself and revise, and where she feels her accent cannot be heard and give her away so easily[32] — she is nevertheless betrayed in her writing as what Kellman refers to as a 'linguistic interloper', for whom, 'some translingual texts expose the accents that their authors never quite discard'.[33] Whilst Siscar is not strictly 'translingual' in the sense implied by Kellman in that she writes in her native tongue, she nevertheless demonstrates the 'code-switching' demonstrated by bilingual speakers and writers who create 'internally translingual texts'.[34] Siscar resolves the problem of representing dialogue in several languages in a Spanish-language text through such code-switching, thus creating a translingual, rather than a strictly monolingual text. When Lucio exclaims '¡Argentina!', he does so 'por fin en nuestro idioma' [at last, in our language] (*SJ*, p. 131), thus designating the language of the dialogue between Lucio and the protagonist up to that point as French (although 'transcribed' in Spanish in the text). Other strategies which convey the linguistic plurality of *La sombra del jardín* are the incorporation of italicised, non-Spanish elements into the text to indicate the language used by the characters, e.g. '*Vous êtes grecque, n'est* [sic] *pas?*' (*SJ*, p. 11), and the narrator's explicit translation of dialogue, e.g. '¿Polaca? Esa fue mi traducción simultánea; la voz grave había dicho: *Polonaise?*] [Polish? That was my simultaneous translation. The deep voice had said, *Polonaise?*] (*SJ*, p. 12). Such discursive strategies point to the linguistic nomadism of the translingual author, uprooted from non-reflective, monolingual language use and relocated in a space of linguistic plurality.

Communication is complicated by written as well as spoken language, as is illustrated by the discourse of indecipherability, both literal and symbolic, in *La sombra del jardín*. As the protagonist travels in the combi van with her companions, she time and again sees 'otro letrero indescifrable' [another indecipherable sign] (*SJ*, p. 28). This disorientation is posited as an inability not only to recognise her physical surroundings, but also an inability to read the codes and symbols by which she is surrounded. These two modes of disorientation are neatly brought together in the image of Miss Poupée's inability to make sense of a map of France as she sets out on the solitary leg of her journey. As she traces her journey across the map's markings she is unable to interpret its cartographic information and ends up metaphorically lost and falling off the side of the map: 'cuando quiero acordarme, estoy cayéndome al mar, me he extraviado en los Vosgos o, del otro lado de cualquier frontera, vacilo en el borde del mapa' [before I realise it, I'm falling into the sea, I'm lost in the Vosges, or on the other side of some frontier, I hover on the edge of the map] (*SJ*, p. 93). Miss Poupée's disorientation can be considered in light of the distinction between French and Latin American cities that is a particuarly salient feature of the experience of exile for Latin Americans, as observed by Vásquez and Araujo:

> Les villes françaises sont devenues des 'villes écrites', où toute information apparaît sur des pancartes ou est symbolisée par des plans: on ne demande pas sa route, on étudie le plan du quartier. En Amérique latine, la ville est plus 'verbale', on parle davantage.[35]
>
> [French towns have become 'written towns', where information appears on signs or is symbolised on maps. One does not ask for directions, one studies the map of the area. In Latin America, the town is more 'verbal', one speaks more.]

In *La sombra del jardín*, Siscar thus also illustrates that the linguistic shift is not only a question of *what* language is used, but *how* language is used. The protagonist's tracing of her name in the snow in the opening scene of the novel suggests her efforts to assert herself in the space and the community around her by adopting the new scriptural linguistic codes. The fact that her symbolic gesture of inscription is interrupted by the sound of her name being called out by her new-found travel companions indicates an affirmative first step in the process of recognition and acknowledgement of her identity. Yet she is all too aware that her lack of linguistic communicative ability prolongs her invisibility as an outsider and anonymous inhabitant of the city, and she remarks that 'si no hablaba, si no me oían hablar, podían pasar los años y sus multitudes sin que una mirada tropezara con la transparencia que era yo' [if I didn't speak, if they didn't hear me speak, the years and their multitudes could go by without anyone laying eyes on the transparency that I had become] (*SJ*, pp. 10–11). The protagonist thus demonstrates a heightened awareness that she must not only adopt the new language and its linguistic codes in order to articulate her identity to others, but also that the expression of her identity in such precarious conditions is the only way to overcome her invisibility and assert her subjectivity both to herself and to others.

Narrative Strategies of Fragmentation and Mobility

Linguistic, communicational fragmentation is paralleled by the inherent narrative fragmentation of *L'Empreinte de l'ange* and *La sombra del jardín*. Both works adopt complex, layered narrative structures, employing shifts in the narrative focalisation and disruption of teleological chronological progression to signal the way in which the past inhabits the present for the recently exiled subject, and the consequently disjointed way in which the protagonists inhabit the present.

L'Empreinte de l'ange is narrated by a self-conscious, third-person narrator who imparts information gradually such that Saffie's past history is only revealed at an advanced stage of the novel, and then only in fragments at a time. The anonymous narrator (of whose sex the reader is not informed) occupies an instrumental role in the telling of Saffie's story insofar as he/she straddles the divide between the hetero- and the intradiegetic. Whilst not a character in the fiction's plot, the narrator takes on the role of an agent of the plot through the characterisation of the narratorial persona as an individual rather than a merely anonymous narrator, and by his/her strong presence in the imparting of Saffie's story. The domineering presence of the narrator only serves to make Saffie's vulnerability upon arrival in exile more evident. The narrator's self-conscious interjections in the narration, and reflections on his/her own role as narrator draw the reader's attention to the text itself as a product of language, asserting the constructed, even contrived feel of the narrative. The narrator coerces the reader through the interpellative use of the first-person plural, soliciting the reader's complicity with his/her role in the reading pact. The implied complicity between narrator and reader is heightened by the narrator's tendency to directly address the reader, for example: 'Venez, [...] Allez, [...] approchez-vous' [Let's go [...], come on now, come along] (*EA*, p. 99). The effect of the assumed readerly complicity is at times cinematic, positioning the reader as an obedient and willing spectator who follows the storyteller round the physical setting of the novel: 'Comme Mlle Blanche est en train de se verser un deuxième pastis et de se perdre dans ses souvenirs, nous pouvons nous rétirer sur la pointe des pieds de sa cuisine orange et kitsch' [Now that Mademoiselle Blanche is pouring herself a second glass of *pastis* and getting lost in her memories, we can tiptoe out of her tacky orange kitchen] (*EA*, p. 75).

Despite the apparent levity of the tone of narration in Huston's *L'Empreinte de l'ange*, the narrator is sternly domineering and acutely aware of his/her commanding position *vis-à-vis* the narrative suspense. He/she repeatedly alludes to his/her hand in orchestrating the plot in an altogether cavalier fashion with interjections such as, 'Donnons un coup d'accélérateur' [Let's speed things up here a bit] (*EA*, p. 79). The narrator's conclusive remark — 'c'est enivrant ce pouvoir' [it's exhilarating, this power] (*EA*, p. 79) — gives a knowing nod towards the commanding authority of the narrator that is also explored elsewhere in Huston's œuvre, and which contrasts with the protagonist's own lack of control and authority. Such self-conscious metafictional narration is characteristic of Huston's fictional corpus as a whole, which gives central importance to the role of the narrator in the telling of fictions, as well as confounding the separation of narrator and author. Huston's multilayered, metafictional novels reflect on the acts of writing and reading fiction through their complex narrative structures and polyphonic narration.[36] The self-conscious, extradiegetic narrator of *L'Empreinte de l'ange* draws attention to Huston's own role as the text's real-life author, and in turn, compels her reader to consider the author's own relationship to Saffie's story of exile.

The anticipation of significant episodes in *L'Empreinte de l'ange*, in the manner of 'c'est ici que commence la fin de cette histoire' [We're slowly approaching the end of the story] (*EA*, p. 297), and the withholding of information from the reader — 'c'est le printemps — pas celui-là, pas celui-là, un printemps d'avant la peur, quarante-deux peut-être, ou quarante-trois' [it's springtime — no, not that springtime, not that one, a springtime before the fear, 1942 perhaps, or 1943] (*EA*, p. 107) — similarly serve to impress upon the reader the all-knowing and all-commanding hand of the narrator. However, if the domineering tone of the narration initially serves to highlight Saffie's vulnerability and inability to assert or even express her subjectivity, she is portrayed as increasingly autonomous as such narratorial control diminishes to the point where Saffie disappears without a trace from Paris, and indeed from the narration itself. Despite the initially authoritative reader–narrator partnership, Saffie manages to acquire a degree of self-sufficiency and escape the controlled and controlling presentation of her identity. She assumes autonomy from the narrator at the novel's conclusion, as illustrated by the narrator's comment, 'Même moi je ne sais pas ce qu'est devenue mon héroïne' [Even I have no idea what became of my heroine] (*EA*, p. 321), ultimately characterising her as an autonomous being who exists independently of the narrator. The fact that this self-realisation is only partial and, like the protagonist of *La sombra del jardín*, results in a further departure, recalls the lived experience of exile as a chronological process as well as a spatial phenomenon. If Saffie and Miss Poupée are shown to have negotiated a way through their initial silence and vulnerability to achieve a degree of autonomy by the novels' conclusions, they have yet to pass through the subsequent stages of expression, and appropriation, of the state of exile.

The development of Saffie's sense of self in displacement is further illustrated by the shifting focalisation of the third-person narrator. Initially depicted as silent, and only vaguely present, Saffie is largely inaccessible to the reader in the early stages of the novel, and only becomes less so as the focalisation of the narration gradually shifts to Saffie's perspective. In the opening pages, a blank, absent Saffie is externally and superficially portrayed 'comme si elle était invisible, un fantôme' [as if she were invisible — a ghost] (*EA*, p. 27). Saffie's initial self-effacement can be explained by a desire to erase the memories and identity of her past, as illustrated by her eagerness to change her papers upon her marriage to Raphaël:

> Dorénavant, Saffie s'appelle: Mme Lepage. Le lendemain même de la cérémonie, livret de famille en main, elle va à l'ambassade de la république fédérale d'Allemagne [...] et fait refaire son passeport. [...] Le nom de son père, le nom de famille qu'elle a porté durant les vingt premières années de son existence, est oblitéré à jamais. (*EA*, p. 65)

> [Now her name is Madame Lepage. The day after the ceremony, her new family record book in hand, she goes to the West German embassy [...] and requests a new passport. [...] Her father's name, the family name she bore for the first twenty years of her existence, has been obliterated once and for all.]

Her metaphoric designation as a blank canvas onto which others (namely Raphaël) project their assumptions and desires for her indicates an initial lack of subjectivity as a result of her complete disorientation, both geographical and linguistic, upon arrival in Paris. The narrator fulfils the role of narratological filter, maintaining Saffie at a distance from the reader, through external focalisation which ensures the reader's lack of insight into her thoughts and motivations.

As the narration shifts to focalisation through Saffie, her increasing autonomy is resisted by the omnipotent narrator, who anticipates the shift and forewarns the reader with the notification, 'Or, sous peu, nous allons justement passer un moment dans la tête de Saffie' [And we shall soon be spending some time in Saffie's mind] (*EA*, p. 101). The narrator's reluctance to relinquish control over his/her protagonist reflects Saffie's struggle in the transition from object to subject. Despite the imposing tone of the narration, Saffie's voice nevertheless develops from a hesitant voice, 'sidérante de fragilité' [devastatingly fragile] (*EA*, p. 25), to an affirmative 'I' of subjectivity, when she explosively objects to András's ideals of violent revolution: 'Oh! J'en ai *marre*! Toujours la guerre, *la guerre, LA GUERRE!*' ['Oh, I'm *fed up*! Always *war, war, WAR!*'] (*EA*, p. 263).

The shifting presence, in Huston's metafictional text, of an authoritative narrator-figure functions to scrutinise the hierarchy that operates in the exchange between the narrator and the protagonist in the telling of the protagonist's story. In contrast with *La sombra del jardín*, where the protagonist tells her own story in the first person, *L'Empreinte de l'ange*'s Saffie is at the outset shown to lack the capacity for self-narration, as symbolically indicated by the lack of mastery of French, and by the narration of her story by an external narrator. By contrast, Siscar's use of a first-person narration constitutes a narrative decision to 'dar toda la dimensión interior del personaje' [give the full interior dimension of the character],[37] thus establishing Miss Poupée's developed sense of individuality, in contrast with Huston's protagonist who is initially pure surface and whose depths are only gradually revealed.

Huston's shifting of narrative perspective likewise allows for the distortion of chronology, a further narrative strategy of fragmentation and a mechanism for representing the silence and vulnerability of her exiled protagonist. On one occasion in *L'Empreinte de l'ange*, as Saffie mentally recalls the past from the safety of her bourgeois lifestyle in Paris, she is abruptly brought back to the present by the evocative sound of the doorbell ringing:

> *Sirène!* Une peur nauséabonde prend Saffie à la gorge et — avant qu'elle ait eu le temps de comprendre, avant que son cerveau ait pu faire la moindre raisonnement en sa défence, paix pas guerre, Paris pas Berlin, adulte pas enfant — elle s'étrangle. Sonnette pas sirène. On va à la porte, on l'ouvre et rien n'explose, personne n'est mort. (*EA*, p. 118)

> [*Siren!* Fear clogs Saffie's throat. Before she's had time to think, before her brain can undertake the least reasoning in her defence (peacetime not wartime, Paris not Berlin, adult not child), she chokes. Doorbell not siren. You go to the door, you open it and nothing explodes, no one is dead.]

Such eruptions of the past into the present, and her withdrawal from the present into recollections of the past, gradually draw out the details of her past trauma and provide an explanation for her unusual behaviour in the present. Saffie's psychological development is signalled by her increasing ability to separate the past from the present, and such instances of chronological confusion become scarcer as the novel progresses.

On a number of occasions the narrator of *L'Empreinte de l'ange* swings intermittently back and forth between different scenes at a vast temporal remove from each other to create dramatic effect, as for example, the implicit continuum of cause and effect that is established between Saffie's childhood and her entry into motherhood by the switching between the image in the present of an immobile Saffie in the corridor outside the sleeping Emil's bedroom, and that of a young Saffie surrounded by her siblings and mother as they hang out the washing. The immense sense of pending tragedy created by this temporal switching is replicated in the narration of Emil's fatal accident. The tension of the scene between father and son in the train is juxtaposed with the sexual passion of Saffie and András, creating a sense of urgency, anticipating the tragic outcome of the adulterous relationship, and insinuating the death of Emil as Saffie's punishment for her involvement in the illicit relationship.

The past is similarly shown to erupt into the present in *La sombra del jardín*, where memory is also foregrounded. Images and circumstances in the present in Paris trigger apparently random connections with events and memories of the past. The sight of a nun's robes in the train evokes memory in this seemingly spontaneous and unexpected way: 'De las rodillas [de la monja] caen los pliegues levemente temblorosos por el zarandeo del tren, levemente, temblorosas, caían en verano las flores blancas del palo borracho, en las baldosas rojas del patio' [The folds, gently swaying from the rocking of the train, fall from the knees [of the nun], gently swaying fell the white flowers from the ceiba tree onto the red tiles of the patio in summer] (*SJ*, p. 96). The past lies just below the surface of the present in the apparently random and disconnected way that scenarios and images draw up memories, revealing the protagonist's difficulty to inhabit the present as she is continually haunted by the past.

Memories also invade Miss Poupée's sleeping hours in *La sombra del jardín*, where the eruption of dream sequences in the narrative is in equal measure poetic and disturbing. Memory blurs with reality in the novel leaving the reader, at times, unable to distinguish between past and present, or between dreams and reality. One particular nightmare sequence sees her dreaming of men in military uniform whilst on a train journey, thus evoking the military authorities of the dictatorship that sent her into exile. When she suddenly wakes (still within the dream) to find the seat next to her, as well as the whole train empty, her nightmare evokes the terror and uncertainty that caused her flight to Paris. Unaware of the train's destination, she alights from the deserted train of her nightmare in order to ask the name of the station, only to be left behind on the platform when it pulls out of the station, taking with it her luggage, still onboard. As the station guard puts on the jacket and hat of his station guard uniform, the evocation of the military that underlies the episode is complete. While this entire sequence seemingly occurs within the confines of her dream, the lack of any further mention of Lina's bag (the significance of which is discussed below) for the remainder of the novel suggests its actual loss by the narrator and confounds the distinction between dream, memory, and 'reality' in the novel.

Indeed, the dreamlike quality of the narration of *La sombra del jardín* is fostered by the text's tendency to switch between past and present, and from dream to reality, and by the legendary tone of the narrative in which unlikely and fantastical events mark the protagonist's quest. The narrator-protagonist's own disorientated state reinforces a sense of the unreal, and in addition to failing to fully interpret visual information, she is similarly unable to keep track of time. During the first leg of her journey in the van, Miss Poupée is not sure if she slept, was pretending to, or was dreaming. The fact that this is not a disturbing experience, but a comforting one due to the reassuring movement of the vehicle in transit suggests the protagonist's drive to escape the traumatic present as well as the haunting past through constant mobility between the two. On the day after their arrival on the first leg of the journey, after what is recounted as an interminable night spent travelling, time ebbs and flows, expanding and shrinking, in the hours spent occupied in communal activities with her travelling companions. The inclusion of a film screening in the narrative expands the range of narrative discourses in the novel, and stages the distortion of time in a very explicit fashion. The Haitian peasant women who appear in the film made by one of the puppet troupe are destined to carry out mundane and repetitive actions over a lifetime which are condensed into the duration of a film: 'El las filmó durante cuatro días, y luego cortó y pegó celuloïde hasta obtener una hora de película' [He filmed them for four days, and then cut up the tape and stuck it back together again to end up with an hour of film] (*SJ*, p. 67). Real time becomes warped into endless, repeated loops as 'la vida reproducía el tiempo de la película' [life reproduced the time of the film] and the present, 'un puro transcurrir incapaz de evolución' [a pure passing of time, incapable of evolution] (*SJ*, p. 69), becomes increasingly absurd. The film thus efficiently represents the way in which time is experienced by the recent exile as distorted: Miss Poupée inhabits a disrupted yet self-perpetuating present which is invaded by the past and fragmented by the disorientating eruption of dreams and memory, presaging the journey to a future in which she will come to accommodate herself within the ongoing state of exile.

The chronological complexity seen in Huston's novel is thus also apparent in Siscar's *La sombra del jardín*, where the teleological progression of time is not a given, and the reader must actively decipher the time span of the protagonist's present in France, and her past before her arrival in Paris. The reader is thus lulled into a sense of disorientation which replicates the protagonist's own disorientation, and must actively resist being mesmerised by the oneiric quality of the narration in order to remain anchored in the present of reading and thus make sense of Miss Poupée's story. The novel's opening paragraph establishes the significance of chronology in the novel from the outset:

> Ahí, en el kilómetro cero de París, lugar de reunión y de partida, se anudaban para volver a desatarse, igual que las vías al entrar y salir de una estación, los hilos de una historia que había empezado a tejerse tres meses atrás, el día de mi llegada a la ciudad. O tal vez mucho antes, con los sucesos que, desde el otro lado del océano, me habían empujado hasta el centro de esa plaza donde estoy a las dos de la tarde de un día de enero, de comienzos de enero, hace años. (*SJ*, p. 9)

> [There, in the official centre of Paris, site of encounters and departures, the threads of a story knotted together only to unravel again just like the tracks in and out of a train station, a story which had begun to weave together three months earlier with my arrival in the city. Or perhaps it began even earlier with the events that, from the other side of the ocean, had propelled me to the centre of the square where I am at two in the afternoon on a day in January, early January, years ago.]

In this initial stage of exile characterised by trauma, mourning and guilt, the novel's protagonist seeks constant onward movement while incessantly haunted by the past, thus denying the present altogether. Where the present in *L'Empreinte de l'ange* is infused by the past, Siscar's protagonist in *La sombra del jardín* barely inhabits the present in her constant drive towards an uncertain future, and her haunting by characters and events from her past in Buenos Aires. The overshadowing of the present by the past in *La sombra del jardín* is symbolised by the rescued objects that the protagonist carries around with her: Lina's bag, a well-thumbed book by Witold Gombrowicz, and a Polish stamp that she finds in her attic room in Paris. Siscar's interest in the commemorative symbolism of objects is a more widespread theme also explored in her other texts, and to greatest effect in *Los efectos personales* [*Personal Effects*], which carries the dedication, 'Dedico este libro a una chica que fui: a ella y sus cosas' [I dedicate this book to a girl I was: to her and her things].[38] Symbolic objects in Siscar's texts function as more than mere symbols, but also take on the function of repositories of meaning and memory which sustain affective and cultural ties to the past. Miss Poupée's repetitive reading of Gombrowicz in *La sombra del jardín* becomes a ritualistic, and thus comforting action which creates a degree of familiarity in a painfully unfamiliar environment: 'Y como siempre, en la pausa abrí el libro, el único libro que había escapado conmigo. Se trataba de un rito. Una vez más relía, fatalmente, los mismos párrafos' [And as always, in the pause I opened the book, the only book that had escaped with me. Like a rite. Once again, fatally, I read the same paragraphs] (*SJ*, p. 12). The book fulfils the function of mnemonic anchoring device to which she turns for sanctuary from her disjointed ties with others, and which offers constancy and reliability in its unchanging paragraphs.

The book by Gombrowicz provides a symbolic and physical link to the homeland: both the object and its historical author have links with Argentina, and Gombrowicz's own nomadic wandering between Argentina and Europe can be compared to that of the protagonist. Gombrowicz (1904–1969) spent many years in Argentina, from 1939 to 1963, when the Nazi invasion of Poland prevented him from returning from a visit to Argentina. He never returned to live in his native Poland: after a brief sojourn in Berlin upon his return to Europe, he settled in the south of France. The inclusion of a figure who represents such a potent symbol of exile in the Argentine cultural imaginary inscribes the narration into a wider history of the Argentine experience of exile that counters the isolated and individual nature of the protagonist's experience of exile. The fact that one of the definitive symbols of exile for Argentines is not, in fact, an Argentine but a Pole reflects changing historical patterns of migration, in that Argentina was largely a country of reception of exiles and migrants up until the mid-twentieth century. Lina's bag, by contrast with the book, evokes the personal toll suffered by the exile when the protagonist remembers and is the constant physical reminder of Lina's traumatic disappearance in Buenos Aires which accounts for Miss Poupée's exile to Paris. The intense guilt of having escaped a similar fate is constantly brought back to her by the physical presence of the bag, and is made clear in the following passage when the protagonist remembers:

> Que ella, Lina, había venido a casa por unos días, en esos días en que arrancaban a la gente de sus casas. Autos y hombres armados recorrían una ciudad marcada, llena de cruces. Una mañana señalaron mi casa, irrumpieron, se llevaron a Lina, yo no estaba. Creo que es de noche cuando regreso; sólo distingo una cosa, una sola cosa reconocible en medio de la destrucción: su bolso, en el suelo, cerca de la entrada. Fue un segundo, atinar a rescatarlo y huir. Ahora, ese bolso es todo mi equipaje. (*SJ*, p. 43)

[That she, Lina, had stayed with me for a few days, during the days in which they dragged people from their homes. Cars and armed men patrolled a marked-up city, full of crosses. One morning my house was targeted, they broke in, they took Lina, I wasn't home. I think it was night when I got home. I only remember one thing, only one recognisable thing in the midst of the destruction: her bag, on the floor, near the entrance. In a second, I managed to snatch it and run. Now this bag is all the luggage I have.]

Lina's bag functions as the physical manifestation of the protagonist's burden of guilt following Lina's disappearance in a raid targeted at herself as its weight bears down on her: 'la correa tirante del bolso se me hunde poco a poco en el hombro como si, tal vez a causa de mi debilidad, empezaran a pesarme mis escasas pertenencias' [the taut strap of the bag digs into my shoulder as though, perhaps due to my weakness, my scarce belongings had begun to weigh down on me] (*SJ*, p. 93). The reference to her 'escasas pertenencias' only highlights the symbolic, rather than the actual weight of Lina's bag. By underscoring the fact that the protagonist has only scarce belongings, the narrator emphasises that Miss Poupée has not only lost her home, her belongings, and any sense of locatedness, but also all the material possessions which represent these things: all that remains to her are the book and the bag. The discovery of the old Polish stamp between the carpet and the skirting board in her attic room in Paris thus signals the beginning of the necessary process of establishing links with her present, where people and objects left behind slowly begin to be replaced with new people, new objects, and new memories.

The powerful emotional force of objects rescued from the past is not lost on the protagonist of *L'Empreinte de l'ange*, as indicated by the inclusion of her mother's prayer book and the rather gruesome poodle-foot amulet alongside the (also rather scarce) items of clothing in Saffie's suitcase on her arrival in Paris. Not a real poodle's foot, but the remnants of a stuffed toy that her father gave her, Saffie's amulet is a link not only to Germany but to her childhood, whereby the past and childhood are inextricably linked for the young woman. Saffie is only able to detach herself from the object by symbolically casting it into the Seine after disclosing her past to András. The release from the grip of the past and the move towards a continuous cycle of ongoing mobility that the symbolic gesture of casting off the symbolic object triggers take place in altogether different circumstances in *La sombra del jardín*. The loss of Lina's bag on the train in the protagonist's nightmare ambivalently suggests both a fear, and a simultaneous and apparently contradictory desire to be rid of the bag, thus enabling Miss Poupée to engage more actively in her present.

The metaphorical weight of Lina's bag implicitly comprises a commentary on the burden of Argentina's recent political turmoil on its survivors, underpinning the novel with a political undercurrent. Likewise, *L'Empreinte de l'ange* is heavily infused with its historical and political backdrop. The narration of Saffie's story is underpinned by a didactic tone which expounds on the historical and political background of the novel's action, which is situated in a precise temporal and spatial setting. The importance of the insertion of the novel's action into a concrete historical and political backdrop is underscored in the text's opening prologue, which provides details of the political fluctuations and economic boom of the post-war years. The Algerian War figures in the novel as the narrator's primary political concern, and he/she frequently interrupts the narration to comment on the situation in Algeria at the time, and on the extended impact of the war on metropolitan France. Torture methods used by the French army in Algeria, bomb attacks by the National Liberation Front, the actions of the Algerian National Movement, the attempted coup of 13 May 1958, de Gaulle's return to power, and the repression and massacre of Algerians in Paris on 17 October 1961 are all extensively documented in the narration.

The novel's contemporary political context sits in dialogue with the political strife experienced by the novel's protagonists in the past. The narration draws links between History and individual histories, highlighting individuals' roles as both agents and victims of History. Along with repeated references to the Algerian War and its impact in Paris at the time, the novel also makes reference to a vast range of other significant events in contemporary world history, placing the French historical backdrop of the novel in a wider, international context. However, if the narrator is highly concerned with contemporary current affairs and politics, the protagonists, Raphaël and Saffie, on the other hand are not, and the narrator condemns them for failing to grasp the significance of the decision to award Albert Camus the Nobel Prize for literature in 1957: 'lorsque [...] le comité Nobel décide de décerner son prix de littérature à Albert Camus, ils ne saisissent nullement la portée politique de ce choix' [when the Nobel committee [...] decides to award its prize for literature to Albert Camus, they're oblivious to the political implications of this choice] (*EA*, p. 81). The representation of French attitudes to recent French history constitutes a challenge by the author, whose display of her own profound knowledge of France's political and historical past gestures towards a greater engagement with French culture than the French themselves, and equally constitutes a criticism of France's failure to live up to its standards of *liberté, égalité, fraternité*. In addition to developing the historical, social and political context of the novel's setting and action, the foregrounding of contemporary French history in *L'Empreinte de l'ange* also situates the author in relation to the events recounted, as both a writer who belongs to the French literary canon, and an outsider to the events of History that she relates.[39] In doing so, she inscribes herself into that history, and lays claim to a voice of legitimacy from which to add to the discourse on the events of French history, from a position outside the (nationally and sexually) hegemonically dominant, as a non-French, woman writer.

The narrator's at times overwhelmingly ironic tone also reveals the author's own voice behind the text. The tongue-in-cheek criticism of French bureaucracy in *L'Empreinte de l'ange*, which echoes many of the arguments of Huston's non-fictional writing, is clear when the narrator states:

> Tout cela a énormément changé depuis, bien sûr. Les employés des mairies et des commissariats parisiens ne se comportent plus avec le mépris, la morgue et la malveillance pour lesquels ils étaient jadis célèbres. De nos jours, dès qu'on met les pieds dans une administration parisienne, on tombe dans un état voisin de l'extase. (*EA*, pp. 61–62)
>
> [Nowadays, of course, all this has changed radically. The employees of Paris town halls and police stations no longer treat people with the condescension, arrogance, and malevolence for which they were once famous. Nowadays, the

minute you set foot in a Paris administrative service, you enter a state not far from ecstasy.]

Furthermore, Huston constantly draws attention to the way in which characters use the French language, highlighting its use in public discourse itself. When the narrator, for instance, parodies the French government's use of the term 'événements' [events] to describe (and deny) the war in Algeria against the backdrop of which the novel is set, Huston's voice is clearly audible in the text.

Siscar demonstrates a similar sensitivity to the ideological resonance of language, which can be traced to the way in which meaning was monopolised and distorted by the military rulers during Argentina's dictatorship, in order to frame the expulsion of 'undesirable' citizens in a discourse claiming the preservation of national 'order' against 'subversive' individuals. The encounter with French institutions is also represented in critical terms in *La sombra del jardín*. Seeking cartographic information upon embarking on her solitary quest, Miss Poupée encounters the condescension of the librarian in Reims: 'No *mademoiselle*, en Francia no tenemos ninguna localidad con esos nombres' [No *mademoiselle*, in France we don't have any places with those names] (*SJ*, pp. 110–11, original italics). The librarian assumes Miss Poupée to be a tourist, and misreads her presence in France as the result of an appreciation and admiration of French culture: 'aquí también tenemos *Les rêveries du promeneur solitaire*... supongo que habra oído hablar de la obra de Rousseau, verdad?' [we also have *The Reveries of the Solitary Walker*... I suppose you've heard of the works of Rousseau, haven't you?] (*SJ*, p. 111). The effect on the protagonist of such encounters, which clearly demarcate lines of inclusion and exclusion, through the use of the first-person plural, and the implicit dynamic of 'we' and 'you' therein, are expressed spatially in the novel in the image of the *cours* in Paris:

> En las inmediaciones del teatro Odeon, penetramos por un amplio portal en una de esas *cours* adoquinadas que muchas veces yo había espiado al pasar, desde la vereda, viéndolas como el recinto sagrado e inviolable de una ciudad fortificada, y que siempre ejercían la fatal atracción del misterio, al mismo tiempo que me confinaban en el sentimiento de estar de paso. (*SJ*, p. 134)
>
> [In the vicinity of the Odeon Theatre, we penetrated the wide doorway of one of those cobbled courtyards of the type that I had only glimpsed from the street many times in passing. Seeing them as the sacred and impenetrable enclosure of a fortified city, they had always exuded the fatal attraction of their mystery, at the same time confining me in a feeling of transcience.]

Her eventual admittance into one such courtyard, so long a symbol to her of exclusion from French society, indicates the first step in the process of overcoming the disorientation and dislocation that are so intensely felt in the first half of the novel.

While *La sombra del jardín* is certainly situated in a suggested temporal setting, given the historical circumstances of the protagonist's departure from Argentina during a military dictatorship, time is on the whole represented as disconnected from any concrete reality. It is characterised primarily by its passing, conveying an atmosphere of legend, rather than being inscribed in a specific historical and political setting as seen in *L'Empreinte de l'ange*. Indeed, Siscar's text takes on the tone of a legendary quest as a means to recover a sense of self that has undergone irreparable damage in exile.

Alternative, Non-linguistic Modes of Communication

If language proves to be a privileged medium through which exiled women writers negotiate and express a way of 'being' in exile, *L'Empreinte de l'ange* and *La sombra del jardín* both formally and thematically demonstrate that it is a highly problematic medium in the initial stage of arrival in exile. Both novels present alternative non-verbal and aesthetic forms of communication — which between them include painting, sculpture, film, theatre and performance, classical music, jazz, dance, and song, as well as gestural and ritual expression — to broaden the aesthetic texture of the narratives and illustrate alternative modes of expression where the obstacles of linguistic difference and the near-impossibility of the verbal representation of past trauma do not obstruct communication. Much emphasis is placed, in both novels, on gestural communication as a form of expression which avoids the problems of hierarchy and the distortion of meaning that are associated with verbal communication. In her study of trauma, language, growth, and development in *L'Empreinte de l'ange* through the illuminating framework of psychoanalytic theory, Loraine Day points out the 'sensorial and multi-dimensional nature of Saffie's rapport with András', demonstrating how, in addition to language, they communicate through silence, laughter, play, and 'through the bodily expression of instinctual needs'.[40] Whilst these gestural forms of communication may be considered a feature of sexual relationships in general, these take on a special significance for the displaced couple of *L'Empreinte de l'ange*, insofar as they provide channels of communication unhindered by the problem that linguistic communication poses.

If non-verbal, gestural communication takes on a special significance for individuals in exile, it offers a way of consolidating group relationships in the transnational, multilingual groups with which Huston and Siscar's protagonists come into contact. Such relationships are particularly important for Siscar's protagonist, who demonstrates a sense of individuality (albeit a precarious sense of individual subjectivity, severely damaged by the severance from the ties — social, cultural, and linguistic — on which her identity was anchored prior to exile) at the expense of the loss of a sense of community through her departure into exile. Miss Poupée's desire to reinstate a sense of 'identidad del conjunto' [collective identity] (*SJ*, p. 30) is of particular significance in the context of the Argentine experience of exile insofar as exile was frequently experienced as an intensely solitary ordeal. Pilar González Bernaldo de Quiros identifies the denial of access to a collective identity as that which characterises exile when she poses the question: '¿Qué es el exilio sino la condena a una exclusión de la comunidad nacional a través de la exclusión del territorio sobre el cual se funda la pertenencia colectiva?' [What is exile but condemnation to exclusion from national identity through exclusion from the national territory on which collective belonging is founded?].[41] Singled out and expelled from the native land, and thus excluded from the collective national identity, individual identity is often the only sense of identity that remains for the political exile. It is indeed the pursuit of reintegration into a collective identity — that which was denied and lost through exile — that initially motivates Miss Poupée's interaction with the theatre group, and it is primarily through gestural and ritual actions that Miss Poupée finds her way back into collectivity. Communal activities are portrayed as feeding her starved sense of collective identity, such as sharing meals, travelling together, and collectively occupying delimited spaces (i.e. the combi van, the cottage, train carriages, and cars). The novel posits the rituals of communal actions as a form of consolidating a group identity:

> Cortar, pinchar, llevarse el tenedor a la boca, masticar, saborear, tragar, beber, llenar de nuevo el vaso, romper con los dedos una rabanada de pan, estos gestos repetidos, elementales, constituyen, al parecer, el lenguage excluyente de este grupo de oficiantes de una ceremonia instintiva y tribal, que se prolonga indefinidamente. (*SJ*, p. 21)
>
> [Cutting, stabbing, lifting fork to mouth, chewing, tasting, swallowing, drinking, refilling the glass, breaking bread, these elementary repetitive gestures seem to constitute the exclusive language of this group of celebrants in an instinctive and tribal ceremony which prolongs itself indefinitely.]

The emphasis on the rituals of eating in *La sombra del jardín* also highlights an initial impulse in exile to provide for physiological demands. The physical necessity of eating, a need certainly far easier to fulfill than that of relocating a sense of identity and purpose in exile, provides an achievable quotidian goal that the protagonist of *La sombra del jardín* relishes: 'la cena nos reclama. Sopa de cebollas, omelette de quesos, borgoña, pan. Bocado a bocado, copa trás copa, esta vez me abandono a la ceremonia muda y gestual' [dinner calls us. Onion soup, cheese omelette, Burgundy, bread. Bite by bite, cup after cup, this time I give myself over to the mute gestural ceremony] (*SJ*, p. 35). These mute, gestural ceremonies are shown to provide a medium of expression which linguistic communication, shown to be problematic and inadequate, hinders: 'Por medio de gestos, y recurriendo finalmente al lenguaje esencial, telegráfico, consigo decir lo que nunca había dicho' [Through gestures, and finally turning to an essential, telegraphic language, I manage to say what I had never said] (*SJ*, p. 22).

If the road to the assertion of identity in exile occurs in the domain of the linguistic and gestural, it also passes through the visual, as the titles of both Huston's and Siscar's novels foreground. Yet the vision that each title expresses is only opaque — an impression (*empreinte*, rendered as 'mark' in the English translation), a mere shadow (*sombra*) — suggesting a drive for self-representation that is manifest but as yet unachievable in the initial stage of exile. The preoccupation in *La sombra del jardín* with the inability to see clearly is reflected in Siscar's predilect image of reflections in train windows, and is used in *La sombra del jardín* to illustrate how the protagonist must first 'recognise' herself, and affirm her own destabilised identity to herself before overcoming her invisibility to others: 'En un lento girar de cabeza, mi mirada se topa con mis ojos mirándome desde el vidrio de la ventanilla que la noche exterior ha vuelto espejo' [As I slowly turned my head, my gaze came across my eyes in the glass of the window which the night outside had turned into a mirror]

(*SJ*, p. 95). Imagery of interior reflections in the windows of moving vehicles recurs in other texts by Siscar — most notably in her most recent short story, *La Siberia* — effectively providing a means by which Siscar's protagonists may see themselves from the exterior, as though through the gaze of others.

Miss Poupée indeed seeks the status of subject in the gaze of others, as illustrated by the description of a boy in the metro who '[l]e miraba con tanta persistencia que [su] cuerpo empezó a modelarse dentro de la ropa' [he looked at her with such persistence that her body began to take shape inside her clothes] (*SJ*, p. 11). The boy's gaze not only confirms her subjectivity but also grants her a physical presence, thus diminishing her perceived invisibility. However, whilst a sense of her own subjectivity may be reflected in the gaze of others, it also poses the risk of misidentification. Insofar as being gazed at is a passive activity for the subject being recognised, it leaves the way precariously open to the imposition of supposed or assumed identities on behalf of the beholder. That Miss Poupée (not yet named as such by this scene in the novel) is misidentified four times in the opening pages of the novel — as Greek (p. 11), Iranian (p. 11), Polish (p. 12), and Italian (p. 19) — indicates that this is a very real concern for the protagonist. We see a similar concern for misrecognition and misidentification in Huston's non-fictional writing, as illustrated by the aforementioned example of Huston's frustration at her misrecognition as an American tourist in Paris. Yet, as this example also illustrates, it is also her white, Caucasian appearance that allows her to 'pass' as French and which distinguishes her from other groups of cultural outsiders. Huston's concern for misrecognition thus takes on selective overtones, as being mistaken for 'une Française' appears less irksome to her than to be mistaken for 'une "Américaine à Paris"'. Such concerns suggest a context in which the destabilisation of identity for exiled women writers drives a constant need to define a sense of self in displacement, and to prescribe their own terms of identification and community.

To return to the wider aesthetic texture of the two narratives at hand, it must be noted that music occupies a privileged role in *L'Empreinte de l'ange*, and functions as a structural narrative device as well as a symbolic device which illustrates the many divisions which operate in Saffie's life in exile, yet it is the use of visual imagery by both Huston and Siscar that I wish to stress here.[42] Raphaël's comparison of Saffie to a Hans Bellmer doll broadens the aesthetic range of *L'Empreinte de l'ange* to include the visual, while propagating, rather than disrupting the misogynistic violence that Saffie herself experienced during the course of the war.[43] Hans Bellmer created his mannequin-like 'dolls' in the 1930s, assembling distorted, abjectly inanimate and mutilated female forms which embody a violent, misogynist objectification and eroticisation of the infantilised female body. Such a comparison not only contributes to Saffie's characterisation as a damaged, distorted object manipulated by male actions and desires but visually symbolises Raphaël's objectification of the young Saffie's body.

La sombra del jardín incorporates an even wider range of creative forms, including music, painting, song, dance, film, theatre, puppetry, and doll-making, as well as thematising the act of writing itself. Siscar's novel also, significantly, includes the theme of dolls in the form of doll-making and, of course, in the protagonist's own nickname ('poupée' meaning 'doll'). The comparison of Saffie to a doll, and the naming of Siscar's protagonist as such by another character signals both protagonists' initial lack of subjectivity and their manipulation by others. The metaphor is extended in *La sombra del jardín* as Miss Poupée also earns this name as she is also a doll-maker. Her stated desire to make dolls is an overt sign of a desire for self-regeneration, but the fact that she does not actually make any dolls over the course of the novel's action bears witness to the difficulties and obstacles that prevent her from actually doing so. In keeping with the segmentation of the stages of exile, whilst the will and desire to renegotiate identity are clearly visible, the means for achieving this are not yet available to her in this early stage of displacement and instability.

Corroborating Miss Poupée's desire to assume a new identity is her obsessive interest in a long-deceased woman named Stella, whose name she finds carved into a tree trunk near the country house where she is staying, along with the date, 22 June 1942, which she eventually traces to a young Polish Jew who lived in hiding in the house and whose paintings she discovers in the attic. Miss Poupée begins to speculate about Stella, and without any real evidence decides that she must have painted under the threat of danger and, for this reason, comes to feel a connection with her. 'Memories' of Stella begin appear to her — Miss Poupée has visions of her running through the forest pursued by men in military uniform and jackboots — suggesting a drive for the sublimation of her own trauma in that of Stella. One painting in particular, a palimpsestic self-portrait, figuratively and literally depicts the fragmented and multilayered identity that Miss Poupée imagines to be marked by trauma and displacement, and she ponders the various 'Stellas' that the self-portrait conceals. The representation of both painting and identity as palimpsest posits the negotiation of identity subsequent to traumatic displacement as an ongoing process: can the top layer of the palimpsestic self-portrait ever be said to be the final one? When Siscar's narrator states, 'La miro. Sé que veo lo que ella veía de sí misma o, al menos, lo que deseaba que de ella vieran los demás' [I look at her. I know that I see what she saw in herself, or at least, what she wanted others to see in her] (*SJ*, p. 60), she is also (knowingly or unwittingly) speaking of herself. The motif of Stella's self-portrait also evokes the same fundamental question of self-representation posed by Huston: when the mechanisms of identity formation and presentation are necessarily and consciously negotiated, can the presentation of identity be considered authentic?

Huston offers a provisional conclusion to this question in the treatment of her position as the real-life author behind the narrative persona, and which is illustrated by the performance of (amongst other aspects of Huston's identity) French cultural citizenship in her text. As a non-native French citizen, Huston's inclusion of an abundance of historically significant dates, facts, and statistics effectively stakes a claim to a rightful place within French citizenry in a performance of citizenship along the lines of May Joseph's 'nomadic citizenship'. Joseph refers to 'a peculiar condition for which theories of citizenship do not adequately account: that of nomadic, conditional citizenship', whereby citizens are required to perform their citizenship in a performance that nevertheless marks them out as inauthentic citizens.[44] Huston's highly conscious demonstration of her knowledge of French culture and history in *L'Empreinte de l'ange* illustrates Joseph's theory of a 'citizenship [that] is not organic but must be acquired through public and psychic participation'.[45] Whilst I would dispute Joseph's notion of 'organic citizenship', in that citizenship (whether of the birth or an acquired culture) is a social phenomenon which always requires performance, she nevertheless makes a valuable point about the performativity of 'nomadic citizenship' that illuminates Huston's narrative strategies. In performing a citizenship that stakes a claim to a rightful place within French culture, Huston highlights the consciousness of that performance, a consciousness that has been remarked upon elsewhere in her corpus. Matthew Manera says of *Cantique des plaines*:[46] 'Specific references to political events may serve to keep the chronology in focus, but Huston's use of them always seem to stand outside the flow of the narrative... They seem too researched, too carefully placed.'[47] In charging Huston with too calculated and contrived a style, Manera echoes Huston's own concern with performativity, and which the translingual, transcultural writer necessarily encounters. I would suggest that Huston addresses this apparent aporia by consciously reminding the reader of her authorial presence behind the text. In citing a criticism frequently levelled at Huston, that by foregrounding her novels' formal architecture Huston has prevented the reader from constructing an illusion of reality, Frank Davey perhaps unknowingly identifies Huston's prime narrative strategy, which is to make visible to the reader the very illusion of reality inherent to writing.[48] This illusion of reality is strikingly similar to the illusion of the 'authentic', self-continuous identity of the monolingual, 'unexiled' subject, who is not made forcibly aware of Said's 'outside' to language and community as is the translingual, exiled subject. Huston thus reminds the reader that the text, as much as an individual's identity, is a construct the contemplation and conscious presentation of which is not, as Mary Besemeres points out, so much an act of inauthenticity, as an act made aware of its own performativity due to the discontinuation of the unquestioned and seemingly authentic self.

The creative and performative nature of the identarian processes of exile are thus enacted and problematised by Huston, and writing is likened to the construction and simultaneous expression of identity in that, like the act of writing, identity undertakes the negotiation of its processes as it is carried out. Despite the importance of alternative, non-verbal modes of communication in *L'Empreinte de l'ange* and *La sombra del jardín*, writing, and ultimately language, remains the privileged medium for combatting the silence, vulnerability, and invisibility of displacement. If exile is absence, and its struggle is the exiled subject's efforts to win their way back into presence, writing is a way of turning absence into presence.

The protagonist's epiphanic decision in *La sombra del jardín* to write her story marks a turning point in the novel's plot, and the end of her wandering quest:

> Entonces ocurre. En este momento, allí, sentada en el suelo a un costado de la ruta, comiendo y esperando que alguien me recoja, hacen contacto en mi mente la burla oblicua de la bibliotecaria de Reims y la exhortación del cartero. Por primera vez, concibo la idea de escribir esta historia algún día. Miro a un lado y otro: nada adelante, nada atrás. (*SJ*, p. 126)

[And then it happened. At that moment, there, sitting on the side of the road, eating, and waiting for someone to offer me a lift, I thought of the inadvertent gibe of the librarian in Reims and the warning of the postman, and something clicked. For the first time it occurred to me to write this story one day. I looked one way and then the other: nothing ahead, nothing behind.]

The decision to inscribe her story finally fixes her in the present ('nada adelante, nada atrás') albeit a transitory present as her subsequent departure into an unknown future indicates. The conclusion to *La sombra del jardín* suggests the close of the first phase of exile and progression towards the second as her resolution to write her story 'algún día' suggests. Siscar describes her own transition from the heightened turmoil of arrival in exile to the relative stability of a period of employment in the French Alps (largely resembling Miss Poupée's own episode in the Alps towards the end of *La sombra del jardín*) which permitted her return to writing, an activity which had been disrupted by her departure into exile.[49]

Siscar describes the kind of 'literary homecoming' that the writing project affords exiled women writers, where the notion of writing itself constitutes a nomadic site of belonging and location of identity for exiled women writers whose sense of self takes leave of fixed national or linguistic identities, to resettle in the 'non-space' of the in-between:

> creo que en el exilio se hizo más claro, que la casa, el lugar de residencia y de identidad, de permanencia, era la escritura, sí... pero una *casa rodante*, al mismo tiempo. Yo digo eso porque es como que esa casa de la escritura al mismo tiempo no es una casa fija, es una casa en movimiento permanente, es una recreación permanente, una refundación permanente.[50]

> [I think that in exile it became clear that home, the place of residence and identity, of permanence, was writing, yes... but, at the same time, a *mobile* home. I say that because it's as though that home that is writing, at the same time, is not a fixed home, it's a home that is in constant movement, a permanent recreation, a permanent resettling.]

Siscar's evocative likening of the space of writing to a home that is mobile, rather than fixed, qualifies the space of 'writing as home' in terms of dynamism and creativity. The scriptive drive expressed by Siscar's protagonist in the novel's closing pages thus prefigures the second stage of exile where the exile, having overcome the silence and vulnerability provoked by the unsettling arrival in displacement, is concerned with expressing the fragmented nature of exiled subjectivity during the period when return becomes conceivable, even possible.

Notes to Chapter 3

1. See, in particular, Emily Vaughan Roberts, 'A Vietnamese Voice in the Dark: Three Stages in the Corpus of Linda Lê', in *Francophone Post-Colonial Cultures*, ed. by Kamal Salhi (New York: Lexington, 2003), pp. 331–42; and Vásquez and Araujo, p. 34.
2. Kaminsky, *Reading*, p. 30.
3. Huston, *Lettres parisiennes*, p. 110.
4. Boccanera, p. 59.
5. Díaz, p. 8.
6. Vásquez and Araujo, p. 71.

7. Boccanera, p. 53.
8. Said, p. 176.
9. Huston, *Désirs et réalités*, p. 202.
10. Huston, *Lettres parisiennes*, p. 11.
11. Elia Geoffrey Kantaris, 'The Politics of Desire: Alienation and Identity in the Work of Marta Traba and Cristina Peri Rossi', in *Forum for Modern Language Studies*, 25 (1989), 248–64 (p. 253).
12. Nancy Huston, *L'Empreinte de l'ange* (Arles: Actes Sud; Montreal: Leméac, 1998) [*The Mark of the Angel*, trans. by Nancy Huston (New York: Random House, 1989)].
13. Cristina Siscar, *La sombra del jardín* (Buenos Aires: Simurg, 1999).
14. Cristina Siscar, 'El andén', published in *Reescrito en la bruma* (Buenos Aires: Per Abbat, 1987), p. 40.
15. Siscar revealed in an interview conducted in Buenos Aires in March 2009 that although published after her return to Buenos Aires in 1987, 'El andén' was the only short story in the collection, *Reescrito en la bruma* [*Rewritten in the Fog*], to have been written in Buenos Aires before her exile to Paris, and was originally titled 'Los que se quedan' ['Those who stay (behind)']. The sense of immobility and disempowerment present in both the original and modified titles of the story denotes a shift from a desire for an empowering yet unattainable mobility (comparable to the sense of entrapment in a military dictatorship from which one is unable to escape, as illustrated by the potent image of Tomás on the platform watching the train pull away) to the accomplishment of the extreme mobility of the protagonist of *La sombra del jardín*. Furthermore, the original title resonates with the burden of guilt which certain of 'those who stayed behind' in Argentina endeavoured to instill in those who opted for exile, and which Siscar was seen to decisively refuse to assume in Chapter 1. See Averis, 'La casa de la escritura'.
16. All primary texts will be referred to with abbreviated forms of the works' titles in parenthetical textual references. See List of Abbreviations.
17. For a paradigmatic example of Huston's meditation on her relationship to French, see her essay, 'En français dans le texte', in *Désirs et réalités*, pp. 263–69.
18. Franco, p. 64.
19. Besemeres, p. 11 (my italics).
20. For a discussion of Huston's sensitivity to the tensions of performative identity and authenticity, see Kate Averis, 'Le "vrai" moi: Nancy Huston's Concern for Authenticity', *Essays in French Literature and Culture*, 45 (2008), 1–18.
21. In the manner of J.L. Austin's 'performative utterances', whereby a sentence uttered performs the act that it names, one pertinent example of which being wedding vows. For further information see Austin.
22. Huston, *Lettres parisiennes*, p. 168.
23. Huston, *Lettres parisiennes*, pp. 169–70 (original italics).
24. Besemeres, p. 32.
25. Huston, *Journal de la création*.
26. Besemeres, p. 18.
27. Huston, *Désirs et réalités*, p. 265.
28. Huston, *Désirs et réalités*, p. 265.
29. Huston, *Désirs et réalités*, p. 264.
30. Siscar's interest in linguistic polyphony is further developed in the eponymous short story of her most recent published work, *La Siberia* (Buenos Aires: Mondadori, 2007), in an inversion of the Latin American exile's encounter with linguistic difference in Europe, where a disparate group of international tourists are drawn together on a bus trip through a desolate and wind-swept Patagonia in southern Argentina.
31. Steven G. Kellman, *The Translingual Imagination* (Lincoln: University of Nebraska Press, 2000), p. ix.
32. Nancy Huston, *Nord perdu: suivi de Douze France* (Arles: Actes Sud; Montreal: Leméac, 1999), p. 38.
33. Kellman, p. 8; p. 10.
34. Kellman, p. 15.
35. Vásquez and Araujo, p. 60.

36. For further paradigmatic instances of Huston's self-conscious narrators, see also *Cantique des plaines* (Arles: Actes Sud; Montreal: Leméac, 1993), *Instruments des ténèbres* (Arles: Actes Sud; Montreal: Leméac, 1996), *Dolce agonia* (Arles: Actes Sud; Montreal: Leméac, 2001), and *Une adoration* (Arles: Actes Sud; Montreal: Leméac, 2003). See also Diana Holmes, 'Écrire est un verbe transitif: Les voix narratives de Nancy Huston', in *Nomadismes des romancières contemporaines de langue française*, ed. by Audrey Lasserre and Anne Simon (Paris: Sorbonne Nouvelle, 2008), pp. 83–91, for an analysis of the narrative voices in Huston's œuvre.
37. In Averis, 'La casa de la escritura'.
38. Cristina Siscar, *Los efectos personales* (Buenos Aires: De la Flor, 1994)
39. Laura Restrepo operates a similar strategy in *La isla de la pasión* (Bogotá: Planeta, 1989) in which she fictionalises a historical event of Mexico's colonial past, and in her more recent *Demasiados héroes* (Bogotá: Alfaguara, 2009), an autofictional account of the experience of a former militant activist (a character based on Restrepo herself) during the early stages of Argentina's most recent military dictatorship. Like Huston, Restrepo also inscribes herself into the literary, cultural, and political histories of the countries in which she has lived.
40. Loraine Day, 'Trauma and the Bi-lingual Subject in Nancy Huston's *L'Empreinte de l'ange*', *Dalhousie French Studies*, 81 (2007), 95–108 (p. 104).
41. Pilar González Bernaldo de Quiros, 'Presentación: Emigrar en tiempos de crisis', *Anuario de Estudios Americanos*, 64.1 (2007), 34–44 (p. 35).
42. For further information on Huston's use of music as a structural and thematic device in her fictional works, see David Powell, 'Dimensions narratives et temporelles du jeu musical dans trois romans de Nancy Huston', *Francophonies d'Amérique*, 11 (2001), 49–64, and Catherine Khordoc, 'Variations littéraires dans *Les Variations Goldberg*', in *Vision/Division: l'œuvre de Nancy Huston*, ed. by Marta Dvorak and Jane Koustas (Ottawa: University of Ottawa Press, 2004), pp. 95–111.
43. The German artist who renounced his German nationality and took up the French after emigrating to Paris in 1938 can also be said to bear a number of parallels with Saffie's own departure from Germany and eagerness to take up the French nationality. For more information on Hans Bellmer and his dolls, see Sue Taylor, 'Hans Bellmer in the Art Institute of Chicago: The Wandering Libido and the Hysterical Body', <http://www.artic.edu/reynolds/essays/taylor.php> [accessed 23 January 2014].
44. May Joseph, *Nomadic Identities: The Performance of Citizenship* (Minneapolis: University of Minnesota Press, 1999), p. 2.
45. Joseph, p. 3.
46. Huston, *Cantique des plaines*.
47. Matthew Manera, 'Plainsong and Counterpoint', *Canadian Forum*, 73 (1994), 36–38 (p. 38).
48. Frank Davey, 'Big, Bad, and Little Known: The Anglophone-Canadian Nancy Huston', in *Vision/Division: l'œuvre de Nancy Huston*, ed. by Marta Dvorak and Jane Koustas (Ottawa: University of Ottawa Press, 2004), pp. 3–21.
49. See Averis, 'La casa de la escritura'.
50. In Averis, 'La casa de la escritura' (my italics).

CHAPTER 4

❖

Writing Home: Malika Mokeddem's *L'Interdite* and Laura Restrepo's *Dulce compañía*

By contrast with fictional accounts of exile depicting an individual's initial disorientation in the new country of residence, such as those seen in the previous chapter, exiled writers, as might be expected, often turn their gaze back toward the birth country once the prospect of return becomes possible or even fulfilled. Rather than focusing on individual accounts of the inner life of the exiled writer in the new country, 'home-based' exile writers (to use a designation coined by Andrew Gurr and introduced in Chapter 1) embed their narratives in the social and historical context of their country of origin in narratives which frequently span both the individual and the collective.[1] Often claiming to occupy an ideal position of distantiation from the object of their critique, such writers can be said to wield the critical distance and intellectual freedom that Edward Said identifies as available to those in exile, which enable a privileged position from which to observe and criticise.[2] If the estranged insider — both native to and distanced from the home country through exile — is well placed to adopt a critical voice, the dual insider–outsider status can equally be experienced as a problematic position, due to the very distantiation from what was once 'home' and as such places the authority and legitimacy of the author's claim to any representative function in doubt. This troubling insider–outsider status is further problematised by women exiles insofar as women, largely responsible for the transmission of traditional cultural values and practices, disrupt this trend through their departure into exile. Malika Mokeddem and Laura Restrepo are two writers who can be considered 'home-based' writers, and whose works deal with the problematic position of the exiled woman writer for whom the possibility or the fact of return casts her in the role of privileged critic of the country of origin.

Despite differences in the duration of the two authors' absence from the birth country (Restrepo has periodically resided in Colombia in the years between her six-year exile and her current residency in Mexico, compared with Mokeddem's permanent departure from Algeria and residency in France), the two writers' circumstances of exile have much in common in that both women left their countries of origin to avoid both threats of violence as well as the mounting difficulty of carrying out their daily occupations. After beginning her medical studies in Oran, Mokeddem left for Paris to complete her degree away from the increasingly oppressive atmosphere in Algeria at the time, which was compounded by the project of Islamisation and its restrictions on and violence towards women. As she explains in her own words, 'J'ai eu besoin d'aller finir mes études ailleurs, de respirer un air ailleurs, d'être plus libre' [I needed to go and finish my studies elsewhere, to take in a different air, to be freer].[3] For Restrepo, it was participation in the peace negotiations between the Colombian government and guerrilla movements that put her personal safety at risk and made it necessary for her to leave Colombia. The imminent danger of her role as a negotiator in the failed peace negotiations made it impossible for her to write her account of the experience free from the threat of attack or attempts on her life, and Restrepo departed for Mexico in order to do so. If the danger was explicit and very real in Restrepo's case, as testified by the violent deaths of key figures who took part in the negotiations, for Mokeddem the climate of Islamisation in post-independence Algeria created by the Islamic Salvation Front (FIS) and other Islamist groups, and the backdrop of increasing violence that would result in the civil war of the 1990s were no less threatening.

Significantly, the experience of exile had a directly causal role in each woman's entrance to literary writing, to which their highly autobiographical first texts bear witness. Both Mokeddem and Restrepo embarked on their literary careers in an autobiographical vein, with first books which vividly recount the circumstances which lead up to and eventually prompted their exiles. In these autobiographical texts, both authors emulate a wider tradition in the literary negotiation of the exiled female subject. Jean Déjeux comments on the frequency with which Francophone North African women writers turn to the autobiographical in their first novels, which he identifies as a gendered strategy for affirming individual, female subjectivity as well as facilitating the entry into writing: 'En effet, voulant sortir de la marginalisation sociale, du silence ou de l'ombre, les auteurs dans leurs premières œuvres veulent s'affirmer, communiquer aux lecteurs leurs expériences, leurs vies, leurs combats *pour être reconnues en tant que femmes*' [In fact, wishing to break out of social marginalisation, silence, or the shadow, these authors want to affirm their identity, and communicate their experiences, their lives, and their struggles *as women* to their readers, in their first works].[4] Déjeux describes a shift from marginalisation and silence to a space of communication and affirmation of identity that Valérie Orlando expresses in terms of migration from the private to the public space, as discussed in Chapter 2. Like Déjeux, Orlando describes women's entry into the public space of writing as fundamental to overturning the roles that have been contrived for them by male oppression within the private sphere of the sexual, familial, and domestic. Orlando also highlights the fact that women's entrance into writing is paralleled by relegation to a new space of marginalisation where their numbers are few.[5] Déjeux's and Orlando's conceptualisation of women's affirmation of subjectivity through the literary inscription of their identity illuminates the understanding of the passage through the autobiographical that is frequent in exiled women writers' first texts. This initial autobiographical impulse is not confined to Francophone North African women writers, but can also be observed more widely in transcultural women writers (and arguably, women writers in a more general sense) who are compelled to inscribe their experience in order to confidently articulate their identity in an environment that has not historically facilitated women's self-assertion. Both Restrepo's and Mokeddem's writing has followed a similar trajectory in terms of its reliance on the autobiographical. The first books of both authors are firmly rooted in the life experiences that lead to their exiles, with an autobiographical drive that has returned in increasing measure in both authors' most recent novels. Whilst diminishing mid-corpus, arguably due to efforts to establish themselves personally and professionally in their respective countries of exile and to distance themselves from a monothematic literary agenda, the overall increasing referentiality of their novels peaks in the recent and explicitly autobiographical *La Transe des insoumis*[6] [*The Trance of the Rebellious*] and *Mes hommes*[7] [*My Men*], by Mokeddem, and *Demasiados héroes*[8] [*No Place for Heroes*] by Restrepo, indicating the degree to which the negotiation of exiled female identity is an ongoing and pressing drive behind their writing projects well beyond the second stage of exile.

This initial 'scriptotherapeutic drive'[9] to inscribe the trauma and adjustments of exile often leads to a continuing literary production which carries over the centrality of displacement into subsequent texts, rendering the experience of exile both the starting point as well as an ongoing drive behind these authors' writing projects. This is particularly striking in the case of authors who carry out their literary activity alongside other professions, as is the case for Mokeddem and Restrepo (who practise, respectively, medicine and journalism alongside their literary careers). This is also notably the case of other displaced women writers of note who have pursued literary careers alongside other professional activity such as Luisa Futoransky, Milagros Palma, Kim Lefèvre, Gisèle Pineau, Ana Vásquez, as well as, to a certain degree, the other four writers of this study whose universally hybrid literary activity covers many different spheres of writerly activity including journalism, teaching, radio broadcasting, and translating. Where their professions become the arena for social insertion and recognition in their adopted societies, literature remains the domain of the continuous negotiation of the exile's location and expression of identity.

Their respective experiences in Algeria and Colombia, and their exiles in France and Mexico, are manifested in their novels to differing degrees, with Mokeddem relying more heavily on the autobiographical than Restrepo. Both authors' protagonists often resemble their creators and share certain biographical similarities with them, yet Restrepo's novels do not resemble the autofictional accounts of exiled protagonists and their negotiation of the in-between space of exile that characterise Mokeddem's œuvre. Remarkable in Restrepo's corpus is the total absence of narratives that explicitly relate the six years that the author spent in exile. She has, however, inscribed the experience of her involvement in left-wing militant organisations opposed to the military dictatorship in Argentina in the more recent *Demasiados héroes*, although the experiences fictionalised in this novel took place before her exile in Mexico, which has not yet been treated in the same way. Restrepo has instead largely produced texts which provide an account of contemporary Colombian society and its struggle to overcome the violence and internal conflict in which the country has been immersed in recent decades. Her novels present depictions of local realities from the dual perspective of one who is both native to, and distanced from the society that she writes about. The autobiographical in Restrepo's novels is present and tangible with narrative themes related to those which have motivated Restrepo's own personal and political activity and protagonists who bear experiential and professional similarities to Restrepo herself, without being first-person narrations of her own experiences. Mokeddem and Restrepo both create texts concerned with the re-encounter with the birth country, and charged with the tensions of return (in the form of periodical visits to Algeria in the case of Mokeddem, and longer periods of residency in Colombia in the case of Restrepo). The texts of Mokeddem and Restrepo can thus be said to illustrate the second, intermediate stage of exile, typically comprising a period of transculturation in which the exiled writer undertakes the discursive realignment of the mooring points of identity. In this stage, writing becomes a priority as it constitutes the very platform on which the renegotiation of identity is performed. Both writers are exemplary of the negotiation of the altered relationship with the home country, of the process of transculturation undergone by the subject in exile, and of the discursive negotiation and realignment of mooring points of identity that typically correlate with the second stage of exile.

If the texts of Mokeddem and Restrepo are underpinned by the personal and the autobiographical through the oblique or explicit inscription of the authors' life experiences in their novels, the novels' contexts are broadened by the representation of the cultural and political life of the native countries left behind. If Déjeux distinguishes a common concern with contemporary history in the texts of Francophone women writers of the Maghreb — 'Un thème précis et particulièrement douloureux, mais glorieux aussi, pour les romancières algériennes est celui de l'histoire immédiate' [one specific and particularly painful, yet glorious, theme for Algerian women writers is that of recent history] — this can be attributed to the fact that recent history has exacted an enormous cost on North African women's agency and freedom.[10] Mokeddem's concern with the treatment of 'l'histoire immédiate' is clear throughout her corpus and serves both a personal and a historical function. The personal drive behind Mokeddem's inscription of her experience of the events of Algeria's recent history allows the author to make sense of her position in relation to a society which forced her into exile, and in which she nevertheless locates an originary site of identification and connection with her ancestral past. The historical drive endeavours to provide an unofficial record of the events of late twentieth-century Algerian history from a non-hegemonic viewpoint, that is to say, from the position of a woman who is a part of, yet who speaks out against the developments of contemporary Algerian society. Mokeddem's corpus is weighted towards the depiction of Algerian society in the context of the violence it has suffered particularly intensely in the 1990s and at the beginning of the twenty-first century, rather than focusing on her experiences in her new country of residence. Restrepo has also consistently engaged with issues pertaining to contemporary Colombian history, as Claire Lindsay notes.[11] In Restrepo's corpus, the near absence of narratives set in the country of exile, which places her in stark contrast with the other five authors at hand, indicates the writer's principal concern with the depiction of the homeland which sent her into exile rather than with her individual experience as an exile. This chapter argues that it is the political and historical circumstances of their exiles, and the socio-historical patterns of the societies from which they were exiled that cause both Mokeddem and Restrepo to cast a critical gaze on the birth country, a gaze that seeks both to analyse and denounce hierarchical social structures and the roles they impose.

Indeed, much of the fictional writing by women exiled from their countries of origin due to social and political turmoil is characterised by a hybrid discourse of denunciation. Frequently incorporating historical and journalistic discourses, the fictional text becomes the generically hybrid vehicle through which such displaced writers both denounce the birth country that exiled them, and attempt to redefine their relationship with it. In their overtly politicised texts, both Mokeddem and Restrepo present their own ideologies and political agendas. Charles Bonn identifies a continuous tradition of a 'discours d'idées' [discourse of ideas] in an earlier generation of Algerian literature in French due to its origins as a weapon against French colonialism in Algeria.[12] Mokeddem thus inscribes herself into a wider tradition of ideological literature in Algeria through her contestatory texts in French, a language which *a priori* bears a political weight in the Algerian context, a weight which, according to Bonn, cannot be avoided by the Algerian writer who chooses to write in French. David William Foster similarly attributes an inherent politicisation to Latin American fiction that bears any claim to realism, stating that 'institutional violence is such an ordinary part of Latin America that one must conclude that its appearance in Latin American literature has been predominantly documentary rather than fictional'.[13] Indeed, a contextual reading of the texts of Mokeddem and Restrepo reveals the extent to which they are infused, even governed, by a political and documentary imperative.

Highly critical of the patterns of violence and the hierarchies of authority of their respective countries, Mokeddem and Restrepo both discursively demonstrate an empathy and solidarity with the female population who, along with other marginalised groups, receive the brunt of that violence and repression. Mokeddem writes from a female perspective to denounce abuse and violence targeted at women by Islamic fundamentalists, and to expose a discourse of an extreme interpretation of Islam imposed on the population. Restrepo's is also a specifically female voice that details the lack of power and consequent difficulties suffered by the female inhabitants of the impoverished communities of Colombia, greatly disadvantaged in a patriarchal society radically divided into rich and poor. Restrepo denounces a political system which denies a voice to a large part of the population and which sanctions the complicity of Colombia's upper classes with the lucrative illegal activities of the criminal underworld. Rather than portraying the purely personal history of the isolated exiled individual who negotiates their identity in the new foreign community, the two authors in question thus seek out a position of collectivity. This collective aim bears certain parallels with the texts by Huston and

Siscar analysed in the previous chapter. Yet Saffie and Miss Poupée, whose sense of collective identity is severely damaged by the highly isolating experience of exile, attempt to reinsert themselves into a group identity, whereas the protagonists of Mokeddem's and Restrepo's texts analysed in this chapter are seen to seek out a position of individuality and leadership within the collectivity as the representative spokesperson. Mokeddem's narrative voice advocates solidarity amongst women in Algeria, a community which Mokeddem herself is both a part of, as an Algerian woman, and distanced from, through her residency in France and her migration from village origins to social as well as geographic mobility. Restrepo also seeks out a representative narrative subject position (crystallised in her narrator's catch-cry, repeated in the text, of 'nosotros los colombianos', to refer to a collective, Colombian 'we'), and whose attempts at simultaneously expressing and forging a collective national identity are explored further below. In evoking a feminine collectivity from the position of estranged insider, these two authors articulate the tensions in the relationship between the exiled woman writer, and the society from which they are exiled. Writing from both within, and outside the collectivity they aim to represent mimetically and politically, Mokeddem and Restrepo address the particularity of women's experience of re-encounter with the native country following the experience of exile, when the native country is one stifled by a patriarchal system that designates restricted roles for its female members. An analysis of the collective, or representative, nature of the narrative voice, and the associated question of readership is one of the main focuses here.

This chapter compares two novels published within two years of each other, Mokeddem's *L'Interdite*[14] [*The Forbidden Woman*] and Restrepo's *Dulce compañía*[15] [*The Angel of Galilea*]. Mokeddem and Restrepo situate these narratives in the specific geographical and historical contexts of their native countries in an attempt to work towards an understanding of the events and conflicts that have dominated these countries' contemporary histories and which directly led to their exiles. In addition, these historically and geographically specific settings also reveal the authors' attempts to negotiate their own relationships to the societies that were once home, and whose 'homely' qualitites have been severely disrupted, necessitating the discursive reconstruction of a space of belonging that may constitute (a) 'home', as this chapter's title reflects. The notion of return is central to both authors' context of writing, as it colours Restrepo's representation of Colombian society, written after her return from her six-year exile in Mexico, and underpins Mokeddem's protagonist's re-encounter with Algeria, which echoes Mokeddem's own return visit to the native village twenty-four years after the departure to France. The central questions this chapter poses are how the generic and discursive hybridity of these works, which span the autobiographical, the historical, the testimonial, and the fictional, illustrates the negotiation of the processes of exile, and the extent to which such hybridity achieves or disrupts the apparent underlying objectives of the writing project. If one of the implicit aims of these works is representativity, as this chapter argues, how then do Mokeddem and Restrepo negotiate the problematic representativity that their exilic alienation both enables and problematises? This chapter concludes with a discussion of the real impact of these texts on the lives of those whom they seek to represent, and whether Mokeddem and Restrepo do, in fact, achieve the objectives which are set out in their texts and which are inextricably tied up with their representative imperatives.

Mobility, Space, and the Structures of Power

Mokeddem's *L'Interdite*, set in the small village of Aïn Nekhla in Algeria's western desert, and Restrepo's *Dulce compañía*, set in the mountain slums of Bogotá, are both located in specific sites that correspond mimetically to each author's own native country and the landscapes of their childhood and adolescence. The positioning and movement of their protagonists within the novels' settings figuratively illustrate the hierarchical structures which govern the power relations of those societies, and the location in these power structures of the protagonists themselves, each of whom bears a strong resemblence to her author. The fictitious Algerian village of Aïn Nekhla (resembling in all but name Mokeddem's own native village of Kénadsa) and the Bogotá slums in which the action of these novels take place are also more broadly situated in the national political and cultural contexts which subtend the novels' plots.

Restrepo's *Dulce compañía* relates in the first person the experience of a magazine journalist from Bogotá, who is sent to investigate the reported appearance of an 'angel' in Galilea, a slum neighbourhood on the city's mountainous outskirts. The neighbourhood, made up of a jumble of precarious dwellings, is located high up in the mountains which form the city's eastern boundary. With no paved roads, electricity installations, transport connections, or reliable telephone lines, the neighbourhood is extremely isolated from the centre of the city, and its substandard living conditions highlight the poverty and marginalisation of its inhabitants. The stranger who appears unexpectedly in Galilea is attributed with the status of an angel due to the 'angelic' traits that the Galileans perceive in him: he is male, characterised as exceedingly beautiful, as exuding an aura of peace, and perhaps most importantly, as unintelligible. Apparently mute, he is unable to provide an account of himself or of his arrival in the neighbourhood. The inhabitants take it upon themselves to provide their own explanation, and the mystery surrounding the character of the angel which constitutes the central narrative intrigue is enhanced by the differing impressions of him that the reader receives, on the one hand, from the reported dialogue of the inhabitants of the village, and on the other, from the journalist's account.

The journalist, whose real name is not given but who is referred to by the nickname — 'la Mona' — conferred upon her by the other characters in the novel (a naming process similar to that of Siscar's Miss Poupée in *La sombra del jardín* and, as discussed in Chapter 5, Linda Lê's protagonist, Sola, in *In memoriam*), moves back and forth between the centre of Bogotá, where she lives and works, and the fringe neighbourhood of Galilea. The trajectory denotes the journalist's movement from the privileged, self-contained, middle-class centre to the distant, precarious, and under-developed neighbourhood high up in the mountains beyond the city's outermost limits. If there is traditionally no movement from slum neighbourhoods such as Galilea towards the modern centre of the city, neither is there any movement in the inverse direction, and the metropolis remains divided into two spaces which, although contiguous, remain hermetically sealed from each other. The polarisation and lack of integrative contact between the two spaces are made clear, for instance, by the absence of any established transport links that might connect them. On the occasions when la Mona visits Galilea, she arrives by her own means, and her access to independent transport contrasts sharply with the inhabitants' lack of the same. The restricted movement of the Galileans within the physical space of the novel's setting metonymically illustrates their social immobility as they are unable to move beyond, or away from, the world of poverty that they inhabit, and only serves to underscore the privileged singularity of the protagonist's movement between the two social spaces.

La Mona experiences Galilea as a place beyond the physical and ideological limits of her own world in the sanctioned social space of the centre of town, illustrating the spatial and psychological displacement that characterises the protagonist's positioning in *Dulce compañía*. Yet she also differentiates, and distances herself from her middle-class peers at the magazine and the community of its readership by ridiculing its trivial content, thus presenting herself as a reliable, unaffiliated observer, well placed to investigate the scoop of the angel with an open mind. Initially sceptical of the appearance of a so-called angel in 'el país del mundo donde más milagros se dan por metro cuadrado' [the country in the world with the most miracles per square foot] (*DC*, p. 19) and where the signs of mysticism are implied to occur most frequently in the slums — 'nadie se imagina la de presagios que se dejan ver a diario por los tugurios' [one can only imagine the number of omens that crop up daily in the shantytowns] (*DC*, p. 17) — she nevertheless approaches the phenomenon with the rationality characteristic of her educational and social background. In response to the claim that the mysterious, mute young man is an angel, the narrator suggests that he is perhaps autistic. Likewise, when it is suggested to her that the makeshift houses of Galilea may be washed away in an apocalyptic flood brought upon them by the angel's fury, la Mona points out that the regularity of torrential downpours in Bogotá would be the more likely explanation. Throughout the course of the novel, her involvement with the people of Galilea and with the young man considered to be the angel eventually lead her to reconsider her scepticism and rationality and to entertain the possibility of an alternative understanding of the events that unfold.

La Mona is guided through her discovery of the alterity of Galilea by a young boy named Orlando, who plays an essential initiatory role in *Dulce compañía*, becoming indispensable to her comprehension of its rites and norms. In response to la Mona's efforts to account for the unexplained events that take place in Galilea, Orlando, 'alzándose de cejas y hombros, como si fuera muy obvio' [rais(ing) his eyebrows and shrugging his shoulders, as if it were obvious] (*DC*, p. 35), explains the reality of the poor neighbourhood as seen by its inhabitants. His at times incredulous tone in replying to la Mona's questions when explaining the workings of life in the neighbourhood conveys his surprise at her difficulty in apprehending what is to him obvious. La Mona's rational approach is thus shown to be ineffectual in Galilea where a different logic operates, and where Orlando's (and the community's) interpretation is depicted as the norm from which the logic of the dominant middle class is a variation. Thus power structures are overturned, and la Mona must rely on the child Orlando to access and understand Galilea, and indeed her increasing reliance on him is apparent when on one occasion she states: 'Me detuve un instante para pedirle su opinión a Orlando, en cuyo criterio había aprendido a confiar' [I stopped a moment to ask Orlando his opinion, which I had come to trust] (*DC*, p. 150). This disruption of hierarchy is consolidated when the marginalised women of Galilea take the fate of their middle-class visitor into their own hands by orchestrating her involvement with the angel. Initially suspicious of her 'intrusion' into their neighbourhood, the neighbourhood women come to consider la Mona to have been sent by divine intervention. They consequently oversee her access to the angel, alternately granting and denying her participation in the neighbourhood's rites and rituals eventually, and somewhat melodramatically, ensuring her impregnation by the angel so as to secure the posterity of his lineage.

The lack of complete identification with her own social group and the repeated journeys between the centre and periphery of Bogotá demonstrate la Mona's physical and ideological access to both extremes of the city's population. Yet if her differentiation from her peers in her native middle-class milieu is based on her self-declared ideological openness, her differentiation from the inhabitants of Galilea operates on several levels, based not only on her class background but also her cultural heritage as manifested in her appearance. She is physically unlike those that live in the slum neighbourhood, to which the nickname they give her testifies. 'La Mona' designates her fair hair which, along with her atypical height, reveals her European ancestry: 'Exótico para estas tierras, mi pelo es — junto con veinte centímetros por encima de la estatura promedio — la herencia que recibí de mi abuelo el belga' [My hair is considered exotic in this corner of the world. That and my height, which is six inches above average, are a legacy from my Belgian grandfather] (*DC*, p. 34).[16] La Mona's European background provides striking evidence of Janet Wolff's claim, discussed in Chapter 1, that nomadic social mobility, rather than being freely and equally available, is in fact largely predicated by one's cultural and social inheritance, thus limiting the possibility for certain individuals to move beyond their own frame of reference in order to adopt an ideal position of critical scrutiny and ideological freedom.

If the narrator frames her physical difference in the eyes of Galilea's inhabitants in terms of exoticism, her description of the neighbourhood and its inhabitants reciprocates with a similar discourse of exoticisation. In his study of social segmentation in *Dulce compañía*, Samuel Jaramillo González refers to the underscoring in sociological studies of the strict segmentation between rich and poor that characterises many Latin American cities and recalls the frequent exoticisation of the physical and social space occupied by the poorest inhabitants by outsiders. According to Jaramillo González, this exoticisation is linked to the temporal association of the two spaces, the rich and the poor, with present and past, or with modernity and premodernity, thus linking the exoticisation of the underprivileged other to a nostalgia for the past:

> Surge la tentación de entroncarlo con otro tiempo: el estereotipo habla de que en las ciudades latinoamericanas coexisten al menos dos ciudades que corresponden a dos épocas, una al presente [...] y otra al pasado. Modernidad y premodernidad, dirían otros, ocupando espacios inmediatamente vecinos.[17]
>
> [There is a temptation to connect it to another time: according to the stereotype, there are at least two cities within the Latin American city which correspond to two eras, the present [...] and the past. Some might refer to modernity and postmodernity, which occupy contiguous spaces.]

The past can be seen to occupy the collective imaginary of the present in more ways than one in *Dulce compañía* as Galilea's community, largely of *mestizo* background, initially treats la Mona with both the admiration and suspicion with which the Spanish were received in the fifteenth century, framing the encounter in the novel in the contradictory terms of both cultural invasion and 'salvation'.[18] La Mona's designation by the inhabitants as the divinely chosen one sent to intervene with the angel reinforces the exoticisation of the Other which occurs in the encounter of the two different 'worlds', reflecting that of colonial discourse, and underscoring the reciprocal 'othering' by both the indigenous and the cultural outsider. Despite the rhetoric of contact and unification that is present in *Dulce compañía*, the effort to breach social and economic divides ultimately fails as la Mona and the Galileans remain irrevocably Other to each other through such reciprocal exoticisation. Unlike the Spanish *conquistadores* la Mona does not, of course, alight in a new country, but rather discovers an unknown side of her own native country, thus placing her encounter with the Other under the sign of 're-discovery' of the familiar which can be considered in terms of Resptrepo's own 're-vision' of the homeland, a vision necessarily altered after her exile in Mexico.

For Jaramillo González, *Dulce compañía*'s portrayal of the segmentation of the city into physical, social, economic, and ethnic extremes is accompanied by radical ideological differences between the protagonist's world and that of the poor inhabitants of Galilea. The appearance of the angel not only creates a point of contact between the two parallel worlds, it also presents their contrasting apprehensions of this event as radically, even incompatibly different:

> estas ciudades paralelas, la que lleva consigo la protagonista y la ciudad de los pobres en la que se aventura, tienen, cada una, una interpretación del mundo radicalmente diversa, en algunos aspectos incompatible. Los mismos hechos se codifican en registros sustancialmente diferentes.[19]
>
> [each of these parallel cities, the one the protagonist carries with her, and the city of the poor into which she ventures, has an interpretation of the world that is radically different from, and in some ways incompatible with the other. The same facts are codified in fundamentally different registers.]

The Galileans' supernatural, or spiritual explanation of events, which posits the appearance of an angel in their midst as entirely plausible, is juxtaposed but not subordinated to a rational interpretation of the unexplained appearance of the stranger. The suspension, indeed the overturning, of her (culturally conditioned) reasoned interpretation of reality is demonstrated when la Mona decides to remove the angel from the psychiatric institution in the centre of town where she had taken him for tests, and to return him to Galilea: 'Me lo voy a llevar de vuelta a su barrio. Allá arriba es un ángel, mientras que aquí abajo no es más que un pobre loco' [I'm going to take him back to his neighbourhood. Up there he is an angel, while down here he is nothing but a crazy idiot] (*DC*, pp. 187–88).

Where la Mona is characterised by her bilateral movement between the two social spheres throughout the course of *Dulce compañía*, the positioning and movement of the protagonist of *L'Interdite* within the novel's setting is complex and multi-dimensional. *L'Interdite* recounts the return of Sultana, a young Algerian doctor settled in Montpellier, to Aïn Nekhla, the village of her birth in the Algerian desert. She returns to the village upon hearing the news of the sudden death of a former boyfriend, Yacine. Her return to the native village in Algeria for the first time since her departure to France fifteen years earlier, is characterised as a spatial and temporal journey between present and past, north and south, city and countryside, and modernity and tradition.

The opening pages of the novel depict Sultana in transit: as she arrives in Algeria she draws gradually nearer to the isolated *ksar* (traditional walled Maghrebi village made of adobe) where she grew up, and moves increasingly further away from her present existence in Montpellier. Her spatial return to the landscape of her childhood is also depicted as a chronological return to her past, leading to the inevitable renegotiation of her past with her present self. Sultana descibes 'un retour qui n'en est pas' [(a) return that isn't a return] (*I*, p. 82), as neither is she the same person as the one who left Algeria, nor is the country she encounters the same as the one she left behind, illustrating the irreversibility of exile highlighted in Chapter 1 whereby the exile will experience herself and her place of origin as irrevocably changed. Sultana's journey is thus one of discovery which undermines any illusory nostalgia that she may have held for her village from the position of exile, and which eventually reinforces the decision to leave made fifteen years earlier. The discovery she makes entails the realisation that her native village has become even more oppressive under the Islamic fundamentalists than the village of her childhood recollections, and that her present identity can no longer be tied to the fixed sites of either Algeria or France, but is only conceivable 'dans le déplacement, dans la migration' [in moving around, migrating] (*I*, p. 161).

These discoveries are made abruptly, even brutally, as her re-encounter with the homeland proves to be immediately hostile. Upon arrival, Sultana is aggressively questioned by a taxi-driver during the journey from the airport to the village. He is visibly outraged by what he perceives as the audacity of a young woman travelling on her own, his character thus anticipating the Islamist stranglehold she will encounter in the village. Sultana's defiance of his imposing authority, in the form of holding his gaze in the rear-view mirror of the taxi, and evading, even ignoring, his questions, is received by the taxi-driver as an unthinkable challenge to the patriarchal power structures of the village and sets the scene for the violent conflict that will erupt between Sultana and the male villagers. Where in the encounter with the cultural Other in the home country, Restrepo's protagonist is confronted with new, unfamiliar norms and codes which she strives to understand and learn from, Mokeddem's protagonist rediscovers codes with which she is only too familiar and which she entirely rejects. These two authors thus portray two key positions of return: one which is framed as a discovery, a 're-vision' of the home country that is only possible through the critical distance that distantiation affords, and another in which the original reasons for leaving are only reinforced and more enduringly embedded. Both positions, however, result in similarly politicised texts and in a similar drive for representation which attempt to take advantage of, respectively, the insightful altered perspective of one, and the dissidence, even anger, of the other.

If Sultana's return to the Algeria of her past from the France of her present is the key trajectory which triggers the action of the novel, her movement within the setting of the village is also disruptive and catalytic. It is initially her movement in the public space which the men of the village perceive as threatening, a space whose strictly encoded gender divisions are all the more striking for her after her long absence. Further exacerbating her effrontery in the eyes of the men of the village, she moves unaccompanied through the public space, or in the company of men who are also outsiders to the village, such as Salah (a Kabyle doctor from Algiers) or Vincent (a visiting Frenchman). Her 'invasion' of male territory however reaches its climax in her professional role: her assumption of the position of village doctor, left vacant by Yacine's death, bestows on her the authority that is attached to the profession, yet this authority is countered by her sex. The men see her above all as a woman and thus 'out-of-place' in her role as village doctor. They are troubled by being seen by a female physician, and do not allow her to examine them on the grounds that she is a woman, illustrated in the protest, and the inappropriately familiar tone of one male villager: 'Tu es une femme. Tu ne peux pas me toucher. C'est péché' ['You're a woman. You can't touch me. It's a sin'] (*I*, p. 125).

It is primarily the visibility of her presence in the public spaces of the village which makes her the target of male aggression and distinguishes her as an outsider, as the women of the village are virtually invisible as well as silent throughout most of the novel. Vincent, the other main character of *L'Interdite* with whom Sultana shares the first-person narration in alternating chapters, reinforces the validity of her narrative perspective as a dissenting fellow outsider by echoing many of the remarks and criticisms that Sultana herself makes. Vincent is particularly struck by the nature of women's fleeting, apologetic occupation of public space, noticing that, 'Pressées, affairées, elles traversent le jour, le temps d'une rue, le temps d'un courage, entre deux bornes d'interdit' [In a hurry, busy, they go through the day, the time to cross the street, the time for some courage, between two markers of the forbidden], before remarking on their disappearance after nightfall: 'Le soir les avale toutes' [The evening swallows all of them up] (*I*, pp. 64–65). Night-time in the village crystallises the essentialised roles designated to women in the village, where the only two spaces conceivably occupied by women are the domestic space of the home or the sexualised space of the brothel.

Complementing Vincent's description of a public space reserved for men, Sultana characterises the streets of Aïn Nekhla as a hostile, male-inhabited environment populated by eyes whereby men occupy the traditionally masculine role of spectator: 'Foule d'yeux, vent noir, éclairs et tonnerres. Je ne flâne plus. Je fends une masse d'yeux' [Crowd full of eyes, black wind, lightning and thunder. I stroll no longer. I cut through a crowd of eyes] (*I*, p. 83). The male body, reduced to a pair of eyes which scrutinise and exert control, has an equally disembodying effect on the female body, which is obliterated and reduced to abstract fear and tension: 'Je marche contre des yeux, entre leurs feux. Et pourtant, je n'ai plus de corps. Je ne suis qu'une tension qui s'égare entre passé et present, un souvenir hagard qui ne se reconnaît aucun repère' [I walk against eyes, between their fires. And yet I no longer have a body. I am nothing but tension losing my way between the past and the present, a haggard memory that recognises no reference point in herself] (*I*, p. 83). The streets which have sprung up (during the years of her absence from Algeria) around the *ksar* where she was born, which itself now lies empty and deserted, are construed as a space once inhabited by the feminine and now invaded and over-run by men and male children. It is a space from which women and female children have been banished, signalling a deterioration of women's political and cultural status since the optimism of the Algerian War where women fought alongside their male counterparts. The suppression of women's right to a public role in the years since national independence, and their confinement to interior, private spaces is a recurring trope also seen in Mokeddem's *Des rêves et des assassins*[20] [*Of Dreams and Assassins*] and *La Transe des insoumis*.

Where the occupation of the public domain of movement and agency in *L'Interdite* is gendered masculine through an exclusively male physical presence, the village itself is gendered feminine through its likening to an exploited and devastated female body, damaged after repetitive pregnancies (somewhat diluted in the English translation due the gender-neutral 'street' in English, and the translation of 'stretchmarks' ['vergetures'] in the original as 'welts'):

> Elle est grosse de toutes les frustrations, travaillée par toutes les folies, souillée par toutes les misères. Soudée dans sa laideur par un soleil blanc de rage, elle exhibe ses vergetures, ses rides, et barbote dans les égouts avec tous ses marmots. (*I*, p. 15)

> [The street is pregnant with every frustration possible, is tormented by every type of insanity and dirtied by all of its misery. Its ugliness hardened by a sun whitened with rage, it exhibits its welts, its wrinkles, and splashes about in the sewers with all of its urchins.]

Mokeddem's metaphor of the ravaged female body reduced to its reproductive function carries an indictment of the curtailing of women's roles in post-independence Algeria to the domestic and the sexual, and certainly draws a link between the confinement of women to a procreative role and the degradation of society.[21] The fact that Sultana resolutely vows never to have children of her own whilst remaining open to the possibility of adoption suggests less a reaction against maternity *per se*, than a rejection of the reduction of women to essentialised roles, and offers an alternative model of femininity beyond that which is available in the re-encountered homeland.

The radicalisation of the existing roles available to women also extends to Restrepo's treatment of maternity in *Dulce compañía*. Restrepo's narrator similarly demonstrates a non-orthodox attitude to child-bearing and -raising that contests the norms of the home society. In the present of writing at the novel's conclusion, la Mona bears a child conceived with the angel in a ceremony orchestrated by the four neighbourhood women who form the self-appointed 'administrative council' of the angel, and who nominate la Mona as the chosen bride to bear the angel's progeny. The angel's lineage is represented as felicitously disrupted by the narrator when the child turns out to be female, and thus unsuitable for carrying on the role of saviour of the people:

> cuando supe que era una niña mi alivio fue inmenso. En cambio la noticia cayó como un balde de agua helada sobre la gente de Galilea: quería decir que no se había cumplido la reencarnación, porque un ángel mujer les resultaba inconcebible. (*DC*, p. 233)
>
> [Of course, I felt infinitely relieved when I found out it was a girl. But the news hit the people of Galilea like a stroke of lightening on a frozen bucket of water. It meant the reincarnation had not taken place: a female angel was inconceivable to them.]

La Mona undertakes to raise her daughter on her own, with the support of Doña Ara (revealed to be the child's grandmother and the mother of the angel) as well as that of the other women of Galilea, effectively creating an all-female nurturing environment for the child and undermining the necessity of any paternal role.

Where Sultana, in *L'Interdite*, experiences the public space as one that is hostile to female presence, the visiting Frenchman, Vincent, experiences the same space quite differently. Unlike Sultana, whose arrival and movement in the setting of the novel is met with aggression from the taxi-driver, insults of 'putain!' [whore!] from the male children in the street, and threatening behaviour from Bakkar, the mayor, Vincent is warmly welcomed in the neighbouring town of Tammar. Despite the fact that foreigners, and in particular the French, were often the target of suspicion and aggression by FIS members, who considered them an unwelcome presence in Algeria, Vincent is befriended by a number of villagers and does not solicit the attacks suffered by the unaccompanied, female Sultana. Her femaleness, along with her dismissiveness of designated gender roles, are perceived by the fundamentalists as a greater threat than Vincent's foreignness. Sultana's disregard of the gendered demarcation of space marks her out as a disruptive element introduced into the town's hierarchy, and leads inevitably to violent conflict with the mayor and his acolytes.

Sultana's behaviour upon returning to her hometown is also perceived by the fundamentalists as a deliberate provocation. Returning as a self-sufficient, unattached woman to the town that she left as a disempowered young girl effectively challenges hierarchies of power in the village. Sultana considers herself beyond the reach of the fundamentalists' misogynist vitriol until the attacks on her turn physically violent, at which point she realises that the stakes of the conflict are still insurmountable and she retreats to France, once again, under the threat of violence. In Mokeddem's autobiographical novels, *La Transe des insoumis* and *Mes hommes*, she employs similarly defiant autobiographical first-person narrators, who testify to Roy F. Baumeister's identarian stategy of the basic human compulsion to define identity by differentiation (as referred to in Chapter 1 and already seen to be a salient feature in exiled women's writing). In negatively defining subjectivity by divergence from existing gender paradigms of the birth country, Mokeddem portrays herself in terms of what she is *not*, thus locating her identity in the interstitial, nomadic space of exile, between sites of belonging, and most importantly, beyond the strictures of the birth community. Yet Mokeddem's autobiographical protagonists push Baumeister's tendency even further, not merely defining subjectivity by differentiation from others, but by *seeking out* difference in a manner similar to that of Nancy Huston when she declares '[je] ne *subis* pas l'écart, je le *cherche*' [I don't *suffer* the margin, I *seek it out*].[22] Nowhere is this more evident than in *Mes hommes* during the protagonist's adolescence, where Mokeddem describes her anorexia, a form of denial which permits her to extricate herself from the social and family body and grants her control of her own body, and thus access to singularity and individuality. The self-denial of food is nevertheless abandoned when it is the very act of eating that marks her difference from others: 'Je mange sur le balcon de ma chambre à la cité universitaire pendant le ramadan. Et quand manger est une victoire sur quelques batailles, je me délecte' [I eat on the balcony of my room in the university residence during Ramadam. And when eating is a victory over certain battles, I relish it].[23]

If Sultana's exile from Algeria was first and foremost a flight from violence and repression, it was fundamentally a flight into individuality. Where la Mona's encounter with the unfamiliar neighbourhood slum in Bogotá is depicted as a fruitful and positive exchange which opens channels of communication and encourages the exchange of ideas between the protagonist and the community, Sultana's return to the setting of her childhood home is a violent encounter which reinforces her alienation from it, and inevitably leads to her departure back to France at the novel's conclusion.

Education and Social Mobility

Both Mokeddem's and Restrepo's protagonists enjoy a high degree of mobility in stark contrast with that of the characters with whom they come into contact, a physical mobility within the novels' settings which is emblematic of their social mobility. Sultana and la Mona are granted the privilege of being able to move back and forth between, in one case, a traditional provincial Algerian village and modern, urban France, and in the other, the urban centre of Bogotá and its underprivileged slums, due to the education they have accessed and their resulting professions. Education and professional achievement are the vehicles which permit this mobility and expand the social space in which the narrators move, but which, as will be seen, also transmit certain responsibilities as well as granting them privileges and freedoms.

In Sultana's case, education leads directly to her departure into exile. Mokeddem describes the commencement of her own university studies in Oran in much the same way as Sultana does the years spent at school in Algeria, as 'les plus beaux moments de mon Algérie' [the most beautiful moments of my Algeria].[24] Sultana portrays school as a site of welcome relief from the suffocating atmosphere of village life under a patriarchal order whose misogyny and violence eventually caused the death of her mother and younger sister, and the definitive departure of her father. The climax of *L'Interdite* reveals her family's violent history, a past that is periodically alluded to but left undisclosed until Sultana suffers a mental and emotional breakdown upon finding herself in the abandoned former family home in the *ksar*. Her bewilderment and catalepsy finally give way to an outpouring when she cathartically recounts her past to Vincent and Salah (who, along with Vincent, is a fellow village outsider and one of Sultana's *confidents*) in a verbal deluge which echoes the aforementioned scriptotherapeutic drive behind Mokeddem's discursive representation of the journey 'home' in *L'Interdite*. Sultana recounts how, orphaned at the age of five when her father violently pushed her mother during an altercation, inadvertently causing her mother's death and her father's ensuing flight and permanent disappearance, she is taken under the wing of a French doctor and his wife. Before their ousting by militant forces, the French couple ensure a place at high school in Oran for the young Sultana, who forevermore associates freedom with education, and with the French language and culture.

The association of (French) education with freedom for women is far from being unusual in North African women's writing, and is clearly articulated across Mokeddem's œuvre. The stakes of education for women in the context of 1990s Algeria are emphasised by the narrator of *L'Interdite*, who stresses the altogether different impact of education for Algerian men through Salah's discussion of Algeria's male university-educated elite. Salah holds this elite (to which he belongs) responsible to the same degree as the male, uneducated poor for the misogynist violence suffered by women, accusing them of superficial liberalism during their university years, which is abandoned upon graduation when the same male graduates ultimately collude with the valorisation of women's submission and docility by marrying the subservient, uneducated brides chosen for them by their parents. This theme is returned to, and with greater emphasis, in Mokeddem's *Des rêves et des assassins*, where two of the main female characters suffer intense emotional trauma when their partners abandon them in order to marry women chosen for them by their parents. The trauma is such that it eventually prompts the departure into exile of Kenza, the novel's protagonist. Describing the dilemma that confronts him and his male peers in *L'Interdite*, Salah declares: 'Nos diplômes, nos vêtements étaient censés être des gages de notre modernité. De fait, la misogynie nous restait chevillée dans l'inavoué. Maintenant, je l'énonce et la dénonce' ['Our diplomas, our clothing were supposed to be the signs of our modernity. But in fact, misogyny clung to us in everything we did not admit. Now I talk about it and I denounce it'] (*I*, p. 52). Higher education alone is thus shown to be insufficient for overturning the precepts of long-standing patriarchy, and can only be effective when combined with an awareness of the educated male elite's own complicity with the misogyny advocated by the Islamists. The character of Salah attests to the difficulty of modifying ideologies upheld as the social standard for generations for men, who enjoy a position of dominance in the social hierarchy and who benefit from the perpetuation of that dominance.

Women's education is thus presented in *L'Interdite* as a key tool for the fostering of a society no longer predicated on women's subordination, for whom it is also a means of escape from the domestic space historically designated as the only space available for women to 'legitimately' occupy. Mokeddem's narrative implicitly suggests that young male students, who already hold autonomy and power by the mere fact of their sex, do not have the same drive as their female counterparts who find in education the only possible route to independence and freedom from an overwhelming patriarchal authority. But if Sultana has benefited from her education to be able to claim a place in public life through her profession (albeit in France), she expresses concern for the manipulation of the institution for ideological purposes in the Algeria she encounters on her return to her native village. Dalila, a young girl whom Sultana befriends during her short stay in the village, cites her teacher when she says that school 'est plus l'espace où on apprend [...] c'est qu'une fabrique d'abrutis et de petits islamistes' [is no longer a place where you can learn [...] it's a factory for morons and little Islamists] (*I*, pp. 90–91). A younger version of the protagonist, the young Dalila provides a dissenting vision of the schooling system in 1990s Algeria that reflects Sultana's own, and she describes its particular difficulties for female students. Instrumentalising the honesty and spontaneity typically associated with a child's voice, Mokeddem expresses a criticism of the educational practices that were the ongoing legacy of Arabisation in post-independence Algeria.[25] The lessons of the denominational village school in *L'Interdite*, and by extension, the Algerian educational system as a whole, are harshly criticised by Dalila, who denounces a system that preaches female submission and obedience to the patriarchal order: 'La lecture à l'école, c'est toujours l'histoire d'une petite fille sage et qui aide bien sa maman alors que son frère, lui, il joue dehors' [The reading at school is always the story of a good little girl who helps her mama while her brother plays outside] (*I*, p. 91). As a result, Dalila seeks an alternative education to the one her school offers her, enlisting the help of Ouarda, her schoolteacher, who tutors her in French outside school hours. The underscoring of Dalila's quest for tuition in French language and culture to counter the Islamist indoctrination she receives at the village school brings Mokeddem's own vision of the advantages of a French education for women in Algeria to the fore in the text.

Dalila's nonconformity with the social order of the village and the restricted opportunities it offers her hint at a similar future trajectory to that of Sultana, who was only able to achieve autonomy through her departure to France. Dalila's older sister Samia, who at the novel's conclusion is revealed to be a figment of Dalila's imagination, incorporates a projected older version of Dalila in the text. In the imaginary Samia, Dalila conjures up an ideal older sister who lives and studies in France, free from the debilitating surveillance of father and brothers, where (as she reiterates several times in the novel) Samia has the freedom to walk unaccompanied in the street, in stark contrast with the aforementioned near absence of women in Aïn Nekhla's streets. Indeed, Dalila and the imaginary Samia can be considered projections of Mokeddem herself in the novel, as they retrace the educational and migrational steps that Mokeddem has taken. The character of Sultana can be said to complete that idealised version of Mokeddem, given the autobiographical referentiality between the two, consequently presenting herself as a role model for a younger generation of Algerian women. The similarities between author and narrator are such that the author is firmly evoked by the narrator-protagonist, whilst not resembling each other sufficiently to provoke more than an autofictional reading of the text. Through her self-styled narrator-protagonists (and indeed, most of Mokeddem's narrator-protagonists can be said to resemble the author to a certain degree), Mokeddem offers herself as a model of the ideal ambitious, liberated woman capable of breaking away from the restrictions placed on Algerian women.

As is frequently the case with Mokeddem's narrator-protagonists, Sultana is portrayed at the heart of a love triangle between two men who vie for her attention, and as such vouches for the desirability of her model of femininity to 'enlightened' male characters who contest her execration by the 'backward' male villagers who would have her banished. Sultana appears as an aberration to the fundamentalists yet a seductive outsider to the like-minded, liberal love interests, Salah and Vincent. Indeed, it is worth noting that Sultana's personal relationships are limited to relationships with men: her relationships with other women characters are limited to that of feminine figurehead and political role model, and rarely extend to relationships of friendship and parity of status. If Sultana is aloof with regard to the two men, refusing to be tied down to either, and her relationships with other women are characterised by distance, she maintains a similar relationship to the reader. In spite of the fact that a greater part of the text is narrated in the first person by Sultana, the reader has very little access to her beyond the expounding of ideological standpoints that comprise much of her narration and dialogues, as the political 'subtext' essentially becomes the 'text' in *L'Interdite*. Mokeddem creates an idealised narrator whose unattainability and partial representation is strikingly replicated in the cover of the 1993 Livre de Poche edition, which depicts a woman at close-range, with her head turned such that only a partial view of her face is visible. The facial expression of distance and aloofness suggests only partial exposure, and there is a general sense of the highly controlled presentation of the self that reflects the narrator's presentation within the text. Like the woman represented on the front cover, Mokeddem literally presents her 'best side' to the reader, evoking the author behind the text as a female role model.

Ambition, such as that demonstrated by Dalila (and by implication the young Mokeddem herself), is thus presented alongside education as an essential requirement for women's liberation, yet it is described as a rare trait among the villagers due to the complacency encouraged in the male population and imposed on the women by the Islamic fundamentalists. The men of the village in *L'Interdite* are characterised as ignorant followers of the Islamists, complicit with the repressive regime largely out of selfish fear of the consequences of sexual equality, and despite any ambition that the women may harbour, the channels for exercising their will and claiming independence are extremely limited. The village women do eventually stage a climactic rebellion in the hospital at the novel's conclusion, instigated by Sultana's reclamation of this public space for them. This collective action suggests, perhaps rather optimistically for reasons discussed below, the attainment of social change that seemingly drives Mokeddem's writing project. If the text calls for ambition in women, it also criticises the responsibility and complicity of women in their own victimisation, as reiterated by Mokeddem herself in an interview:

À la décharge des hommes, je crois qu'il ne faut pas être trop manichéen, ce sont les femmes qui transmettent les traditions [...] c'est de la bouche des femmes, d'abord la grand-mère, puis la mère, ensuite les sœurs aînées, les tantes etc. que les petites filles reçoivent leur première leçon de soumission et les petits garçons leur première leçon de machisme et de misogynie.[26]

[In men's defense, I don't think we should be too Manichaen. It's women who pass on the traditions [...] it's from women, via grandmothers, mothers, older sisters, aunts, etc., that little girls receive their first lesson in submission, and little boys their first lessons in chauvinism and misogyny.]

L'Interdite can be said to militate for a radical change to the social dichotomisation of women into either the domestic or sexualised role, and as Mokeddem's declaration reinforces, presents as crucial to this project women's renunciation of complicity in their own subordination.[27]

Given the autobiographical traces of both *L'Interdite* and *Dulce compañía*, Sultana's (and by inference, Mokeddem's) upward social mobility can be compared and contrasted with la Mona's (and Restrepo's) social mobility. Sultana's distantiation from her family and social environment is extreme: she is doubly removed by virtue of her education and professional status, and by her permanent departure to France. Yet where medicine brings Sultana back into contact with the estranged social group of which she was once a part, la Mona encounters an entirely different social milieu and one with which she was previously unacquainted. In an interview with Jaime Manrique that is worth quoting from at length, Restrepo sheds light on the origin of her high degree of social mobility, which can be said to share many parallels with that of la Mona. Describing the catalytic event of her entry into teaching when still an undergraduate at university in Bogotá, Restrepo recalls the access that her position as a university student and high-school teacher gave her to social groups beyond that of her own middle-class upbringing:

[E]stando en segundo de carrera, me recibieron como maestra de literatura en una escuela pública para varones, a donde corría a repetir a las once de la mañana lo que acababa de aprender a las nueve. Los alumnos, de estrato bajo, eran mayores que yo, sabían más que yo, habían vivido más que yo [...] y de ellos aprendí una lección inquietante, que habría de cambiarle el rumbo a mi vida: aprendí que más allá de mi cerrado núcleo familiar, y de esa caja de prodigios que era el arte y la cultura, había todo un universo por explorar, ancho y ajeno, feroz y apasionante. Como si me hubieran propuesto un viaje a Marte me lancé con avidez a la exploración por los barrios populares de mi ciudad y los campos de mi país, por la mentalidad y las costumbres de gentes distintas a las mías; por el universo hasta entonces desconocido para mí de la sexualidad; por el horror y el dolor de una sociedad marcada por la desigualdad y la injusticia; por los sueños de quienes luchaba por hacerle cambiar.[28]

[When I was in second year at university, I began to teach literature at a state secondary school for boys, where I would run to teach at eleven in the morning what I had learnt at nine. The students, from a low socio-economic background, were older than me, knew more than me, and had lived more than me [...] and from them I learnt a troubling lesson that would change the course of my life. I learnt that there was a whole universe, broad and alien, ferocious and fascinating, to explore beyond that of my restricted family circle, and beyond the treasure trove that were to me, art and culture. As though I'd been offered a trip to Mars, I threw myself into exploring the disadvantaged neighbourhoods of my city and the rural areas of my country, the mentality and customs of people different from me, the world of sexuality (until that point unfamiliar to me), the horror and pain of a society marked by inequality and injustice, and the dreams of those who fought for change.]

The cultural crossings that are described here are manifold. As a young, middle-class woman at university, Restrepo enters into the masculine, working-class environment of the boys' school to discover a previously unimagined parallel system of values. She describes her students as older and more worldly than her, thus contrasting the valorisation of formal, academic knowledge with that of life experience, granting both equal validity as systems of knowledge. She furthermore refers to the lesson she learns from her students, thus reiterating an interest in disrupting hierarchies of power, as seen in *Dulce compañía*, by inverting the hierarchy between the students and herself.

This extract also unequivocally conveys Restrepo's sense of responsibility towards her country and fellow nationals. Her journey of discovery through 'los barrios populares de mi ciudad' and 'los campos de mi país' designates the disadvantaged areas of the city with the polite euphemism 'popular', and the rural areas of the country, both of which delimit spaces in the national geography at the greatest remove from Restrepo's own experience. Yet she nevertheless reclaims these spaces as her own through the use of the possessive pronoun, calling upon a shared national and cultural identity which impels her to access and interact with the disenfranchised. The discovery of the cultural Other within her own country is framed as a political and social awakening from a middle-class slumber, and one that she feels compelled to act upon, given the social and educational tools that she possesses. Although aiming to emphasise her eagerness to discover spaces vastly different from her own through the comparison with Mars, the exoticism present in *Dulce compañía* is nevertheless also present here when she compares the 'barrios populares' and the 'campos' to Mars. For Restrepo then, education has functioned as a means of access to a vast and unfamiliar world ('universo') beyond the limited confines of her own experience ('mi cerrado núcleo familiar') whose alternative systems of value and discourse she nonetheless valorises.

In light of Restrepo's own experience, we can see la Mona's outward social mobility (which leads her into contact with the inhabitants of Galilea) as a journey which reflects Restrepo's own discovery of the poor and the political left as a result of her education and nascent role as a teacher. La Mona, like Restrepo, is driven to represent and legitimise the poorest sectors of Colombian society, and reveal the effects of poverty and marginalisation on those who suffer the brunt of society's inequalities and injustices: impoverished women and children, and particularly those of indigenous descent. The women of Galilea are shown to be empowered by the myth of the angel and gain a status not previously available to them through their entrepreneurial administration of the angel's appearances. The forces that these women are shown to struggle against are principally the Church, its representative in the neighbourhood, Father Benito, and the band of thugs who make up part of the priest's flock and refer to themselves as the M.A.F.A., 'Muerte al Falso Angel' ['Death to the False Angel'] recalling the real-life M.A.S., 'Muerte a Secuestradores' ['Death to Kidnappers'], a paramilitary group which first appeared in Colombia in 1981. Signalling the triumph of the women of Galilea, the final chapter returns to the present of writing and conveys, in cinematic style, the eventual fate of Father Benito — whose retribution is to suffer a heart attack and die — and the M.A.F.A., which disbands and sees its members decamping to Medellín where they become involved in the illegal drug trade. The association of the Church's representative with what is essentially a band of hired assassins and the absence of any figure of state authority in Galilea creates an implicit indictment of the complicity of the Church, the State and the powerful criminal element, and depicts women and children as those who suffer the brunt of the resulting violence.

However, whilst la Mona's access to the slum community of Galilea is characterised as an openness to a different reality and way of life, Jaramillo González points out that the exchange is rather one-sided, and that at the novel's conclusion social hierarchies remain unchanged: 'el acontecimiento del ángel pasa y cada uno de los personajes retorna a su lugar — la periodista a su cotidianidad de clase media, los pobladores del barrio a sus destinos precarios de habitantes populares' [the episode of the angel passes and each of the characters returns to their place — the journalist to her daily middle-class life, and the residents of the neighbourhood to their precarious destinies as slum-dwellers].[29] Despite the brief phase of interconnectedness between the two opposite poles of the city and the eradication of the nefarious forces from Galilea, la Mona's privileged mobility proves more advantageous for la Mona and fairly inconsequential for Galilea's marginalised inhabitants whose material circumstances are hardly changed, thus raising the question of the real impact of the drive for representativity of politicised women's exile writing.

Representation and Readership

The negotiation of identity in the protagonists' re-encounter with the homeland is explored in *L'Interdite* and *Dulce compañía* along affiliations of nation, class, ethnicity, and gender. Like identification with the nation, seen in Chapter 1 to bear few rewards for women, class and ethnic affiliation are likewise revealed as offering few advantages for the protagonists of the two novels at hand. The overriding axis of identification in both novels is staked firmly along gender lines, and both main characters articulate a rhetoric of solidarity and collectivity with the other women characters, and gender solidarity is foregrounded over national, class, and ethnic affiliations, creating a tension between the strong sense of individuality of their protagonists and each's aspiration to a collective, or representative voice.

Latin American literary criticism tends to view Restrepo as representative of a certain sense of national identity, and she has been described as 'una de las escritoras más representativas de Colombia y Latinoamerica hoy' [one of the most representative (women) writers of Colombia and Latin America today].[30] Such claims have been made, however, without adequately posing the question of whom she seeks to represent, and without sufficiently problematising her labelling as such by academics from a similar social milieu to Restrepo herself. The claim of representativity, whether made by critics, readers, or writers themselves, is a highly charged one, both in terms of the political meaning of representation — to 'speak for' or 'stand in for' — and the mimetic sense of representation — to 're-present' or 'provide a true image of' — and thus demands a closer consideration of claims for Restrepo's representativity and the author's own apparent project of representation. The Colombian scholar Carmiña Navia describes a representative and didactic purpose at work in Restrepo's fiction in general which, she claims, allows Colombians to better understand Colombian reality through its literary inscription.[31] She cites Restrepo's *Delirio*[32] [*Delirium*] as best exemplifying the way in which 'la autora contribuye esta vez a un universo ficcional en el que colombianos y colombianas nos podemos mirar, descubrir y entender' [the author contributes this time to a fictional universe in which Colombian men and women can see, discover and understand themselves].[33] Navia endows Restrepo's writing with a mimetic function which reflects a true image of Colombian reality to her Colombian readers, revealing to them a truth that is made more accessible through literary representation, and which is thereby implicitly posited as less readily available in the direct experience of Colombian reality. This thesis is supported to some degree by Juana Suárez's analysis of the public perception and understanding of contemporary Colombian history as almost entirely mediated through the television, which creates a reiterative and simplified discourse of violence without however offering the critical tools for an analysis of the strategies of presentation.[34] Navia's use of the first-person plural in her discussion of the elucidating effect of Restrepo's writing on a Colombian readership is reflective of a wider trend in Latin American criticism, as well as reminiscent of Restrepo's own use of the same in her narrator's catchcry, 'nosotros los colombianos' [literally, 'we the Colombians'] (see, for example, *DC*, p. 20). There is a certain degree of opacity as to whom this latter phrase refers, given the insuperable divide which exists between the two worlds depicted in *Dulce compañía* and which the text ultimately represents as resolutely separate. The enunciation of a collectivity ('nosotros') could be said to be an effort to bring about a 'nosotros' where no such collectivity exists, and the novel can be seen as an attempt to override differences and create a sense of unity and solidarity through an appeal to a cohesive national identity. However, the novel's permeation by different axes of differentiation and segmentation — the upper and lower classes, men and women, the 'people' ('el pueblo') and those in positions of power (State authorities, the Church and illegal groups that wield power) — make this goal seem hardly plausible.

Restrepo's assertion of a collective voice can be problematised on various other accounts. Firstly, Navia's assertion of the mimetic representativity of Restrepo's writing begs the question of who is seeing and discovering themselves in her texts, in turn raising the important question of Restrepo's readership: representativity and readership are, after all, two sides of the same coin. Given the low rates of literacy and/or readership in the poorer sectors of Colombia's demographic, it seems unlikely that a significant part of her readership comes from communities such as the fictional Galilea. If Restrepo's readership is largely made up of middle-class readers, it follows that her representation of Colombian reality would be recognisable to a middle-class readership and academic audience located in a similar sociocultural position to Restrepo herself. Her attempt to revalidate the disempowered and underrepresented in Colombia through a destabilised narrative perspective, the disruption of power hierarchies between her narrator and other characters, and representative strategies which valorise a non-hegemonic interpretation of reality places Restrepo in the problematic position of replicating a tradition of speaking about, and on behalf of, the voiceless.

Restrepo's problem(s) of representation and readership are similar to many of those which John Beverley describes in relation to the testimonial genre, or *testimonio*.[35] Indeed, *Dulce compañía* can be said to share many of *testimonio*'s features, including constituting a narration in the first person in which the narrator is also the protagonist of the narration, which is itself the account of a particularly significant event driven by the urgency of a situation of repression or marginalisation, and which is inherently political. Yet, unlike the testimonial 'author' who is excluded from the spheres of journalistic and literary production because typically illiterate and therefore reliant on an external transcriber, compiler, or editor to discursively record his or her verbal account (and indeed the degree to which this mediation influences or even shapes the testimonial narration constitutes the most debated aspect of *testimonio*),[36] Restrepo is of course at the very centre of these discursive practices. If, however, *Dulce compañía* shares only a certain number of the diegetic characteristics of *testimonio*, it entirely complies with *testimonio*'s ideological criteria: an underlying moralising intent, the presentation of a problematic social situation that is shared by a group, and a confounding of genres which presents a challenge to the limits and functions of fiction and non-fiction. *Dulce compañía* also resonates with testimony's tendency to evoke a poliphony of other possible voices insofar as, in recounting her encounter with the poor of Galilea, la Mona attempts to present the Galileans' experience of the angel as much as her own account of that experience. Therein lies the problematic aspect of Restrepo's representation: the collective which she seeks to represent (in both the political and mimetic senses mentioned above) is one that she has adopted and speaks for as an outsider. Rather than signalling the failure of the representational intention of *Dulce compañía*, the problems and difficulties it shares with the testimonial genre bear witness to the ongoing debate surrounding testimonial, literary, and anthropological accounts, whereby the paradox of representing the Other has yet to be resolved.

The presence of an extranational body of readers is also inferred in the phrase, 'nosotros los colombianos': if on the one hand, the enunciation evokes national cohesion, on the other it suggests the presentation of an outwardly-projected image of national cohesion for non-local audiences. As Nora Eidelberg aptly puts it: 'El escritor [exiliado] se encuentra en una encrucijada. ¿Para quiénes debe escribir, para el público de su país de origen o para él del nuevo país?' [The (exiled) writer finds him/herself in a dilemma. For whom must he or she write: for readers in the country of origin or those in the new country?].[37] Indeed, many indices in *Dulce compañía* suggest a didactic function aimed at informing international audiences of Colombian reality, such as a paragraph in the opening pages of the text which describes the idiosyncracies of the Colombian national character, and begins: 'Colombia es el país del mundo donde más milagros se dan por metro cuadrado' [Colombia happens to be the country in the world with the most miracles per square foot] (*DC*, p. 19). If the project of literary representation appears problematic, Restrepo's engagement with issues associated with contemporary Colombian history suggests a political drive which circumvents the problem of her 'legitimacy' as a voice of the underrepresented. Restrepo's engagement with such issues has been a consistent feature of her fictional and non-fictional writing and can be related to her writerly origins in journalism and her involvement in the political life of Colombia. In *Dulce compañía*, the gendered narrative voice denotes a strategy for commenting on women's position in Colombian society, in an attempt to draw out similarities while accounting for differences.

The gendered focus of Mokeddem's and Restrepo's writing, which foregrounds the politicisation of women organised in women's groups, features female characters who are marginalised from sites of power and who occupy some of the lowest rungs in the social hierarchy. The social reality of disempowered women is represented in both novels in an attempt to open channels for women's self-representation in order to bring about change in societies where women are frequently the target of political and social violence. There is, however, a tension between the collective aim of each author and the quest for women's solidarity as a means to overcoming patriarchal hierarchy, and the highly individualist stance of their protagonists, particularly in the case of Mokeddem's texts whose protagonists are seen to participate in very few relationships with other women. Whilst *L'Interdite* and *Dulce compañía* both offer models of female solidarity and political organisation (in the women's uprising against misogynist violence and repression at the conclusion of *L'Interdite*, and the combining of forces of the narrator and the neighbourhood women against both legitimate and illegitimate power-wielding authorities in *Dulce compañía*), their protagonists' adoption of the singular representative voice of the collectivity somewhat undermines this solidarity. Like la Mona, Sultana faces similar problems as an outsider to the community of Aïn Nekhla in *L'Interdite*. Directly related to her exile, her alienation from the community is exacerbated by her long-term absence from Algeria as well as the shift from being a daughter of the village to becoming a member of the professional middle classes in France. The question of Sultana's representativity is explicitly raised in the novel, as while the village men see her as foreign and contaminated by Western 'immorality', the women actively seek her (political) representation at the novel's climax. Sultana's sensitivity to the problematic nature of her representativity is manifested in her declining to become the head of the projected women's movement in the village. Sultana (and thus by extension Mokeddem) demonstrates a vivid awareness that her criticism of Algerian society and the lifestyle that she once fled is problematised by her distantiation from this society, and there is an absence of the interpellation of overarching belonging present in Restrepo's narrative.

In her discussion of *L'Interdite*, Valérie Orlando emphasises the symbolic, rather than actual, nature of Mokeddem's discourse of representativity, describing how 'L'histoire de Sultana montre une femme qui fait face à son destin tandis que, symboliquement, elle lutte pour le destin collectif des femmes algériennes piégées dans un monde hyper machiste' [the story of Sultana shows a woman standing up to her destiny while, symbolically, she fights for the collective destiny of Algerian women trapped in a hyperchauvinist world].[38] That Sultana's representativity tentatively takes on a symbolic, rather than an actual role of representation addresses Mokeddem's own problematic suitability as a representative voice of Algerian women. Whilst not renouncing an ambition to give a voice to the voiceless, Mokeddem is cautious in assuming this role, as Sultana's declining of their request for representation indicates. Orlando identifies a coincidence between the political drive behind Mokeddem's narrative and that present in much Francophone North African women's writing:

> Les œuvres francophones féminines n'amènent pas seulement à une réflexion sur la condition de la femme au Maghreb, mais permettent aussi de cultiver un activisme nouveau qui va créer une solidarité féminine capable de changer le statut social et politique de la femme.[39]

> [Francophone women's writing leads not only to a reflection on the condition of women in the Maghreb, but also to cultivating a new kind of activism which nurtures women's solidarity and which is capable of changing the social and political status of women.]

Thus, according to Orlando, texts such as Mokeddem's *L'Interdite* have real power to bring about actual social and political change in the lives of North African women through the prompting of political engagement, a claim which calls for a more thorough investigation of the way such change might, in actual terms, be achieved. The key to this engagement is identified by Orlando as the promotion of women's solidarity and their access to the social and political arena. Such a reading of Mokeddem would seem to coincide with the literary project that the author sets herself, and a brief glance at Mokeddem's early bibliography sheds light on the evolving motivations behind the writer's project. Her first two novels, *Les Hommes qui marchent*[40] [*The Men Who Walk*] and *Le Siècle des sauterelles*[41] [*Century of Locusts*] present autofictional accounts of the author's personal history which attest to an individual need to contemplate her displacement through a revisitation of her past. Her two subsequent works, *L'Interdite* and *Des rêves et des assassins*, described as novels written 'dans un état d'urgence' [in a state of urgency],[42] are a virulent response to the violence that peaked in the 1990s in Algeria, which Mokeddem, unable to remain silent, was impelled to represent and denounce.[43] *L'Interdite* incorporates both of these driving forces — of personal discovery and political engagement — by depicting the protagonist's reflection on her sense of identity and belonging after fifteen years of exile, against the backdrop of her re-encounter with the culture that she rejects and denounces.

If Mokeddem undertakes the project of writing to fulfil these two internal needs, she also identifies a further need that she attributes to her public, as she described in an interview: 'Les lecteurs [...] éprouvent le besoin de lire, d'entendre ces voix authentiques pour comprendre la complexité des situations' [Readers feel the need to read, to hear, these authentic voices to understand the complexity of situations].[44] Mokeddem's reference to 'voix authentiques' somewhat jeopardises her cautious positioning of Sultana as symbolically representative, in implying her narrative voices to be well placed to represent complex situations to a readership that is eager to understand them, despite Sultana's hesitation in *L'Interdite* to adopt this role. In this way Mokeddem makes a distinction between the politically, and the mimetically, representative role. While through the character of Sultana we can deduce that she is hesitant to take on the former, she appears committed to a responsibility towards the latter. Mokeddem does not expand on who the readers she refers to might be, although the implication that they need to read about, in order to understand, a complex reality suggests an audience unfamiliar with the contemporary history of Algeria. Indices within the text, such as extensive footnotes and intratextual clarifications to explain Arabic terms and concepts, further indicate that Mokeddem writes with a non-Algerian audience in mind, and the fact that she writes in French certainly gestures towards a French (as well as a wider French-speaking) readership. The apparent divergence between Mokeddem's implied readership and those who stand to benefit from the political agenda expounded in her texts renders Orlando's claim for the revolutionary potential of texts such as Mokeddem's somewhat questionable.

The linguistic narrative devices employed by Mokeddem recall Steven G. Kellman's 'literary translingualism' which was also seen to characterise the writing of Nancy Huston and Cristina Siscar. Mokeddem's incorporation of Arabic expressions and turns of phrase includes phrases directly transcribed in italicised Arabic in the text and left untranslated, or which are translated into French and appear in italics in the narration, such as *'une seule main ne peut applaudir'* [*One hand alone cannot applaud*] (*I*, p. 145). It also includes the phonetic rendering of characters' French neologisms, notably Dalila's: 'Nous dans le désert, on est pas "parabolé". –Parabolé? — Oui, c'est quand tu as l'antenne qui te branche sur Lafrance' ['We here in the desert, we're not "paraboled". 'Paraboled'? 'Yes, it's when you have the antenna that hooks you up to the LaFrance'] (*I*, p. 72). Here Mokeddem demonstrates the kind of translingual 'code-switching' that signal what Réda Bensmaïa refers to as the reterritorialisation of French.[45] According to Bensmaïa, such reterritorialisation attempts to resolve the dilemma of all Algerian Francophone writers, which is to represent, in a monolingual text, a social reality that is enacted in various languages (amongst which, French, Arabic, Kabyle, Touareg, and Mozabit), and to do so to an ever-diminishing French-speaking local audience in Algeria. As Jane E. Evans explains, 'What is problematic for writers such as Mokeddem is that French in Algeria has been reduced to the status of a foreign language, whereas Arabic has become the required language of study in national schools.'[46]

A discrepancy can be noted, then, between the object of the campaign expounded in her texts for Algerian women's solidarity and political mobilisation, and the reader that is actually addressed. If Mokeddem reaches a wider readership outside Algeria than within its borders due to linguistic and cultural reasons, Orlando's assertion of the revolutionary power of Mokeddem's writing once again seems less plausible. If her novels are only read by a privileged few within Algeria — and not by those who stand to benefit from their revolutionary potential — there is a sense in which she is preaching to the converted. In stating that 'Mokeddem sets out to draw the reading public's attention to the ongoing sociocultural and political strife of a country laid to waste by inner conflict, factionalism, fundamentalism, and abuse of human rights', Orlando also refers to Mokeddem's reading public without explicitly expanding on who this might include and, like Mokeddem, evoking an uninformed, international (non-Algerian) readership.[47] In this sense, Mokeddem and Restrepo both face a similar dilemma in the discrepancy between the imagined, and the actual reader. For their self-designated literary projects to be fulfilled, it would seem crucial that the subjects who are the objects of the texts are also their readers. A sense of responsibility towards a reading public is indeed shared by both Restrepo and Mokeddem and can be said to epitomise one of the key dilemmas of the returned exile. Where Mokeddem describes the author's responsibility from the perspective of the readers' need to 'understand the complexity of situations', scholars attribute Restrepo with a sense of responsibility that is the result of her privileged educational and cultural position. Gabriela Polit Dueñas describes this motivating force as a responsibility that Restrepo feels towards her reading public, stating: 'la responsibilidad del escribo de poner en papel la historia, de darle racionalidad, es la que Laura Restrepo asume frente a la realidad colombiana' [in the face of Colombian reality, Laura Restrepo takes on the responsibility of the scribe to record and make sense of history].[48] The use of the neutral 'escribo' to define Restrepo's role, however, somewhat effaces the author's agency in recording the events of contemporary history, and overlooks problems of mediation. As women exiles from countries governed by a strong patriarchal order, Mokeddem and Restrepo demonstrate a sense of responsibility that extends to denouncing gender inequality, as the drive for feminine solidarity in their works demonstrates.

A sense of responsibility toward the reader which derives from a perceived need to reveal complex national realities through the representational voice of the author also risks permeating the text to such an extent that its political impetus overshadows its literary aesthetic, and its political 'subtext' arguably surpasses the 'text' in *L'Interdite*. The expounding of ideological standpoints that comprise much of the narration and dialogues in *L'Interdite* reveals the strength of the ideological presentation in the text, which is driven by an urgency on part of the author to respond to the mounting religious fundamentalism in 1990s Algeria. Mokeddem denounces such fundamentalism in narrative passages as well as through the dialogue of her characters Sultana, Salah, and Dalila. The character of Vincent also provides an alternative perspective: whilst Sultana (through close autobiographical referentiality) can be considered to present Mokeddem's own views as a woman exiled from her native Algerian village, Vincent's character (male and French) serves to offer a perspective far removed from that of Sultana. Vincent's perspective unfailingly complements and validates Sultana's views as, despite their differences, they are aligned through a shared status as outsiders to the village. The use of dialogue for the staging of criticism of the political upheaval in Algeria is nowhere more apparent than in the initial dialogue between Sultana and Salah which covers a broad range of topics including love, freedom, the protagonist's split, exiled identity, her alienation from the birth society, a criticism of her 'Western' behaviour, the misogyny of Algerian society and its male elite in particular, and the Algerian diaspora of the 1990s.

The author's voice is equally discernable in the text in narrative passages, focalised alternatively through Sultana and Vincent. Indeed, the tone of dialogues and narrative passages are frequently indistinguishable, reflecting the extent to which Mokeddem's own ideology and arguments pervade the text. Mokeddem appears to knowingly acknowledge this fact, and pre-empts possible criticism of her dominant authorial voice, having Salah comment to Sultana, 'Tu parles comme un livre. Tu dissertes!' ['You talk like a book. You're giving a lecture!'] (*I*, p. 47).

Ferdinand Mount has commented insightfully on political fiction in an article that asks: 'Are there artistic dangers when you preach to the converted?'[49] Addressing both the 'over-inking' of the political at the cost of the aesthetic, and the question of whether political fiction actually reaches its target audience over which it admittedly aims to have an effect, Mount concludes that 'an essential condition for turning politics into literary art [is] that our affections have to be engaged, even against our best intentions' and that 'the politics must somehow be absorbed for the piece to succeed as a work of art'. If Sultana's characterisation results in a protagonist who is only partially revealed to the reader and only superficially represented, as I would argue, this could be attributed to the force of the documentary and ideological drives behind *L'Interdite*, written in a state of urgency and defined by the overwhelming need to denounce the violence which instigated Mokeddem's departure from Algeria and which had, at the time of writing *L'Interdite*, reached her in France.[50]

In Restrepo's literary writing, driven by investigation and journalism, there is a similar documentary drive that, as David William Foster observes, has a long tradition in Latin American writing and which foregrounds 'attention to the relation between writing and reality, between narrative and fact, between detached novelist and involved participant'.[51] At the heart of Restrepo's journalistic fiction the question of objectivity is equally present, receiving mixed responses from critics. Elvira Sánchez-Blake commends the objectivity of Restrepo's hybrid writing style — 'Su obra combina el reportaje con la ficción desde una perspectiva objetiva de los conflictos que vive Colombia' [Her work combines journalism with fiction from an objective perspective of the conflicts that Colombia is experiencing][52] — whereas in the same collection of essays Mery Cruz Calvo describes the journalistic partiality at work in *Dulce compañía*: 'la reportera toma partido, se pone del lado de los mas débiles, rompe la premisa de que la objetividad-neutralidad existe' [the journalist takes sides, that of the weakest, breaking the premise that objectivity-neutrality exists].[53] Restrepo's own handling of the notion within her texts suggests scant concern for objectivity, and even an assertion of the impossibility of discursive objectivity. Whilst claiming a journalistic basis and methodology to her writing, Restrepo constantly reminds the reader, through narrative interjections, that she is writing fiction, thus accounting for both the reliable, historically referential nature of her texts, as well as her own personal involvement in the writing. La Mona states in *Dulce compañía*, 'los colegas siempre me han achacado falta de profesionalismo por mi incapacidad de mantener la objetividad y distancia frente a mis temas' [my colleagues have always accused me of lacking professionalism because of my inability to maintain the appropriate objectivity and distance from my subjects] (*DC*, p. 89), and goes on to give examples of becoming personally involved in her stories (a lack of distance and objectivity which certainly reaches its climax in her emotional and sexual involvement with the angel). In this way, not only does Restrepo elucidate her own particular writing style, which fuses fiction with journalism, but also provides a pre-emptive response to any potential criticism for lack of objectivity.[54]

Restrepo's style of representation that shuns claims for objectivity in the pursuit of reliable historical representation as seen from a particular subjective position recalls the link that feminist theory draws between the theoretical and the fictional, between claimed 'objectivity' and subjectivity, and illustrates the hybrid nomadic style which Rosi Braidotti articulates in terms of theorising fictions, and fictionalising theories and which is prevalent in exiled womens' texts. Restrepo's style similarly bears certain parallels with Mokeddem's representative fiction driven by the political and the personal, in that the political, in the cases of both Restrepo and Mokeddem, is personal. Their writing projects are both tied up with the contemporary histories of their countries, and with their own personal histories which have been profoundly affected by these. Mokeddem has demonstrated an ongoing compulsion to react against the circumstances that forced her from Algeria and which have continued to aggravate her relationship to the country. Restrepo's long-standing political activism has found its expression in journalism, literature, and political activity, and can be considered the motivating force behind the evolution of her writing from the journalistic to the fictional. Her literary project thus forms part of a wider political project and is a vehicle for the dissemination of a vision for Colombia which she has both expressed politically and manifested in her writing:

> Yo hice política mucho tiempo y en la política lo que quieres siempre es llegarle a la gente. Esa actitud de que no te importa si la gente te lee o no, no viene al caso cuando se trata de política y para mí los libros siempre han sido un puente hacia la gente. Tengo un gran interés en no hacer algo que deje a la gente por fuera.[55]
>
> [I was in politics for a long time, and in politics you always want to reach people. The attitude of not caring if people read you or not doesn't come into play when it is a question of politics and for me books have always been a bridge to people. I have a real interest in not doing anything that leaves people out.]

A symptom of their exiles, their texts are unreservedly personal, and neither author apologises for the strong textual authorial presence therein. Placing themselves at the centre of their texts would seem to be unavoidable in their exilic writing positions where their writing is aimed at both denouncing the failures of each society to provide for all its members and particularly its female population, as well as negotiating the alienation from the home country. The reader is constantly reminded in both Mokeddem's and Restrepo's texts that alongside the 'literary', lie the discourses of exile and politics. These distinct discourses, intertwined in the texts of both authors, lead to hybrid narratives that bear witness to their authors' literary, political, and personal imperatives, and to their occupation of an interstitial space between the birth and adopted countries, between literary and professional occupations, and in Mokeddem's case, between languages. The struggle, typically associated with the second stage of exile, to give expression to and locate a sense of divided subjectivity in displacement gives way to the experience of exile as an existential position and a cradle for a nomadic sense of identity in the ongoing state of exile, which is the focus of the next chapter.

Notes to Chapter 4

1. Gurr, p. 9.
2. Said, p. 186.
3. Chaulet-Achour and Kerfa, p. 30.
4. Déjeux, pp. 116–17 (my italics).
5. Orlando, *Nomadic*, p. 10.
6. Malika Mokeddem, *La Transe des insoumis* (Paris: Grasset, 2003).
7. Malika Mokeddem, *Mes hommes* (Paris: Grasset, 2005) [*My Men*, trans. by Laura Rice and Karim Hamdy (Lincoln and London: University of Nebraska Press, 2009)].
8. Laura Restrepo, *Demasiados héroes* (Bogotá: Alfaguara, 2009) [*No Place for Heroes*, trans. by Ernest Mestre-Reed (New York: Nan A. Talese and Doubleday, 2010)].
9. Suzette Henke coined the term 'scriptotherapy' to describe 'the process of writing out and writing through traumatic experience in the mode of therapeutic re-enactment' that she observes occurring with notable frequency in twentieth-century women's life-writing. A similar process can be identified in the recent autobiographical writings of exiled women writers, particularly in terms of the 'repressed trauma' and the resultant 'psychological fragmentation' that Henke observes in a large number of twentieth-century women's autobiographies (Suzette Henke, *Shattered Subjects: Trauma and Testimony in Women's Life-Writing* (New York: St Martin's Press, 1998), p. xii).
10. Déjeux, p. 157.
11. Claire Lindsay, '"Clear and Present Danger": Trauma, Memory and Laura Restrepo's *La novia oscura*', *Hispanic Research Journal*, 4.1 (2003), 41–58.
12. Bonn, p. 16.
13. David William Foster, 'Latin American Documentary Narrative', *PMLA*, 99.1 (1984), 41–55 (p. 47).
14. Malika Mokeddem, *L'Interdite* (Paris: Grasset, 1993) [*The Forbidden Woman*, trans. by K. Melissa Marcus (Lincoln and London: University of Nebraska Press, 1998)].
15. Laura Restrepo, *Dulce compañía*, 2nd edn (Bogotá: Alfaguara, 2005) [first edition: 1995] [*The Angel of Galilea*, trans. by Dolores M. Koch (New York: Crown, 1998)]. All references to and citations from the text refer to the 2005 edition.
16. 'Mona', meaning 'blond' in colloquial Colombian Spanish, is commonly used as a nickname for women with fair hair.
17. Samuel Jaramillo González, 'Segmentación social e imaginación', in *El universo literario de Laura Restrepo*, ed. by Elvira Sánchez-Blake and Julie Lirot (Bogotá: Alfaguara, 2007), pp. 149–56 (pp. 151–52).
18. The term *mestizo* denotes mixed racial background. In the Latin American context, this most commonly refers to people of mixed European and indigenous ancestry. Like *métis* in French, the term is unsatisfactorily rendered in the English approximations 'half-breed' and 'mixed blood' due to their negative overtones, and to the different trajectories of colonialism and racial mixing in English-, Spanish-, and French-speaking nations, thus the Spanish has been retained here. For a discussion of the subversive potential of the concept of *métissage* as a critical and writerly position from which to challenge the blindspot of the English language's inability to positively accommodate miscegenation, see Françoise Lionnet, 'The Politics and Aesthetics of Métissage', in *Autobiographical Voices: Race, Gender, Self-Portraiture* (Ithaca, NY: Cornell University Press, 1989), pp. 1–30.
19. Jaramillo González, p. 152.
20. Malika Mokeddem, *Des rêves et des assassins* (Paris: Grasset, 1995) [*Of Dreams and Assassins*, trans. by K. Melissa Marcus (Charlottesville: University of Virginia Press, 2000)].
21. The narrator of Nina Bouraoui's *La voyeuse interdite* (Paris: Gallimard, 1991) [*Forbidden Vision*,

trans. by K. Melissa Marcus (Barrytown, NY: Station Hill Press, 1995)] describes her native Algiers in remarkably similar terms, noting the same absence of women in the street which is itself also described as a female body, exhausted and despoiled by repetitive pregnancies, indicating a wider concern in contemporary Franco-Algerian women's writing with maternity as the default feminine role.

22. Huston, *Lettres parisiennes*, p. 210 (original italics).
23. Mokeddem, *Mes hommes*, p. 56.
24. Chaulet-Achour and Kerfa, p. 23.
25. The project of Arabisation, initiated after national independence from France in 1962, advocated breaking away from the legacy of French colonisation and recuperating a lost ancestral patrimony by curbing the perpetuation of the French language and promoting the use of Arabic, and reached a period of particular intensity during the civil war of the 1990s. Superimposed on Arabisation was a project of Islamisation which was reinforced through various measures, though most notably through the educational system where 'the only kind of school that existed was denominational' (Stora, p. 171), and whose ideology is summed up in the words of Islamic scholar Adelhamid Ben Badis: 'Islam is my religion, Algeria is my nation, and Arabic is my language' (quoted in Stora, p. 206). For further information see Gordon, 'French as Problematic', pp. 147–74, and Stora, 'Society and Culture in Algeria (1962–1982)', pp. 163–77.
26. Quoted in Helm, p. 45.
27. The culpabilisation of older generations of women for their complicity in women's repression is also highlighted in Bouraoui's *La voyeuse interdite*, referred to earlier.
28. Manrique, p. 356.
29. Jaramillo González, p. 155.
30. Elvira Sánchez-Blake, 'Introducción', in *El universo literario de Laura Restrepo*, ed. by Elvira Sánchez-Blake and Julie Lirot (Bogotá: Alfaguara, 2007), pp. 11–17 (p. 17).
31. Carmiña Navia, 'El universo literario de Laura Restrepo', in *El universo literario de Laura Restrepo*, ed. by Elvira Sánchez-Blake and Julie Lirot (Bogotá: Alfaguara, 2007), pp. 19–37 (p. 29).
32. Laura Restrepo, *Delirio* (Bogotá: Alfaguara, 2004) [*Delirium*, trans. by Natasha Wimmer (London: Harvill Secker, 2007)].
33. Navia, p. 29.
34. Juana Suárez, *Sitios de contienda: producción cultural colombiana y el discurso de la violencia* (Madrid: Iberoamericana, 2010).
35. John Beverley, 'Introducción', *Revista de crítica literaria latinoamericana*, 18.36 (1992), Special Issue: 'La voz del otro: testimonio, subalternidad y verdad narrativa', 7–19.
36. John Beverley, 'Anatomía del testimonio', *Revista de crítica literaria latinoamericana*, 13.25 (1987), 7–16.
37. Nora Eidelberg, 'Roma Mahieu y el desarraigo en el exilio', in *Extraños en dos patrias: Teatro latinoamericano del exilio* (Frankfurt am Main: Vervuert, 2003), ed. by Heidrun Adler, Adrián Herr, and Almuth Fricke, pp. 48–65 (p. 49).
38. Valérie Orlando, 'Écriture d'un autre lieu: la déterritorialisation des nouveaux rôles féminins dans *L'Interdite*', in *Malika Mokeddem: Envers et contre tout*, ed. by Yolande Aline Helm (Paris: L'Harmattan, 2000), pp. 105–15 (p. 107).
39. Orlando, 'Écriture', p. 106.
40. Malika Mokeddem, *Les Hommes qui marchent* (Paris: Ramsay, 1990).
41. Malika Mokeddem, *Le Siècle des sauterelles* (Paris: Ramsay, 1992) [*Century of Locusts*, trans. by Laura Rice and Karim Hamdy (Lincoln and London: University of Nebraska Press, 2006].
42. Yolande Aline Helm, 'Préface', to *Malika Mokeddem: Envers et contre tout*, ed. by Yolande Aline Helm (Paris: L'Harmattan, 2000), pp. 7–20 (p. 9).
43. Mokeddem has referred to her fifth novel, *La Nuit de la lézarde* [*The Night of the Crevice*], as an attempt to move away from writing violence and despair, and to reclaim a literary space that is not dominated by politics. Her return to a tone of denunciation and critique in the later novels, *La Transe des insoumis* and *Mes hommes*, however, denotes Mokeddem's difficulty in creating a literary universe that does not arise from a preoccupation with the social and political violence of Algeria.
44. Quoted in Chaulet-Achour and Kerfa, p. 29.

45. Réda Bensmaïa, 'Nations of Writers', in *Experimental Nations, or The Invention of the Maghreb*, trans. by Alyson Waters (Princeton: Princeton University Press, 2003), pp. 11–26.
46. Jane E. Evans, 'Accommodating Arabic: A Look at Malika Mokeddem's Fiction', in *The Selected Works of Jane E. Evans* (2005), <http://works.bepress.com/jane_evans/22> [accessed 23 January 2014] (p. 9).
47. Orlando, *Nomadic*, p. 200.
48. Gabriela Polit Dueñas, 'Sicarios, delirantes y los efectos del narcotráfico en la literatura colombiana', *Hispanic Review*, 74.2 (2006), 119–42 (p. 121).
49. Ferdinand Mount, 'The Power of Now: The Tricks and Traps of Political Fiction', *The Guardian*, Review supplement (4 July 2009).
50. Mary Jean Green and Yolande Helm both provide accounts of the death threats Mokeddem received in France from Islamic fundamentalists before the publication of *L'Interdite* (Mary Jean Green, 'Reworking Autobiography: Malika Mokeddem's Double Life', *French Review*, 81.3 [2008], 530–41, and Helm, 'Préface' to *Malika Mokeddem: Envers et contre tout*, pp. 7–20).
51. Foster, p. 42.
52. Sánchez-Blake, p. 11.
53. Mery Cruz Calvo, 'La construcción del personaje femenino en *Dulce compañia*', in *El universo literario de Laura Restrepo*, ed. by Elvira Sánchez-Blake and Julie Lirot (Bogotá: Alfaguara, 2007), pp. 135–47 (p. 140).
54. For further paradigmatic examples of Restrepo's hybrid fictional style see, in particular, *La isla de la pasión* (Bogotá: Planeta, 1989); *La novia oscura* (Bogotá: Alfaguara, 1999); and *La multitud errante* (Bogotá: Alfaguara, 2002).
55. Julie Lirot, 'Laura Restrepo por sí misma', in *El universo literario de Laura Restrepo*, ed. by Elvira Sánchez-Blake and Julie Lirot, pp. 341–51 (p. 343).

CHAPTER 5

❖

Alternative Femininities: Linda Lê's *In memoriam* and Cristina Peri Rossi's *Solitario de amor*

Of the six authors analysed here, Linda Lê and Cristina Peri Rossi are the only two to have lived uninterruptedly in their countries of exile after political and social turmoil compelled their departures from their birth countries in the 1970s. Born in countries whose political tensions would drive them to relocate and redefine themselves in metropolitan cities of Europe, they both share an extreme sensitivity to the dynamics of exclusion and alienation characteristic of politically motivated exiles. Both women can be considered to form part of the diasporas that the peoples of their respective countries suffered as a result of political turmoil in the late twentieth century. Despite the generational and cultural differences that distinguish the two writers, their works demonstrate similar thematic concerns and narrative strategies for scrutinising the configuration of women's identity in displacement and the negotiation of that identity against stipulated norms for women's sexual, social, and domestic roles — both the norms of the birth country and the adopted country of residence. Throughout their works the border between inclusion and exclusion, and between belonging and 'non-belonging', drives their thinking on the workings of gendered identity. Lê and Peri Rossi both disrupt conventional notions of the feminine in their fictional texts (where these are defined by traditional private, domestic, and sexual roles) through the representation of female protagonists who offer alternative embodiments of femininity situated on the margins of these historical ideals of womanhood. Their representations of femininity beyond that which is commonly considered appropriate or desirable for women is most apparent in their contestation of the permanence and fixity of categories of identity, in particular, those of gender and sexuality, in a way that is commensurate with the nomadic subjectivity facilitated by displacement into exile.

This chapter firstly examines the ways in which Lê and Peri Rossi contest a limited set of traditional domestic and sexual models of women's identity and sexuality by privileging ambiguity and diffuse boundaries. The analysis of Lê and Peri Rossi's presentation of alternative contructs of femininity, which disrupt historical ideals of femininity and gender in general, is followed by a discussion of the narrative devices that each author uses in her reconfiguration of gendered identity, and the striking absence or presence of the female body in the text. I suggest that this concern with the rethinking of gendered identity and the reconfiguration of femininity beyond the limitations of historical representations can be read in light of their experiences of exile and alienation. Their continued occupation, indeed appropriation of the transient, marginal space of exile is commensurate with the third stage of exile typically occurring after the exile has opted either to return 'home' or to remain in geographical displacement, and where exile is experienced as an ongoing, existential position.

In common with Laura Restrepo, Nancy Huston, Malika Mokeddem, and Cristina Siscar, both Linda Lê and Cristina Peri Rossi attest to feeling alienated in their home countries even before their displacement into exile, raising the question of whether a sense of alienation, as well as a symptom of exile, may also to a significant degree be considered one of its original contributing factors. For the young Lê, it was French education in the Vietnamese setting that set her apart from others and initiated the feeling of estrangement that would accompany her into, and become more pronounced during her exile to France. For Peri Rossi, who left Uruguay for Spain at the age of thirty-one, a sense of marginalisation was already present in her divergence from the limited range of approved behaviours and roles for women, as well as her left-wing political affinities in the increasingly conservative and repressive cultural and political environment of Uruguay of the late 1960s and early 1970s. This chapter also argues that a sense of alienation from social and cultural norms, and in particular, nonconformity to a certain ideal of femininity in the birth country even before exile, is a factor as much as a symptom of these women's departures into exile, and examines how this long-standing sense of alienation can be said to impact on their present nomadic identities as exiled women writers.

The œuvres of these two authors demonstrate the particularity of employing both explicit depictions of geographical displacement, and more implicit strategies of the representation of the marginalisation and alienation characteristic of exile. This chapter analyses two texts by Lê and Peri Rossi which employ the latter implicit strategies of the representation of feminine exiled subjectivity through isolated female protagonists who are represented in highly ambiguous terms in their rejection of fixed, static identity categories. These two female protagonists exist on the margins, or beyond the limits of identity markers of gender, sexuality, nationality, and, indeed, of most kinds of affiliation. The two works that form the focus of analysis here, Peri Rossi's 1988 novel, *Solitario de amor*,[1] [*Solitaire of Love*] and Lê's more recent *In memoriam* (2007),[2] are particularly illustrative of the way in which both authors highlight the inadequacies of established categories of identity to account for women alienated from such constructions of identity — a social alienation that is paralleled by their authors' geographic alienation. This chapter also draws on Peri Rossi's *La nave de los locos*,[3] [*The Ship of Fools*] and Lê's *Lettre morte*[4] [*Dead Letter*] and *Les aubes*[5] [*Daybreak*] to further illustrate their representations of the transient, diffuse boundaries of nomadic, exiled identity.

For both Lê and Peri Rossi, exile is key to their writing project, and both write from a position of exile where they positively construe the marginal literary space of the exiled woman writer as a privileged site of creativity. Both authors approach writing as a productive site for the expression of a marginal identity, parallel to the way in which the liminal space of exile provides an environment for the exploration and reconfiguration of personal identity where familiar social and cultural constraints are distanced and thus less binding. In contrast with preceding chapters, this chapter examines, in turn, each novel's vastly different representation of radicalised femininity, beginning with *Solitario de amor* and followed by *In memoriam*, before comparatively analysing the impact of corporeality in the two works, and concluding with a discussion of the ways in which Lê and Peri Rossi positively appropriate the space of marginality and alienation they inhabit as exiles, and write from an explicit, gendered position of exile to create a transient, nomadic sense of belonging.

Recodification of Gender in *Solitario de amor*

Solitario de amor is the first-person narrator's retrospective account of the love affair with his female lover, Aída, from a point in the present of narration after the relationship has ended. Very little action actually occurs in the present of narration, as the narrator, who remains nameless throughout, remembers the affair in a text whose production is never actually accounted for within the fiction of the novel. The reader is invited to conclude that he embarks on this writing project as he departs, at the end of the novel, on a train journey following the unbearable break-up of the relationship, yet this is not explicitly stated in the text. The narrative of the relationship is entirely centred around the narrator's absorbed attention in Aída and his obsessive contemplation of her. While the relationship lasts, the narrator is unable to exist on any other plane than that of his involvement with Aída, an involvement mirrored in the narrative structure which almost entirely consists of descriptions of Aída, Aída's body, and the narrator's gaze upon and contact with her body. The text portrays the narrator's obsessed state to the reader, who is swept along and almost bewildered by the intensity of the lover's gaze. In the complex narrative structure of the novel, the narration relates a retrospective account of the relationship through several different 'presents' which swing back and forth, merging into one another and creating the effect of a continuous present. The effect of such a narrative strategy is to convey an intimate vision of Aída in extreme close-up, whilst she remains at the same time inaccessible to the reader as her perspective of the relationship remains undisclosed: it is the male narrator's perspective that commands the reader's field of vision.

While centring on the contemplation of Aída, these various 'presents' convey different aspects of the narrator's relationship with his lover: the timeless, descriptive present details the narrator's passion for Aída; the narrative present recounts details of Aída's relationship with the narrator; and descriptive passages provide accumulative details of the outside world beyond the confines of the passionate relationship. Much like the non-teleological present of Cristina Siscar's *La sombra del jardín*, time is portrayed as fragmented and discontinuous, with the incorporation of the different strands of narration in the present disrupting any sense of the linear progression of events in the narrative. Despite the narrator's affirmation that the relationship lasts approximately three years, there is no sense of progression or development throughout its duration, but rather a general sense of the narrator's inability to function in the world outside the relationship, which, of course, *is* directed by the teleological progression of time. 'Being' for the narrator is thus portrayed as fragmented and simultaneous through the destabilisation of narrative time and the absence of a stable, singular present. Where in Siscar's novel the present is overwhelmingly invaded by the past and constantly deferred in an onward movement toward the future as the protagonist's persistent wandering conveys, Peri Rossi's protagonist is, by contrast, fully anchored in the present, albeit a multiple and shifting one.

The apparent reiteration of the heterosexual relationship of patriarchal discourse that privileges a male gaze directed at a silent, inaccessible and objectified female beloved, is radically disrupted by a contextual awareness of the author behind the text. The reader's assumptions and interpretations of the characters and gender positions they inhabit are radically altered by the extratextual awareness of Peri Rossi as a lesbian writer. It has been suggested that *Solitario de amor* can be read as a queer text that aims to disrupt culturally dominant heteronormative thought patterns and to unsettle readers' assumptions of the free-standing text regarding, for example, the correlation between the first-person narrator and the author.[6] In what seems to be yet another instance of a heterosexual masculine gaze objectifying a female body, Peri Rossi in fact highlights and contests culturally dominant sexual hierarchy and heteronormativity in *Solitario de amor*, presenting a challenge to gender assumptions through her adoption of a masculine narrative voice. The apparent investment in a phallogocentric ideal in the novel's central sexual relationship is turned on its head by Peri Rossi's female presence behind the text. Arguably, such a reading relies somewhat precariously on the reader's extratextual awareness of the author behind the text, without which *Solitario de amor* does to a certain extent risk falling back into the discourse of patriarchal logic. The novel's subversive potential is only fully revealed when factors of the text's production and reception are taken into account, thus vouching for the kind of contextual approach, advocated in Chapter 2, that highlighted the loss of meaning that occurs in the absence of an awareness of a text's historical, cultural, and political context. Without such contextualisation Peri Rossi's disruptive intent certainly risks becoming obscured. The informed reader is thus forced to consider his or her part in the text's production of meaning and their potential investment in a normative heterosexual reading or, alternatively, in a reading that takes into account the implied incongruence of the author and the first-person narrator. The narration up-ends narrative conventions in that the author constructs an apparently conventional narrative structure only to collapse it and reveal the cultural assumptions on which such conventions rely.

Indeed, one of the main concerns in scholarship on *Solitario de amor* is with the identity and subjectivity of the narrative voice. The work has alternatively been credited as an indictment of obsessive, narcissistic male love[7] and as a veiled homoerotic text. Consuelo Arias sees the male narrator as an androgynous figure, whose androgyny leaves the text open to a homoerotic reading of the love relationship by encoding lesbian eroticism in the male gaze and voice.[8] Peri Rossi's project here appears far more radical than Arias allows for, and that more than merely implicitly eroticising the heterosexual love relationship between Aída and the male narrator as veiled lesbian desire given the presence of the lesbian author behind the text, I would argue that the author advances new modalities of masculine desire which rely on the characterisation of the male lover and speaker as precisely that — male — and not diffused into a homogeneous, undifferentiated androgyny. The gender project that Peri Rossi implicitly advocates in *Solitario de amor* relies heavily on the play between the maleness of the first-person narrator, and the femaleness of the author, and is incommensurate with a homoerotic reading of the text.

Parizad Tamara Dejbord comments on literary criticism's attempts to reconcile Peri Rossi's frequent use of male narrators and constructions of women as objects of desire with Peri Rossi's radical stance on gender identities and sexualities: 'la crítica literaria ha considerado problemática la frecuente textualización de un yo masculino en los textos de Cristina Peri Rossi que construye a la mujer exclusiva y unidimensionalmente como objeto del deseo' [literary criticism has considered problematic the frequent inscription of a masculine 'I' in Cristina Peri Rossi's texts, which depict women, exclusively and one-dimensionally, as objects of desire].[9] Dejbord attempts to explain this apparent contradiction by highlighting that Peri Rossi's characters rarely fit squarely into stable conceptions of sexual and gender identity. Although taking into account Peri Rossi's radical attempt to deconstruct gender and sexual identities, such a conclusion still fails to fully account for the use of the narrative voice, along with other narrative devices, as modes of de- and recodification of sexual desire. Such recodification is enacted in several ways in *Solitario de amor*. Firstly, as already mentioned, in the tension between the identities of the narrative and the authorial personæ which highlight and disrupt conventional sexual hierarchies. Secondly, heterosexual male desire is recodified in the novel by the incorporation of stereotypically feminine impulses, gestures, and modes of participation in heterosexual relationships, such as, for example, the characterisation of the narrator's love for Aída as a type of illness, a disabling passion that disrupts his ability to function in society and causes him to suspend all activity that is not related to his contact with her. This passivity, along with his dramatic loss of appetite due to the all-consuming nature of his passion for Aída, highlight and 're-gender' behaviours stereotypically associated with women's involvement in passionate relationships. Finally, the recodification of masculine participation in heterosexual relationships is envisaged in the narrator's desire for subsumption of the self into the body of the beloved, thus overturning entrenched notions of masculine authority and feminine passivity. The narrator makes frequent reference to a fantasy that he harbours for symbiotic unification with the beloved, which rather than resembling a morphing of the two into one, is imagined as a dissoluton of the male self into the female beloved. This loss of self into the other can be linked to the treatment of sexual penetration in the novel, which is reworked as the penetration of the male by the female through the female to male transmission of bodily fluids as Arias notes: 'it is the male who is penetrated and contaminated [by the woman], but willingly so'.[10] Penetration is depicted as an act committed by the female body's fluids and emissions which are represented as invading and occupying the male body and thus inverting the external genital penetration that commonly characterises heterosexual intercourse. Once again, we see how Peri Rossi constructs her narrative on a foundation of historical assumptions regarding gender identity and behaviour which are inverted or disrupted to voice new possibilities for men and women's participation in heterosexual relationships.

Solitario de amor not only expounds at length on paradigms of masculinity in the context of heterosexuality, but foregrounds an alternative model of femininity through the characterisation of Aída, despite the apparently paradoxical fact that her voice remains largely silent throughout the novel. In fact, Aída's agency is never in doubt: despite her silence, she is far from passive. Within the restricted space dedicated to the depiction of her public role in society and away from the narrator, she is portrayed as an independent woman with a productive role in raising her young son and pursuing a career. Her participation in the sexual relationship is described as one aspect of a vigorous, dynamic life — 'Sale del amor con un extraordinario vigor para las cosas cotidianas' [She comes away from love with an extraordinary vigor for common things] (*SA*, p. 9) — unlike the narrator who has difficulty conceiving of his existence, and indeed of his very identity, away from Aída. It is this more than anything else which explains the restricted scope of Aída's representation in the novel: if Aída's portrayal is limited to her relationship to the narrator, this is precisely because of the obsessive nature of his participation in their relationship, and his difficulty in conceiving of her beyond her relationship to him. Her representation in the novel is more indicative of the narrator's character than of her own. Indeed, the fact that it is Aída who ends the relationship suggests that it was conducted more on her terms than on his.

Peri Rossi reminds the reader that our conceptualisation of gender roles and relationships are historically and culturally constructed, and that, although they are determined by these factors, they are not therefore immutable. The historical power hierarchy that exists in the conventional heterosexual couple is demonstrated as an aspect which can be modified to include a more diverse range of possibilities of heterosexual relations. Peri Rossi does not advocate the dissolution or eradication of heterosexuality in favour of a homosexual egalitarian utopia — she does not argue the inherent incompatibility of the sexes — but merely the inequality and violence of heterosexual relations that are the product of a patriarchal society inscribed in the logic of a masculine sexual economy. This is particularly salient in the Latin American context where gender roles are heavily invested in the myth of masculine dominance and authority, and where adherence to the social norm is strictly policed by different strains of pervasive misogyny that Helena Araújo refers to as 'machismo clásico' [classic chauvinism] and 'machismo interiorizado' [internalized chauvinism].[11] According to Araújo, this is an endemic *machismo* that cuts across regional and class boundaries, and to this extent touches all Latin American women. Tracing its origins to a Catholic tradition of what she refers to as 'the cult of Maria', Araújo suggests that the subordination of women in Latin America can be attributed to the revered feminine model of the Virgin Mary which privileges female obedience, silence, and compulsory motherhood: 'Recordemos, la Virgen nunca habla ni discurre. Solamente oye, escucha órdenes de la divinidad o súplicas de pecadores. Y como madre se prodiga y se sacrifica [...] el silencio es la condición misma de la madre sufriente' [Remember that the Virgin never speaks or discusses. She only hears, listens to divine orders or pleas from sinners. And as a mother she gives of herself and makes sacrifices [...] silence is the very condition of the suffering mother].[12] In her seminal work, *La Scherezada criolla,* Araújo identifies in Peri Rossi a writer who reconfigures such traditional paradigms of femininity in Latin America, both politically and socially as well in terms of gender identity and relations.

In order to illustrate Peri Rossi's recognition of the centrality of gender identities in Latin American identity politics, Elia Geoffrey Kantaris describes how Peri Rossi's *La nave de los locos* places 'sexual identity as the disavowed absence at the problematic centre of national and political identity posturings'.[13] The understanding of the prominence given to gender identities in *La nave de los locos* is illuminated by Kantaris's observation that the 'desire to reimpose "traditional" strong Catholic patriarchal values by projecting a system of social organization predicated on naturalized gender stereotypes' was fundamental to the military ideology during the military dictatorships of the 1970s and 1980s in Latin America's Southern Cone.[14] Diana Taylor reinforces this notion when, in her study of gender and nationalism during the military dictatorship in Argentina in that period, she refers to 'the erasure of the "feminine"' and other gender identities outside the masculinity embodied by the military 'which must be suppressed or repressed for the misogynist version of nation-ness to work'.[15] The military junta in Argentina, similarly to that in Uruguay, represented itself as an authentic model of citizenship, embodying a certain kind of masculinity against which all 'inauthentic' citizens, considered enemies of the state, were feminised and attributed with a range of stereotypically feminine traits (such as weakness, complacency, and guilt). In this way, all unassimilable identities were persecuted and punished, including homosexuals, indigenous people, Jewish people, and women who did not conform to the Marianist model referred to by Araújo. Peri Rossi's configuration of gender can be seen as a response to such violent repression of nonconforming gender and sexual identities in the context of the military dictatorship in Uruguay as well as a reaction to a more generalised enforcement of restricted gender identities both in the Southern Cone at the time, and their ongoing policing during her exile in the tail-end and aftermath of Franco's authoritarian regime in Spain.

Seemingly paradoxical in Peri Rossi's apparently optimistic project of presenting, through the heterosexual couple of *Solitario de amor,* new paradigms that deconstruct the imposed sexual roles that she sees as the cornerstone of women's social and political marginalisation, is her apparent view of sexual relationships as essentially destructive. Peri Rossi emphasizes the paradoxical nature of sexual relationships, stating in an interview:

> I have accentuated the destructive element of love, because love is not only one thing. It is sensual pleasure, communication, but it is also a terrible struggle between two identities which lose their individualities and enter into conflict. The only way out of this situation is the survival of one of the two.[16]

For Peri Rossi, sexual relationships based on a gender hierarchy necessarily involve the annihilation of one of the parties. The trope of the intimate and exclusive sexual relationship as the scene of power struggles is present throughout Peri Rossi's corpus, and is most particularly evident in three of her earlier short stories: 'Historia de amor'[17] [Love story], 'La naturaleza del amor'[18] [The nature of love], and 'La destrucción del amor'[19] [The destruction of love] (where Peri Rossi's use of the term *amor* narrowly refers to love in passionate, sexual relationships). These stories make a number of claims about the debilitating and destructive nature of exclusive, hierarchical sexual relationships. 'Historia de amor' asserts the inevitable and reciprocal disabling of each lover by the other, and the subsumption of one into the other as a necessary condition of exclusive passionate relationships. 'La naturaleza del amor' upholds the destructive nature of passive misogyny by illustrating the fantasised harmony, plenitude, and equality of heterosexual sexual relationships based on gender inequality as a logical fallacy and thus an illusion. Finally, 'La destrucción del amor' presents the ultimate incompatibility of men and women in male-dominated heterosexual relationships, within which men's destructive character, and women's reproductive (and creative) function mutually prohibit any meaningful relationship. Peri Rossi's reiterated denunciation of the reliance of exclusive heterosexual relationships on gender imbalances represents a denunciation of the unattainability of harmonious, heterosexual relationships modelled on contemporary gender paradigms which are based on an entrenched gender hierarchy.

Certainly the relationship between Aída and the narrator epitomises all three of the above scenarios as a strategy for showing up the destructive nature of such interpersonal relationships in order to suggest alternative possibilities based on heterogeneity and reciprocity. In *Solitario de amor*, the narrator is entirely alienated and rendered unproductive by his love for Aída. He is portrayed as being incapable of conceiving of a sense of identity away from the object of his passion: his sense of self is completely destabilised and reduced to definition within the confines of his relationship with Aída. In this way, the amorous relationship is portrayed in similar terms to the state of exile, inducing a sense of profound rupture between past and present, alienation from the public world beyond the private sphere of the relationship, and the loss of a sense of self: the narrator describes himself as '[un] viajero extraviado en una tierra colonizada por otros' [a lost traveller in a land colonized by others] (*SA*, p. 11) and 'un hombre de ningún lugar' [a man from nowhere] (*SA*, p. 21). Love is portrayed as an exilic state as it deprives the individual of all reference points of identity and leaves him disorientated and in a permanent state of limbo. The scriptive drive expressed by the narrator at the novel's conclusion — 'El tren está a punto de arrancar. He comprado un cuaderno negro donde empezar a escribir' [The train is about to depart. I've bought a black notebook to begin my writing] (*SA*, p. 147) — implies a similar need for the kind of discursive interrogation of self and of one's place in the world to which much exile writing bears witness.

The comparison between passionate love and the state of exile is furthered in *Solitario de amor* with the narrator's insistent interrogation of self throughout and beyond the duration of the relationship. The narrator appears narcissistically obsessed with his love for Aída, rather than with Aída herself, and the object of his obsession appears to be his own state of being in love and the alienation that this produces, as she points out to him: 'No me amas a mí, amas tu mirada' [You don't love me, you love your own vision] (*SA*, p. 21). In this respect, his very identity is based upon his state of being in love, and of the suffering that this induces, thus wilfully locating his identity in a state of alienation. Much as the exile has been shown in previous chapters to wittingly locate identity in the non-belonging of exile, so too does the narrator define himself by his location in the alienation of passion. In the state of his passion for Aída, the narrator can be seen to seek out a sense of self defined by isolation and alienation, even from Aída herself, as his claim for their inherent linguistic and corporeal incommunicability suggests: 'hablo una lengua que no conoce, puesto que mi cuerpo es diferente al suyo' [I speak a language she doesn't know, because my body is different from hers] (*SA*, p. 29).[20] In effect, Aída ceases to be the centre of his amorous passion, and his intensity is directed toward clinging on to this passion which eventually provides him with a measure against which to define his identity. Indeed, having aligned his sense of self to the space of alienation provided by the relationship, he is reluctant to relinquish this anchoring, and dreads the idea of reverting to being a 'normal' man — of being 'like' others — rather than being defined by his differentiation from others. If identity, as Roy F. Baumeister affirms, is defined as much by differentiation from, as by identification with other individuals, we see how the narrator embraces, and eventually seeks to preserve the alienation which differentiates him from those around him, and which eventually affords him a space in which to anchor his identity.[21] Similar processes can be seen to operate for exiled individuals who initially experience estrangement from other individuals and from society as a highly traumatic experience, and subsequently come to embrace this alienation which defines them as Other, thus allowing them to recuperate a defined and singular sense of identity that was lost in the anonymity of displacement.

If the passionate relationship is portrayed as a state of exile, banishment from the relationship is likened to a second exile (recalling Mario Benedetti's notion of 'desexilio', or the experience of reverse exile upon repatriatriation following exile which is characterised by a new process of adaptation and an ongoing state of marginality).[22] After the rupture of their relationship, the narrator is seen to embrace the state of banishment for the differentiated identity that this confers upon him. He does not wish to resolve the trauma that the end of the relationship occasions, as he does not want to suffer the fate of Aída's former lovers who are no longer defined by their suffering of the loss of Aída, and thus to lose an identity defined by his relationship to her. In his continuing state of 'exile' following the end of the relationship with Aída, the narrator seeks to remain differentiated by this very state of non-belonging, remaining 'unlike' rather than 'like' those around him, an identarian strategy seen to be widely shared by exiled women writers. He prefers the pain and limbo of abandonment by Aída to a return to 'normality' in which he would be indistinguishable from others: 'Pero yo no quiero que pase [el dolor]. No quiero dejar de amarla. Prefiero este dolor agudo, esta angustia agobiante al tedio del desamor, de la normalidad' [But I don't want it to pass. I don't want to stop loving her. I prefer this sharp pain, this crushing anguish, to the tedium of lovelessness, of being normal] (*SA*, p. 143).

If the metaphoric exile of the passionate relationship is experienced as debilitating and alienating for the narrator, Aída, however, seeks out dynamism in the liminality which the narrator suffers as disenabling. Aída demonstrates a predilection for 'lugares de paso' [places of transit] — train stations, airports, and hotels — that represent empty spaces in which she is unmarked and 'unlocated'. Her recurrent dream of finding herself in a hotel located in an empty street, in a strange city, and in a foreign country, is not represented, as one might expect, as disconcerting or frightening. Rather, in this dream she relishes the opportunity for identity to be self-identical, and to inhabit a space in which her identity is absolute, marked neither by culture, nor by language. The discourse of absolute self-identity that is unmarked by culture is also present in reflections upon the distorting effect of language, and cultural markers such as clothing. Upon waking from an instance of her recurrent dream, she realises the difficulty of obtaining such distance and alienation: it is only a dream, and her embedding in culture is revealed to the extent that she expresses a desire for an ideal of 'casas fijas' [permanent houses] (*SA*, p. 19), the plural of which conveys the idealistic nature of this desire, in that, reinserted back into society after the dream, it is not a longing for *a* fixed home that Aída craves, but for an abstract notion of *fixed homes*, and for an abstract space of fixity rather than a particular given site of fixity. Peri Rossi's expression, through Aída, of the desire for unconstrained fixity is commensurate with the kind of nomadic location and belonging frequently sought out by women exiles. Not a desire for an entirely disconnected, unbound being but for a sense of location and belonging in mobility itself, Peri Rossi's female protagonist's metaphor of 'casas fijas' expresses the kind of belonging that is not defined by a singular place, but by a singular state: that of mobility.

For Lê too, sexual relationships, and indeed personal relationships more generally, are characterised by their mutually destructive nature. This is particularly evident in Lê's portrayal of domestic heterosexual partnerships, where traditional power relationships between husbands and wives are inverted, with the wives/mothers carrying out the financially and socially dominant roles historically occupied by their male counterparts, as particularly evident in Lê's *Lettre morte* and *Les aubes*. Husbands/fathers are portrayed as emasculated and ineffectual, often becoming subsumed by the relationship if not eventually committing suicide. Sexual relationships are very rarely, if at all, portrayed as positive harmonious accords, but rather are violent and doomed to mutual destruction, as has also been seen in the case of Peri Rossi's texts. The relationships conducted by the offspring of such conflictual domestic arrangements are modelled in opposition to the paradigms of their progenitors, and are frequently characterised by the isolation of the individuals intent on maintaining a distance from both their own sexual partners as well as from such models of conduct, as is the case in *Les aubes* and *In memoriam*. This is accompanied in Lê's fiction by the rejection of traditional gender roles in a move towards asexualised models that refuse either to inhabit or invert gender roles, preferring to negate them altogether, and to locate identity in a third space beyond binary distinctions. Most notably, it is Lê's female characters who predominantly resist subsumption into the domestic, heterosexual unit, and who define their gender in alterity through asexualised models of gender identity. Rather than merging sexual behavioural characteristics, as seen in the case of Peri Rossi's characters, Lê's female characters attempt to efface the traces of gender altogether as a way of defying gender norms.

Effacing Gender in *In memoriam*

In memoriam, like *Solitario de amor*, retrospectively recounts the past love affair between the first-person narrator and a character named Sola that ended not with the rupture of the relationship, but with the suicide of Sola as the outcome of what appears to be severe mental illness. Like Peri Rossi, Lê adopts a male narrator, a despairing writer who finally meets Sola, a successful novelist, in a chance encounter after fruitlessly endeavouring to contact her through her publisher. The meeting takes place in a bookshop in which the narrator happens to come across Sola, and a tormented relationship is initiated which lasts approximately two years until Sola's suicide. A number of Lê's predilect themes resurface in this novel, including debilitating mental illness, alienation, despair, and suicide. Like *Solitario de amor*, *In memoriam* also portrays exclusive heterosexual relationships as inherently stifling, unfulfilling, and conflictual, as brought to the fore in Sola's inclusion of the narrator's brother and life-long enemy in what becomes a triangular love relationship.

The extreme isolation common to the individuals of Lê's fictional universe is manifested in *In memoriam* by Sola's highly symbolic name, meaning 'alone'. As also observed to be the case of Siscar and Restrepo's protagonists, this too is a name conferred on her by another character, yet in contrast with Siscar and Restrepo's narrator-protagonists, it is in the case of Sola, the first-person narrator who designates her as such. Thus, like *Solitario de amor*, the reader's direct access to the female protagonist is shown to be limited as her representation is highly mediated by the narrator. He similarly reduces Sola's identity to the one-dimensional whilst denying her the same multiplicity with which he characterises himself when he evokes his own complexity, using the first-person plural to refer to his own duality of body and mind: 'Nous l'appelions Sola parce qu'elle était solitaire et seule, d'une solitude souveraine' [We called her Sola because she was solitary and singular, of sovereign solitude] (*IM*, p. 9). The plurality of 'nous' contrasts sharply with the solitary nature of Sola, who occupies an isolated space within the fictional world of *In memoriam*. Like Aída's representation in *Solitario de amor*, Sola's representation remains almost entirely confined to the space of her relationship to the narrator, and she is seen to participate in very few other personal relationships. In contrast with Aída, Sola is thus portrayed as an extremely isolated individual, and there are only scarce references to participation in the public sphere beyond the private world of the relationship that are underscored in the representation of Aída.

In addition to the narrator's confinement of Sola to a one-dimensional representation, Sola also voluntarily distances herself from those around her, as illustrated by having published her first novel under a pseudonym, and thus further confounding the notion of naming to designate a singular, static identity. The motivation behind using a *nom de plume* is attributed to her eagerness to distance herself from family ties: 'Elle avait, quand elle publia son premier livre, choisi un pseudonyme, ce qui en disait long sur sa volonté de déracinement' [When she published her first book, she had taken a pseudonym, which spoke volumes of her wish to uproot herself] (*IM*, p. 28). If Sola distances herself from the father by symbolically resisting the inheritance of the patronym, her mother, referred to only as 'une Nantaise' [a woman from Nantes], is practically disowned, being referred to but once in the text. The almost entire effacement of the mother, along with the complete absence of any other significant relationships with women (or indeed, to all but the fleeting presence of any other women characters in *In memoriam*) suggests, on the one hand, that Lê's project is more preoccupied with the displacement and alienation of the (ungendered) individual at odds with their social and cultural surroundings than with an explicitly gendered project concerned with the representation of women. Or rather, that such an absence of gender only makes the concern with gendered identities all the more present: it is, after all, upon a female protagonist that Lê enacts the effacement of gender. Such de-prioritisation of gender, however, does risk collapsing into a conventional representation of an explicitly ungendered but implicitly male individual which somewhat troubles such a strategy of 'un-gendering' the characters (and the question of whether Lê ultimately inscribes herself into such a masculine literary tradition is indeed explored in this chapter's conclusion). Yet Lê's circumvention of gender appears a deliberate gesture in itself, and an attempt not merely to hierarchise alienation and marginalisation over gender, but to move away altogether from the primacy of gender of the alienated exiled subject.

Lê's more widespread representation of isolated and marginalised women characters as ungendered suggests, moreover, a resistance to orthodox representations of gender. The representation of Sola in *In memoriam* suggests a reappropriation of women's identity that disturbs historically conventional paradigms which define women within domestic, heterosexual arrangements as she is shown to strongly resist such identification. Sola's symbolic name, despite being externally granted and not of her own invention, can equally be considered a strategy on the part of Lê herself to define the female protagonist's identity in and of herself, rather than measured against the masculine Other, be it the father or a sexual partner. As in many of Peri Rossi's texts, symbolic naming is widely used in Lê's narratives to portray her characters less as the bearers of a singular, designated identity, than as alternatively constituted subjects defined by the characteristics that they enact. These characteristics often describe a mental or psychological state, or a gestural characteristic that identifies the character and suggests an aspect of their personality. Lê avoids historical, geographical, and familial markers of identity, a stylistic trait reflected in Emily Vaughan Roberts' observation that in the naming of her characters Lê privileges identity characteristics that are rooted in the present, thus '[placing] the narrative within the "state of the exile", which does not encourage the growth of roots in the shape of clearly defined allegiances or loyalties'.[23] As exemplified in Sola's adoption of a publishing pseudonym, these symbolic names replace pre-existing markers of identity in such a way that also allows Lê to free her characters from intransitive, imposed identities, leaving the way open for the redefinition of identity in the present. If the feminine nickname 'Sola' apparently designates the protagonist as female, the fixity of the notion of femininity is however contested by the alternatively constructed, ambivalent femininity that she embodies. Peri Rossi's symbolic naming of her characters goes even further than that of Lê, as in the case of the protagonist of *La nave de los locos*: the all but nameless 'Equis' [Ecks] is placed under the ultimate sign of anonymity and ambiguity by his symbolic naming such that he is solely identified by his exilic wandering. *La nave de los locos*, Cristina Peri Rossi's best-known and most widely studied work, is a reworking of the medieval metaphor of the 'Ship of Fools', a closed and marginalised community of fools, criminals, and outcasts who are ejected from the community and society, and cast out to sea in an aimless voyage of endless exile. The novel presents Peri Rossi's most developed exploration of exile and identity and the heightened sense of marginality that, for Peri Rossi, lies at the intersection of the two notions. Exile in *La nave de los locos*, as for Peri Rossi herself, is not only the result of political dissidence and estranged national identity, but is also inextricably tied up with sexuality. In this novel the author's political and sexual concerns converge, outlining the degree to which the two are implicated with one other.

Sola's symbolic, evocative name in *In memoriam* contrasts starkly with the narrator's namelessness, which coincides notably with Peri Rossi's similarly nameless narrator in *Solitario de amor*. Like Aída's lover in *Solitario de amor*, the narrator of *In memoriam* remains nameless and faceless, and the reader learns very little of his history beyond his relationships with Sola and his brother. For both Lê and Peri Rossi's male protagonists, the sexual partnership is imagined as a constructive space for the affirmation of personal identity. The perception of this space as one of identification is vigorously resisted by both of the female characters, who seek to define their identity on their own terms, and not solely within the limits of the relationship. In this way, Peri Rossi and Lê both question the scope of hierarchical, male-dominant, heterosexual relationships as fruitful spaces for self-realisation for women, depicting them as hindering women's inhabitation of a fully realised, multi-faceted identity. The in-between space of exile can be seen to offer the woman exile a measure of distance from such hierarchically defined relationships which defined and structured identity in the birth country, not because such gender hierarchies do not exist in the country of exile — where they most certainly prevail, in a potentially altered form — but due to the disruption of the exile's ties to surrounding societal structures and their hold over her through the fact of displacement. Female exiles are not bound in the same way by behavioural expectations as are women who live 'at home', and are thus more readily able to adopt new behaviours by virtue of their occupancy of the margins. The unevolving namelessness of the two novels' male protagonists, and the departure of both female protagonists from the relationships at the end of each novel, reveal the illusory nature of the two male protagonists' quests to achieve the fulfilment of a partial or incomplete sense of identity through a complementary relationship with the female Other. Sola and Aída's resistance of definition by the male Other displaces historical representations of women's roles that are defined by the domestic, familial, and/or sexual ties to either the father or the sexual partner, and presents new paradigms for woman's participation in the heterosexual couple. Sola offers a particularly ambivalent model of femininity, both in terms of her individual subjectivity, and her identity in relation to the male lover. In Sola, neither masculine nor feminine traits are emphasised and gender specificity is denied, offering a model of femininity defined by a kind of 'asexual androgyny' that seeks to altogether efface, rather than combine and blur, the traces of gender.

Sola's androgynous femininity is not the only ambivalent aspect of her characterisation, as very little is known about her background (by either the reader *or* the narrator). Virtually the only information that either possesses, apart from the fact that she is a writer, concerns her apparently rootless identity, as a result of the bicultural heritage of a French mother and an Iranian father: 'La France n'est pas mon pays, l'Iran n'est plus ma patrie [...] mon penchant m'incline au flou' [France is not my country, Iran is not my homeland either [...] I have an inclination for vagueness] (*IM*, p. 53). The reader learns that her father emigrated from Iran to Paris at twenty, where he married 'la Nantaise' with whom he fathered Sola, before committing suicide when his daughter reached the age of five. The trauma of this episode is manifested in Sola's withdrawal and isolation from both the narrator and society around her — 'elle était étrangère au monde réel' [she was a stranger to the real world] (*IM*, p. 13) — and in her reluctance to commit to the type of normative heterosexual relationship that the narrator desires with her. It is precisely her vulnerability resulting from her rootlessness and alienation from the world around her that attracts the narrator to her. He interprets her psychological fragility as proof of her reliance on him during periods of crisis, in turn making him believe he is indispensable to her in helping her pull through such crises. Sola's inaccessibility as a result of her psychological alienation is in equal measure appealing and disturbing for the narrator, who assumes that he is able to 'rescue' her, but is shocked when his assistance does not prevent her suicide. Indeed, the fact that on the eve of her suicide she chooses to contact his brother Thomas instead of turning to him, suggests that Sola's reliance on him is more a construct of his own imagination than a reality. The narrator clearly defines the link between the allure of Sola's psychological instability and the symbiotic relationship that he envisages:

> j'avais même espéré que ces laps de temps où elle chavirait parviendraient à créer la symbiose dont je rêvais, et que je n'obtendriais autrement: quand elle était ainsi, elle ne se fiait qu'à moi, j'étais le seul messager du monde extérieur. (*IM*, p. 132)
>
> [I had even hoped that these moments when she lost her balance would eventually lead to the symbiosis that I dreamt of, and that I wouldn't otherwise obtain. When she was like that, she only trusted me, I was the only messenger from the outside world].

He thus illustrates how he seeks to resolve his divided, incomplete sense of self through fusion with the other in an exclusive, mutual dependency.

The trope of partiality and incompletion that is present in *In memoriam* is also evident across much of Lê's writing, suggesting an underlying discourse of a conflicting desire for reconstruction or completion of a fragmented self, that is countered by a refusal of completion. The repeated theme of the double that frequently appears in the form of a lost or dead twin (such as the mentally ill uncle and his long-deceased twin sister in *Calomnies*[24] [*Slander*] and la Manchote's similarly long-deceased twin brother in *Les Trois parques*[25] [*The Three Fates*]) or the father's uncompleted artistic œuvre (as seen in the unaccomplished artistic careers of the painter-fathers in *Lettre morte* and *Les aubes*) which recalls Lê's own father, a painter, left behind in Vietnam upon the family's departure for France, hint at a fundamental absence at the heart of Lê's œuvre which can be linked to the rupture occasioned by Lê's own distantiation from Vietnam and her father at fourteen. Lê's own symbolic representation of her relationship with the distant country of birth, as described in an interview, of carrying Vietnam inside her like a dead foetus, is the epitome of the central absence that haunts Lê's fiction.[26] The image of the deceased baby as taken from her own personal imagery is countered by Lê's repeated literary symbol of incompletion *par excellence* — the burnt manuscript — suggesting a resistance against the trauma of absence that the anguishing image of the lifeless foetus conveys, in that once completion is achieved the manuscript is immediately burnt, and thus the corrosive effect of absence is sustained and perpetuated, leading to an eternal instability that drives the oscillation between the trauma of absence, the desire to fulfil this absence and achieve completion, and the determination to remain in eternal impartiality and lack of resolution.

The narrator thus finds Sola appealing as a self-contained ideal (an ideal which is of course belied by her suicide), and he makes constant reference to her as the missing and desired other half, describing her repeatedly as 'un miroir' [a mirror] (*IM*, p. 13; p. 78) and 'mon double' [my double] (*IM*, p. 72; p. 94), and frequently referring to her — as in other works by Lê mentioned above — as a long sought-after 'twin'. Yet Sola is described as resisting this symbiotic desire, and refuting any kind of resemblance they may bear to one another, effectively destroying the narrator's 'rêve de toujours, celui de [s]'allier à un alter ego' [lifelong dream, to ally [him]self to an alter ego] (*IM*, p. 14). The narrator eventually realises that Sola sees the kind of alliance that he seeks as an undesirable subsumption of the self into the other:

> Je mis du temps à admettre qu'elle se protégeât de toute relation fusionnelle. Elle craignait d'y être engloutie, et cette crainte l'amenait à se partager entre Thomas et moi, à délaisser l'un pour l'autre, puis à fermer la porte à tous deux afin de tenir conciliabule avec les personnages de son invention. (*IM*, p. 15)
>
> [It took me a while to realise that she was protecting herself from any fusional relationship. She was afraid of becoming engulfed, and this fear led her to share herself between Thomas and me, to abandon one for the other, and then to close the door on both of us to hold counsel with the characters of her own invention.]

As this passage makes clear, he also posits his persistent desire for symbiotic unification with Sola as the justification for her turning to his brother Thomas, who embodies an alternative to the narrator and who does not make such demands on her. Ultimately, Sola rejects both Thomas and the fusional identity the narrator proposes, and is represented as already brandishing a complete and coherent, albeit wounded, sense of identity that is divided between her private self and her public authorial self.

Despite her apparent psychological fragility, Sola thus enacts a fragmented yet independent identity that rejects the narrator's desired fusion and attempts to warn him 'contre la tentation de [se] fixer comme unique but [leur] amour' [against the temptation to fix on [their] love as his sole aim] (*IM*, p. 127). Curiously, the narrator does not rail against Sola's resistance towards him, or even reproach her for her infidelity. Instead he acknowledges her desire to escape the stifling nature of the relationship. Ironically, Sola ends up deflecting the narrator's symbiotic desire back onto him, instead supplanting his brother into the role of the other half that the narrator so longs for: 'L'ironie voulut que mon frère, en commettant une scélératesse, me devint plus proche [...]. Nous étions plus que des rivaux, nous croyions tous deux en Sola' [Irony would have it that my brother, in committing a heinous act, would become closer to me [...]. We were more than rivals, we both believed in Sola] (*IM*, p. 162).

(In)corporeality in *Solitario de amor* and *In memoriam*

Where Lê's narrator's desire for symbiotic unification with the female other is depicted in terms of psychological dependency, Peri Rossi's narrator figures a similar desire for symbiosis with Aída as a quest for physical reunification with the maternal body, echoing a dominant tendency in the Uruguayan author's novel to emphasise the novel's focus on the corporeal. More than a desire for fusion, the narrator of *Solitario de amor* expresses a desire for absorption into the body of Aída, expressed both in terms of the novel's treatment of sexual penetration, and in the conventional association of the female with the home and the uterus. Aída is compared to both throughout the novel, in contrast to which the narrator is described as a subject cast adrift, denied access to either.

For these two writers, exile is as much an embodied as a psychological phenomenon, as the physical displacement is primarily experienced through the body, which becomes as important a vehicle as writing for negotiating the relocation of self in exile. Peri Rossi places the body at the very centre of her texts, overcoming the imposed absence of exile with bodily presence, and re-presenting the female body as a key device in her construction of alternative femininity. Lê, on the other hand, emphasises the absence of the marginal body in exile, attempting to efface all traces of the corporeal from her novels, preferring instead to emphasise the psychological, rather than the physiological processes of her female characters. Lê's texts contain very few textual references to bodies (either female or male) and the few descriptions of female bodies which do appear firmly emphasise their physical frailty which is metaphorically represented in terms of immateriality. Both authors, in their different ways, deterritorialise the representation of women defined by the conventional tropes of appearance, exteriority, and surface, and relocate such representation in women's biological (in the case of Peri Rossi) and psychological interior (in the case of Lê). If exile permits Lê and Peri Rossi a critical distance from which to reassess and reassert a sense of self and belonging, the representation of the female body is key to their renegotiation of a revised notion of femininity.

The narrator of *Solitario de amor* establishes the terms for the representation of the female body early on in the novel with the declaration of the intention to abandon euphemisms — 'Nazco y me despojo de eufemismos' [I am born and I strip myself of euphemisms] (*SA*, p. 13) — thus announcing an effort to avoid the idealisation and mythologisation that have historically characterised both social and aesthetic representations of women. Peri Rossi's erotic descriptions of the female protagonist of *Solitario de amor* use meticulous, anatomically correct terminology to emphasise the biological and physiological reality of Aída's body, without thereby dehumanising it, since the female body which is the focus of *Solitario de amor* remains the sum of its parts rather than an objectified, depersonified physique. The narrator's contemplation of Aída is intense and penetrating, as he looks *into*, as well as *at* her, describing the interior workings of her organism. Less interested in its superficial outward appearance, the narrator emphasises the biological, visceral truth of the female body:

> no amo su cuerpo, estoy amando su hígado membranoso de imperceptible pálpito, la blanca esclerótica de sus ojos, el endometrio sangrante, el lóbulo agujereado, las estrías de las uñas, el pequeño y turbulento apéndice intestinal, las amígdalas rojas como guindas, el oculto mastoides, la mandíbula crujiente, las meninges inflamables, el paladar abovedado, las raíces de los dientes, el lunar marrón del hombro, la carótida tensa como una cuerda, los pulmones envenenados por el humo, el pequeño clítoris engarzado en la vulva como un faro. (*SA*, p. 13)

> [I do not love her body, I am loving her membranous liver and its imperceptible heaving, the white sclerotic of her eyes, the bleeding endometrium, the pierced ear, the lines of the fingernails, the small, turbulent intestinal appendix, the tonsils red as cherries, the hidden mastoid prominence, the creaking jaw, the meninges that may become inflamed, the arched palate, the roots of the teeth, the hazel-coloured mole on her shoulder, the carotid artery as taut as string, the lungs poisoned by smoke, the tiny clitoris clasped to the vulva like a beacon.]

Descriptions of Aída's body constitute a large part of the narrative, and like this one, are detailed, repetitive, reiterative and accumulative. The eroticisation of the body through such an excess of detail has the effect of granting the lover's body a solidity and presence that contest the female body of contemporary aesthetic ideals which admire superficiality, lightness, and ethereality. Aída is extremely present in the text not only due to the foregrounding of her physical description, but also because her physique is described as heavy and ungainly: 'La veo moverse, caminar con torpeza, como un gran animal del Mesozoico' [I see her moving, walking clumsily, like a great Mesozoic animal] (*SA*, p. 18). The eroticism of the female body, of its organs and their biological functions, as well as the very solid presence of the female body in the text revokes the idealised female body of patriarchal eroticisation, with an emphasis, in particular, on the biological processes of the female reproductive system which diverges from an idealised, abstract representation of maternity. The narrator imagines the physiological processes of Aída's body during pregnancy and childbirth, emphasising the physical aspect of maternity (such as the lengthy description of Aída's pregnant body, and the birth and breast-feeding of the child on pages 54–55) that is often glossed over to idealise maternity's abstract qualities of caring and nurturing in contemporary textual representations of maternity.

The eroticisation of Aída's strong, child-bearing body reinforces the image of Aída's body as an active, productive one that is also a far cry from the submissive, frail, essentially decorative body favoured by contemporary ideals of female beauty and eroticism. Peri Rossi's language constructs a female body that bears greater resemblance to actual female bodies, and belies historical representations which efface the biological and the anatomical in order to suppress those elements which patriarchal discourse has found unpleasant, unattractive, or even repugnant. Through her narrator's declaration to avoid euphemisms in the representation of the female body, Peri Rossi stakes a claim for the authenticity of such representations in the novel, and suggests the possibility of divergence from a male tradition of euphemistic language in reference to female physicality. The unorthodox eroticism of *Solitario de amor* has been claimed unconvincingly heterosexual by critics, thus provoking readings, such as that of Arias referred to earlier, of the novel as a veiled homoerotic text. That some readers have found it improbable or difficult to imagine the female body described in *Solitario de amor* as the object of a desiring male gaze certainly attests to the radical nature of Peri Rossi's gender project, in that the revisions she suggests for depictions of the female body and heterosexual desire are not readily recognisable within contemporary paradigms of gender and sexual attraction.

Much of the confounding of gender categories in *Solitario de amor* is reinforced by the incorporation of the masculine into the feminine, and vice versa, in a strategy that disrupts the dichotomisation of two distinct genders. Whilst being described as excessively biologically female, Aída's body also incorporates physical characteristics more frequently associated with the male body, i.e. 'no tiene cintura' (literally, 'she has no waist') (*SA*, p. 9).[27] In a similar gesture, the narrator refers to the cohabitation of the feminine and the masculine in his own sense of self: 'te miro desde mi avergonzado macho cabrío y desde mi parte de mujer enamorada de otra mujer' [I look at you from my ashamed 'macho' animal-self and from the part of me that is woman in love with another woman] (*SA*, p. 10). In a move to disrupt binary gender structures and disturb clear delimitations, Peri Rossi posits gendered identity along a continuous spectrum of masculinity and femininity, demonstrating how both may coincide in the same individual. Unlike the neutral, androgynous configuration of masculinity and femininity in Lê's writing, the notion of androgyny does not however adequately account for the merging of genders in Peri Rossi's text. Despite its apparently radical nature, androgyny nevertheless relies on and sustains a fundamental binary opposition between masculinity and femininity. A more helpful way of illuminating Peri Rossi's gender project is through the lens of Judith Butler's questioning of the neat correlation of sex and gender that relies on a binary gender system: 'even if the sexes appear to be unproblematically binary in their morphology and constitution [...] there is no reason to assume that genders ought also to remain as two'.[28] Peri Rossi's radicalisation of gender, it would appear, is made possible by the very fact of her exile, in that notions of gender and appropriate gender behaviour are culturally situated. When it becomes possible to separate understandings of gender from the historical and cultural intersections in which they are produced, such as in circumstances of exilic displacement, the rethinking and renegotiating of gender norms also becomes possible. As Butler states, 'When the relevant "culture" that "constructs" gender is understood in terms of such a law or set of laws, then it seems that gender is as determined and fixed as it was under the biology-is-destiny formulation. In such a case, not biology, but culture, becomes destiny.'[29] It follows that if gender is not the manifestation of a sex, but a convergence of culturally and historically specific sets of relations, departure from a particular historical and cultural context permits the consideration of gender in radically altered ways. Where the articulation of gendered identity within available cultural terms forecloses in advance, or at least hinders, the possibility of thinking of gender in new and productive ways, Peri Rossi demonstrates that removal from a given cultural environment enables a renegotiation of conceptualisations of gender. It is thus the combination of the radical change in her cultural surroundings through exile, as well as an already-present nonconformity with the cultural attitutudes of the home country previous to exile, which results in Peri Rossi's particular construction of femininity as expressed in her texts. The very excess of language and textuality in *Solitario de amor* impresses the visibility of the female body upon the reader, who is forced to contemplate the revised representation of women that Peri Rossi envisages. The excessively present, monumental, sexual body that Peri Rossi presents can be compared with Lê's painstaking *in*corporeality as highly contrasting ways of achieving a similar aim: that of exploding traditional representations of the female body which confine femininity to paradigms of passivity and superficiality.

If Peri Rossi is at pains to emphasise the biological physicality of the female body in *Solitario de amor*, Lê on the contrary strives to efface the traces of corporeality in order to emphasise the psychological condition of her protagonists. The representation of the (absent) female body in exile thus consolidates the effect of psychological characterisation performed by her symbolic naming. Lê emphasises Sola's wounded psychological state, and references to the body, when they appear, serve primarily to reinforce her psychological description. On the infrequent occasions when Sola is described physically, her outward appearance evokes psychological traits rather than providing a precise account of her physical attributes. In fact, the reader is hard pressed to conjure up a mental image of *In memoriam*'s heroine. Sola bears this physical absence in common with most of Lê's female characters throughout her œuvre, who are frequently described as slight, frail, weightless 'feu follets' [will-o'-the-wisps]. Such a representation of women reaches its most emphatic expression in the character of Forever in Lê's 2000 novel, *Les aubes*. In the first-person retrospective account of his childhood, the narrator of *Les aubes* describes the guardian angel-like figure of Forever as barely physically present, almost incorporeal. Always dressed in white, she is described as a light-footed silhouette and portrayed as a 'fée tombée de je ne sais quel ciel' [a fairy fallen from I don't know what sky].[30] Her vague presence is reinforced by her habitation on the absolute margin: she lives by the sea on a cliff, in a fisherman's cottage that faces the horizon. Forever's anorexia is for the narrator but another sign of her immateriality and distances her from the physical world she inhabits, projecting her into a spiritual realm:

> Forever avait aussi ceci d'une fée: elle se nourrissait peu, d'une tranche de pain ou d'un biscuit sec. Cette abstinence était pour moi une preuve de son immatérialité et non le symptôme de la maladie, l'anorexie, dont elle était affligée depuis ses quinze ans. Pour l'heure, la maigreur de Forever était à mes yeux comme le signe de sa sainteté.[31]

> [Forever shared another trait with fairies: she ate very little, a slice of bread or a dry biscuit. This abstinence was proof for me of her immateriality and not the symptom of her illness, anorexia, which had afflicted her since she was fifteen. At the time, Forever's thinness was, in my eyes, the sign of her saintliness.]

The desire to efface the body through the denial of food is shared by many of Lê's protagonists. Like Forever, who only consumes 'une tranche de pain' or 'un biscuit sec', the protagonist's mother in Lê's short story 'Vinh L.' 'n'avalait que quelques grains de riz' [swallowed but a few grains of rice].[32] The physical self-harming in the form of anorexia in *Les aubes* is countered by an intellectual drive in which Fortune seeks to express herself and locate a sense of self that her physical reality appears to obstruct: 'Le refus de la nourriture s'accompagnait chez Forever d'une boulimie d'études' [Forever accompanied by the refusal of food with a bulimia of studies].[33] Like Forever, Sola replaces food with words, and physical sustenance with intellectual sustenance, such that 'Sa chair, son sang étaient faits de la matière même de ses livres' [Her flesh, her blood, were of the same matter as her books] (*IM*, p. 176). The body of writing comes to figuratively replace the biological body when their writings are all that remain and attest to Forever and Sola's existence after the body is eliminated through suicide.

Indeed, the female characters throughout Lê's corpus of novels can be said to be largely interchangeable: firstly, they are all physically frail and show signs of suppressing their physicality (eating disorders, dressing in black, hiding behind long hair and fringes); secondly, they are on the whole displaced, alienated women who occupy liminal spaces; and finally, they adjust to their displacement by voluntarily assuming occupancy of the marginality to which they have been relegated. In this sense they are not individualised or physically distinguishable, but the embodiment of characteristics which serve to highlight their vague presence on the margins. Like Fortune in *Les aubes*, Sola is described as eternally dressed in white (the colour of mourning in Lê's native Vietnam) and deathly pale, thus presaging her suicide — already intimated in the novel's title — at the novel's conclusion: 'Elle portait une robe blanche, simple et stricte. Son teint était très pâle. Dans la pénombre du lieu, cette extraordinaire pâleur lui donnait l'aspect d'une revenante' [She wore a simple, strict white dress. Her complexion was pale. In the half-light of the place, this extraordinary paleness gave her the appearance of a spirit] (*IM*, p. 68). Her diaphanous presence and physical frailty are early on established in the novel when she is likened to 'une plante anémique' [an anaemic plant], 'une enfant arriérée' [an underdeveloped child], and 'une vieillarde impotente' [a helpless old man] (*IM*, p. 18) — everything but an able-bodied woman. Sola's frequent comparison to a bird and her description in terms of bird-like qualities further emphasise her frailty, and above all, her mobility: 'je ne cessai pas de la comparer à un oiseau de paradis, planant très haut dans le ciel et qui mourrait s'il frôlait le sol' [I always compared her to a bird of paradise, gliding high in the sky and which would die if it touched the ground] (*IM*, p. 71). In addition to emphasising her frailty and vulnerability, the likening of Sola to 'un oiseau perdu dans une bourrasque' [a bird caught in a gust of wind] (*IM*, p. 89) provides evidence of the narrator's difficulty in being able to tie her down, and accounts for his failure to confine her in the kind of contained, interdependent relationship he envisages with her. Sola continuously dodges and evades him, resisting the identity and the symbiotic relationship he attempts to impose on her. The comparison furthermore serves to locate her identity in transience: far from having her feet planted firmly on the ground, her psychological isolation and her alienation from such defining markers of identity as national or familial heritage place her representation in the realm of the in-between. If her elusive physical presence is representative of a lack of engagement with the physical space that she inhabits and a preference for the liminality of the margins, this is not portrayed as a space of suffering but rather one which is sought out and voluntarily occupied. Throughout Lê's corpus there is an insistence on the productive location of otherworldly, incorporeal identity located on the margins, and a refusal to pursue a sense of belonging in the mainstream.

The lack of engagement that Lê's female protagonist demonstrates in connecting with the outside world or with opening herself to others can be considered in light of Lê's exile at age fourteen. Lê's discursive denial of corporeality signals a stagnation that is expressed in her writing by the suppression of the physical signs of femininity — those which are associated with changes the body undergoes in puberty — and the retention in her protagonists of the signs of the prepubescent body. Lê's privileging of a gender-neutral androgynous female body suggests a desire for non-progression past the narcissistic adolescent phase of the moment of her departure from Vietnam. Unlike her departure as an adolescent from Vietnam, which was involuntary, the exercise of controlling the physical self — the body — indicates an exercise of will, where the attempt at preservation of the body in a prepubescent stage of development makes up for the lack of autonomy exercised in the departure into exile. By retaining the female body in a permanent state of underdevelopment, Lê effectively stops time at the moment of departure from Vietnam. This departure and the ensuing state of limbo is lived out time and again in Lê's novels in the repetition of interchangeable female characters in marginal and extremely unstable scenarios bearing witness to an inability to surpass the traumatic moment of exile.

The treatment of the theme of maternity indicates another significant way in which the physical signs of femininity are suppressed and incorporeality is foregrounded in *In memoriam*. If *Solitario de amor* places great emphasis on Aída's child-bearing function and her reproductive body, quite the opposite is true of Sola. In fact, it is the possibility of maternity, through Thomas's expression of his desire to have a child with Sola, that initiates the final mental breakdown which culminates in her suicide. The question of Sola's potential maternity, referred to as 'cette féminité qu'elle refusait' [this femininity that she refused] (*IM*, p. 176), is a decisive one which disrupts the relationship between Thomas and Sola. Through her treatment of Sola's outright refusal of maternity, Lê presents an alternative vision of femininity beyond 'cette féminité' (amongst others) that Sola refuses. In consideration of Lê's own decision not to have children,[34] parallels can be drawn between the protagonist and the author, and indeed, in a dizzying *mise en abîme*, both Sola, and Sola's own characters mirror Lê's refusal of maternity: 'Les livres d'elle, que précisément éludaient toujours la question, mett[ait] en scène des personnages sans descendance, [...] la procréation devenait alors un tabou inviolable' [Her books, which precisely always evaded the question, present[ed] characters without descendants [...], procreation thus became a sacrosanct taboo] (*IM*, p. 182). As well as suggesting a voluntary choice, Lê's aforementioned reference in an interview to 'le Vietnam que je porte comme un enfant mort' [the Vietnam that I carry in me like a dead child] suggests if not a physical, then a psychological inability to bear children, given that this role has been usurped by the memory of Vietnam that she envisages as a physical inhabitation.[35] If bearing children in circumstances of displacement and alienation, and establishing the ties with society that this entails is considered a common and effective way of setting down roots in a new environment and anchoring a sense of belonging,[36] Lê's alienated and isolated protagonist, like Lê herself, rejects both maternity and its potential for anchorage. Rather, Lê's protagonist turns to writing as a means of willfully inhabiting her situation of alienation, literature having for her an 'importance vitale', replacing not only physical sustenance, as already seen, but also providing her with a space in which to locate and express her dislocated sense of self.

Lê's discursive refusal of maternity through the character of Sola can furthermore be seen as not only a refusal of the body, but a refusal or denial of the mother, a figure already seen to be almost entirely absent in *In memoriam*. The eschewal of the maternal role proposed by Thomas constitutes another way in which the figure of the mother is effaced, suggesting a resentment towards Lê's own mother who took her into exile in her childhood, away from Vietnam, and away from the father. The fact that Lê's exile was not her own choice, but that of her mother accounts for the (perhaps inevitable) idealisation of the father left behind and the apparent resentment towards the mother. Lê's literary output is haunted by the spectre of the father as a symbol of the immense and ongoing guilt felt towards the real-life (and now deceased) father. If the narrator can be considered a father figure in *In memoriam*, then the end of the relationship becomes a foregone conclusion, insofar as the father represents an eternal absence, a sense of incompletion which, as observed above, Sola has no desire to fill. Such a refusal of maternity can then be seen as both a denial of female corporeality, as well as a rejection of the figure of the mother and the traditional female maternal role. Seen as a creative act, maternity is repudiated by Sola, and literature is posited in the novel as a creative alternative to maternity which fulfils a similar drive for self-realisation. Whilst Thomas attempts to project his desire for her maternity onto her — 'il avait essayé de graver ceci dans son esprit: elle ne se reconcilierait pas avec elle-même tant qu'elle ne serait pas mère' [he had tried to engrave this in her mind: she would not be reconciled with herself as long as she wasn't a mother] (*IM*, p. 184) — the narration describes how she shies away from this imposed role which is already fulfilled for her through writing and literature.

Nomadic Belonging

For *In memoriam*'s protagonist, as for Lê herself, the writerly project itself comes to constitute her sense of identity, and literature consequently takes on the character of a site of belonging, or rather, of 'non-belonging'. Whereas Sola rejects social, familial, and national spaces of belonging, she embraces writing as a privileged site for the expression and realisation of her individuality and subjectivity. Writing constitutes a way in which Sola is able to achieve her own sense of agency and authority, normally problematised by her failure, or inability to engage with the world around her in other ways. The central themes of the literary project and the act of writing are also the plot devices through which the two protagonists of *In memoriam* encounter and relate to each other, and there is an overarching commentary throughout the novel on writing, and its relationship to the discursive construction of identity.

The narrator encounters Sola through his status as both a reader and a writer: he 'reads' Sola before actually encountering her in 'real' life. If initially she is known to him as the unseen, unembodied author behind the text, she remains to a large degree unattainable after he makes her acquaintance as her physical presence proves to be insubstantial, and her psychological instability keeps her similarly distanced from him as the text between them once did. Their acquaintance within the interpersonal dynamic of reader and writer hierarchises their relationship from the outset. The narrator and would-be acclaimed writer is implicitly placed in a subordinate position as reader and admirer of the successful author's texts. This hierarchisation of the relationship is consolidated by the narrator's belief that Sola is by far the more talented of the two writers, having published three much-lauded novels with a fourth coming out during the timespan of the action of the novel. This is in stark contrast with the narrator's efforts to write something which he considers noteworthy whilst earning a living as a proofreader at a publishing company. The perceived hierarchy between the protagonists gives rise to jealousy on behalf of the narrator on several accounts. Not only 'jaloux des heures qu'elle dédiait à ses manuscrits' [jealous of the hours she dedicated to her manuscripts] (*IM*, p. 142) and that keep her absent from him, the narrator also appears jealous of the texts which she is capable of writing and which he struggles to produce. In order to assert some claim to authority in their relationship, he imagines himself to be her ideal reader: 'Il y avait, dans les trois romans que Sola avait publiés, un appel qui, croyais-je, m'était adressé, à moi seul' [In the three novels that Sola had published, there was a call which, I believed, was addressed to me, to me alone] (*IM*, p. 77). Later in the novel he attempts to transform this imagined role into a reciprocal one when he projects Sola into the role of his 'première lectrice': 'Je lui envoyais les chapitres au fur et mesure que je les terminais, et recevais ses commentaires comme si je n'étais entré en littérature que pour être lu par elle' [I would send her my chapters as I finished them, and I would receive her comments as though I had made my entrance into literature only to be read by her] (*IM*, p. 130).

Through the representation of the narrator as a reader and aspiring writer, the reader gains an insight into Sola's role as a writer, and the value that the writing project holds for her, alongside which Lê also emphasises the necessary role of writing for *In memoriam*'s narrator. Writing is attributed with a very pragmatic role for the narrator, as established in the novel's opening line: 'Je serais devenu fou si je n'avais pas écrit ce livre' [I would have gone mad if I hadn't written this book] (*IM*, p. 7). The absent project at the heart of the narrative, paralleled by the missing manuscript that Sola was working on at the time of her death and is nowhere to be found, is the text which the narrator declares to have written in response to Sola's death, entitled 'Tombeau de Sola' [Sola's Tomb], and which may or may not be the text which the reader has in his or her hands. In the opening pages of *In memoriam*, the narrator refers to the text he wrote in the aftermath of Sola's death '[qui] s'intitulait *Tombeau de Sola*' [(which) was called *Sola's Tomb*] (*IM*, p. 9, original italics), and which he describes burning upon completion, suggesting that the manuscript was thus forever lost and is not the text that the reader is currently reading. There is, however, a play of referentiality at work in that the text that the reader has before him or her greatly resembles the manuscript referred to intratextually, both in title and content. Having discovered literature's power to bring the dead back to life when he writes a short fictional narrative of the last days of Sola's father's life before his suicide, the narrator declines to put Sola's memory to rest by writing her obituary when invited to do so (although by whom is not specified in the novel). He prefers, instead, to 'élever un *Tombeau* à Sola' [to erect a *Tomb* for Sola] (*IM*, p. 20, original italics) in the form of a text, as a repository for her memory where she will remain alive and present to him. The tomb that is metaphorically evoked by the title of his text suggests a site where the absent deceased is rendered present, both as a repository for the memory of the deceased, as well as a site of visitation of that memory. Typically, the project fails when he realises that it is only during the writing process, in other words, in the act of writing itself, that this objective — of rendering Sola present — is fulfilled. Once the writing is over he is plunged back into the darkness of the void that Sola left in the wake of her suicide.

The erection of fictional mausoleums, the representation of the writing project as a means of catharsis, and the motif of the burnt manuscript are notions that are repeated throughout Lê's œuvre, and most notably in *Lettre morte*. In Lê's 1999 novel, the narrator appropriates the narrative to resolve feelings of guilt induced by her abandonment of the father and native country at a young age. This is apparent in the self-centred, even self-indulgent nature of the text, which is repetitive and reiterative, suggesting in itself a compulsion to repetition as a result of trauma. Similarly to *Lettre morte*, the commemorative text written by the narrator of *In memoriam* is more a desperate act to help bring about his own salvation, as illustrated when he states 'Il ne me restait qu'une seule issue: écrire sur elle' [I had only one way out: to write about her] (*IM*, p. 23), than the homage to Sola that the title suggests. He finally concludes, or rather admits to himself, 'je n'avais pas tracé le portrait de Sola pour la ressusciter, mais pour me l'approprier' [I hadn't traced a portrait of Sola in order to resuscitate her, but to reappropriate her] (*IM*, p. 24).

The act of writing, then, can be seen as a self-preservational response to the narrator's unbearable situation of loss, as foregrounded in the opening line of *In memoriam*, cited above. Through his 'scriptotherapeutical' engagement with literature,[37] the narrator seeks to appease his sense of loss, and resolve the identity problems that ensue as a result, through the dissolution of his identity into writing: 'j'aspirais à me fondre dans ces pages pour n'être plus rien' [I yearned to dissolve myself into these pages so as to no longer exist] (*IM*, p. 8). Sola's suicide leaves the narrator bereft as it places in doubt his understanding of literature as 'une planche de salut' [a lifeline] (*IM*, p. 8). Evidently, writing does not fulfil the same function for the narrator as for Sola in that he writes '*Tombeau de Sola*' in order to get over the traumatic ending of the relationship which took place with Sola's suicide. On the other hand, Sola commits suicide despite having written '[l]es deux livres' [the two books], according to the narrator, '[qui] auraient dû signer sa victoire sur le néant' [(which) should have declared her triumph over the abyss] (*IM*, p. 12). Sola's writing project can be seen, then, less as a means to work through trauma toward the resolution of crisis, than as an end in itself. There is a clear absence of a drive for resolution in Sola's attitude to writing, and in its place a desire to locate herself and her sense of identity in the space of both writing and trauma that can be compared to Lê's own approach to writing from a position of exile, where the primacy of the *process* of writing is privileged over the completed *product* of writing. This is underlined in *In memoriam* when the narrator describes how he wrote '*Tombeau de Sola*' very quickly, in only three weeks following Sola's death, and that he did not re-read the manuscript before burning it. Having fulfilled his objective in writing the text, the final text is no longer significant in itself, as demonstrated by the act of burning the manuscript, leaving behind no trace of its existence. Here Lê's novel foregrounds writing as mode and process, rather than as a means to the production of literary works. This treatment of writing can be related to Lê's identarian project as a whole, where she is evidently more interested in identity as a process of configuring and expressing a sense of self, than arriving at a point where identity becomes fixed and static. Rather than seeking to define the self by fixed categories of identity, Lê is more interested in positing identity as mobility, uncertainty, and marginality. If anything, she appears to eschew the quest for the 'resolution' of the displaced and alienated identity of the exile: like Sola, she seeks out that space where identity is unresolved and unsettled, as though denying the very possibility of a securely located identity.

Like *In memoriam*'s recollective writing of the past love affair, the narrator of *Solitario de amor* writes an account of his relationship with Aída in order both to bring it back to life, and to appropriate the representation of Aída, in her absence, on his own terms. In the present of narration at the conclusion of both novels, the narrators describe the decision to mourn the departure of their lovers and resolve their absence through the literary inscription of their memory. Like *In memoriam*'s narrator, *Solitario de amor*'s narrator's decision to construct a discursive account of the relationship similarly aims to keep the beloved present and to counteract the corrosive effect of time on her memory: 'He de escribir cada uno de nuestros recuerdos. Condenado al olvido [...] seré el escriba de este amor' [I must write down all our memories. Condemned to being forgotten [...] I shall be the scribe of this love] (*SA*, p. 147). The writing project is also a central focus of Peri Rossi's novel, where the narration centres on both the representation of Aída, and the very production of that representation. The narrator simultaneously creates Aída as he describes her, producing a strong connection between the aesthetic and the linguistic: language is shown not only to describe or communicate what is already there, but to bring reality into existence. For Peri Rossi, language is the prime site where meanings are inscribed and either perpetuated or disrupted, and as such the disruptive quality of language and literature can be exploited due to its subversive status as 'a site of a battle for meaning, as a simultaneously personal and social sphere where both complicity and resistance are engendered'.[38]

Peri Rossi's radical perception of language to question its assignation of meaning is most apparent in her use of literary techniques. For Peri Rossi, social and political power is closely linked to language and discourse, and language plays a key role in the political and sexual revolution that she advocates. In *Solitario de amor*, linguistic play serves a fundamental role in the author's questioning of male and female roles and behaviours. Peri Rossi takes phallogocentric language and exposes it as such by using descriptions and metaphors which rely on traditional associations. Peri Rossi appears to be describing her own linguistic agenda when her narrator states 'el lenguaje convencional estalla' [conventional language explodes] (*SA*, p. 12). The text reappropriates phallogocentric language, dispossessing it of its masculine authority by referring to language as an act which creates, rather than an act which names that which already exists. In this way, language is likened in the novel to the female creative acts of birth and creation, restricting male access to the appropriation of such processes: 'el lenguaje lo inventaron las mujeres para nombrar lo que parían' [women invented language so they could name their offspring] (*SA*, p. 16).

The stereotypical association of certain tropes and images with the feminine is highlighted on several occasions in *Solitario de amor*, such as, for example, in the narrator's association of his lover with flowers. The narrator describes Aída's love of flowers with characteristically Latin American baroque literary language, subsequently developing an association between Aída and flowers. Peri Rossi's voice can be heard behind Aída's response to the narrator's association when Aída reproachfully highlights the distinction between 'flores de laboratorio' [laboratory flowers] and 'flores naturales' [natural flowers], thus distinguishing between 'el cultivo — la cultura' [cultivation — culture] (*SA*, p. 20) and nature. The symbolic association between 'flower' and 'woman' is extended to incorporate a discourse on the claimed perverse effect of culture on nature, reinforcing Peri Rossi's account of the mutating effect of culture on women's (and indeed men's) identities. The narrator's description of Aída's body provides Peri Rossi with further scope for drawing attention to the signifying mechanisms of language and reconfiguring the ways in which these function: in naming Aída's body parts, the narrator uses the verbs 'discover', 'name', and 'conquer', placing the encounter in a matrix of the masculine *conquistador* of a passive feminine territory. The emphasis on the masculine drive to appropriate and possess, as codified in the language that the narrator uses, recalls Hélène Cixous's theorisation of the masculine desire for possession which contrasts with the feminine lack of concern for possession:

> ce qui est nôtre se détache de nous sans que nous redoutions de nous affaiblir: nos regards s'en vont, nos sourires filent, les rires de toutes nos bouches, nos sangs coulent et nous nous répandons sans nous épuiser, nos pensées, nos signes, nos écrits, nous ne les retenons pas et nous ne craignons pas de manquer.[39]

> [that which is ours breaks loose from us without our fearing any debilitation. Our glances, our smiles, are spent; laughs exude from our mouths; our blood flows and we extend ourselves without ever reaching an end; we never hold back our thoughts, our signs, our writing; and we're not afraid of lacking.][40]

Indeed, Peri Rossi's use of language suggests an awareness of and an affinity with the theorists of 1970s French feminism of sexual difference which resists the discursive and ideological construction of femininity disseminated by androcentric culture. Peri Rossi's linguistic project can be seen to intersect with that of the proponents of sexual difference and *écriture féminine*, who link women's language with women's bodies in a bid to express the specific rhythms and sexuality of femininity. For Peri Rossi, like for Cixous, women approach language from an oblique perspective which offers the capability of exposing the underlying hierarchical premises of language, much in the same way that the exile's oblique perspective provides the tools for laying bare the mechanisms of inclusion and exclusion of linguistic and cultural communities.

Stylistically and syntactically, Peri Rossi incorporates fragmentation and multiplicity into the text by the merging of various presents and through her repetitive descriptions and sentence structure. Descriptive passages frequently repeat phrases, and sentences often begin with the same opening locutions in such a way that disrupts linear, teleological chronology and maintains the narration in a multi-dimensional present. The prose is saturated with a sense of the narrator's stagnation in 'el presente eterno de la obsesión' [the eternal present of obsession] (*SA*, p. 45)[41] so that the reader is led to sift through the text in order to glean Aída's thoughts and feelings, which are significantly silenced by the narration. While language and imagery upon first encounter seem to take themselves quite seriously, and to replicate patriarchal discourse, upon closer inspection they seem ironic, as though the mechanism of the use of conventional tropes and language by an author who places herself outside of them were sufficient to show them up. For Peri Rossi, the use of long-standing literary conventions, such as the masculine narrative viewpoint and the representation of masculinity and femininity in terms of agency and passivity, are in part inherited from the literary tradition to which she belongs, yet they are also a means to their subversion by their very incongruence in Peri Rossi's radicalisation of gender.

There is indeed a strong tradition in Southern Cone literature throughout the twentieth century of the contestation of language's function as a regulating mechanism of society. This is evident, for example, in the discursive representation of virulent misogyny in works by Juan Carlos Onetti, such as *El pozo*[42] [*The Pit*] or the regendering of discourse in the writing of Luisa Valenzuela who, in *Cola de lagartija*[43] [*The Lizard's Tale*], inscribes 'an attempt at finding an alternative feminine voice with which to construct a discourse that questions the strident, dominant language of the military dictatorship'.[44] Inscribing herself into such a tradition, Peri Rossi calls for a recodification of language in order to undermine traditional power structures and contemplate the possibility of greater individual freedom through greater linguistic freedom. The silencing of Aída's voice behind the male narrator's is in keeping with the tendency visible throughout Peri Rossi's œuvre to firstly codify representations in accordance with what Frederic Jameson has coined the 'cultural dominant logic or hegemonic norm' to refer to the dominant structures of cultural production, so as to contest the validity of such representations.[45] Such a strategy operates on the premise that 'the very mechanisms of reiteration and inscription that produce and fix sex allow for their destabilization',[46] and Peri Rossi herself confirms her use of strategies of reiteration and inscription of cultural models in order to expose and contest them, affirming that she takes advantage of writing within a literary tradition in which the conventions are already in place.[47] Peri Rossi uses the existing tropes and conventions of the representation of women as objects of desire in ways that profoundly challenge these conventions.

Peri Rossi's critique of gender subordination is thus closely linked to language and its revolutionary potential to open new possibilities for women's representation and self-assertion of identity. Her resistance to binary representations of identity, and her challenge to normative heterosexuality and the roles for women that these impose, are linguistically and syntactically manifested in her texts. In Peri Rossi's œuvre the reflection on 'being woman' is persistent, and she celebrates plurality and multiplicity as a response to reductive models of behaviour, in open-ended narratives which provide scope for the imagining of alternative patterns of thought which place the limitations and restrictions of conventional language in the spotlight. Peri Rossi criticises the linguistic, cultural, and social mechanisms involved in the normalization of rigid gender categories and the policing of practices defining proper sexual behaviour in ways that have also been identified in Lê's fiction. Much in the same way that language is manipulated by Peri Rossi to disrupt its patriarchal purchase, Lê too has been seen to wield the act of writing in her texts as device for reconfiguring identity and belonging.

Lê and Peri Rossi's contribution to feminist thinking on the renegotiation of women's identity in the context of exile is however somewhat troubled by an apparent deference in both authors' œuvres to a masculine European literary tradition which could be said to uphold the kind of gender norms and disparities that the two writers attempt to revoke. Despite the clear gender projects outlined in their texts, which challenge and disrupt conventional representations of gender and sexual identities, and the avoidance of identities circumscribed by fixed, historical categories of identity, Lê and Peri Rossi nonetheless appear to aspire to belonging within the very literary canon whose conventions they manipulate and disrupt.[48] They have both demonstrated a deference to a phallogocentric literary tradition, and could be accused of adopting the historically masculine figure of the isolated and tormented literary genius insofar as their reiterative narratives return time and again to the isolation of a central protagonist struggling, and often failing, to come to terms with his subjectivity in a hostile world. Claire Lindsay observes, in the case of Peri Rossi, that 'This notion of the artist as a distanced, isolated figure is one that is reiterated in Peri Rossi's accounts of her own early experience.'[49] Peri Rossi's adoption of the role of tormented literary genius is characterised by Lindsay as a rebellious occupation of a traditionally masculine terrain: 'Peri Rossi appears to be assuming an author function of "creative genius" which has for so long only been the privilege of her male counterparts'.[50] Peri Rossi has explained her rebellious position within an otherwise masculine literary tradition in terms of the inherently feminist position of the woman writer in the Latin American socio-cultural context, as discussed in Chapter 2, insofar as it is capable of disrupting the norms of expected and accepted women's behaviour. Given the context in which Peri Rossi began writing and publishing in the 1960s in Uruguay, the mere fact of being a woman writer would indeed have heralded a degree of spontaneous feminism. If Peri Rossi's apparent aspiration to the ideal of tortured literary genius has been associated with the early stages of her literary career, Lê is also known to have publicly disowned the first three books she published, *Un si tendre vampire*[51] [*Such a Tender Vampire*], *Fuir*[52] [*Flee*], and *Solo*[53] [*Alone*], for the intimidation, respect, and submission with which they approach both the French language and the French literary tradition. Lê's relationship to the French literary canon can also be described as ambiguously paradoxical as she, on the one hand, shows a distinct deference to the French language and masculine literary tradition, and, on the other hand, manifests an explicit expression of resistance to them inasmuch as Lê reclaims and reinvents the French language in order to create her own literary space and tradition. This seemingly contradictory position may be considered in terms of Lê's 'colonisation' (or rather, 'counter-colonisation') of the French language and literary canon: Lê infiltrates a lengthy tradition of French literature from beyond its national, linguistic, and gender frontiers, thus appropriating the canon, and reshaping it to include the margins that she occupies. In Lê's self-consciously literary project writing becomes an end in itself, and she perceives the very codes and institution of literature as constituting a sense of belonging. Lê's gradual 'infiltration' into the the canon of French literature from the national, linguistic, and gender margins becomes increasingly evident over the course of her literary career, and if any doubts remain about any lingering deference to a patriarchal tradition, they are readily dispersed upon consideration of what Lê refers to as 'littérature déplacée', as described in the conclusion to *Tu écriras sur le bonheur* [*You Will Write of Happiness*], a compilation of prefaces written by Lê when she was employed as a preface editor at Hachette in the 1980s.[54]

By way of conclusion, I draw on Lê's notion of 'littérature déplacée' ['displaced literature'] as a paradigm of nomadic, exiled women's writing, which, rather than demonstrating a restorative intent, manifests an altogether more creative process of reconciliation of the spatial and chronological ruptures of exile in contemporary women's writing. Via her trademark device of incorporating anecdotes and *faits divers* into her writing, Lê describes the principal qualities of 'littérature déplacée': firstly, as 'paroles d'exil' [words of exile], a literature forged through displacement and the inherent duality therein; secondly, as a literature which inhabits the in-between ('qui ne trouve pas sa place' [which is out-of-place]); and finally, as a literature which is permanently 'out-of-place' and thus disruptive, 'inconvenante' [unsettling].⁵⁵ I would argue that these characteristics, as identified by Lê in her conceptualisation of 'littérature déplacée' — 'in-betweenness', permanent impermanence, and disruptiveness — deftly capture the tendencies and aims of exiled women's writing as demonstrated in the cases of the six writers at hand, and are central to women's configuration of identity in exile. Audrey Lasserre and Anne Simon also point to a comparable kind of writing in what they refer to as nomadic literature, which spans and binds the ruptures of women's exile, and which can be considered key to the way in which contemporary exiled women's writing negotiaties the distinction between the fact of exile and the manner in which it is inhabited: 'le nomadisme choisi peut venir contre l'exil subi, *via* une écriture qui arpente un impossible ici comme un impossible ailleurs' [chosen nomadism can provide a response to imposed exile, via a writing that spans the distance between an impossible here and an impossible elsewhere].⁵⁶

Like the Deleuzo-Guattarian notion of a 'minor literature', Lê's 'littérature déplacée' is also a disruptive literature which imposes itself on a major tradition and language: 'elle perturbe l'ordre naturel des choses. Elle cherche à rompre avec l'autorité. L'autorité du pays quitté. L'autorité de la langue empruntée. L'autorité de la tradition littéraire dans laquelle aucune place ne lui est réservée' [it troubles the natural order of things. It seeks to break from authority. The authority of the country left behind. The authority of the borrowed language. The authority of the literary tradition in which it does not have a rightful place].⁵⁷ As a literature of the in-between, it disrupts the polar distinction between here and there, and locates itself in the unsettling in-between. Described by Lê as bearing similarities to a self-propagating plant, 'littérature déplacée' also operates in the dynamic, non-hierarchical way of the Deleuzo-Guattarian 'rhizome' with which Rosi Braidotti compares the configuration of nomadic subjectivity in that the rhizome is organised around multiplicity, heterogeneity, and connectedness, and brings about new forms and structures of consciousness, rather than replicating or tracing existing ones.

Lê's notion of 'littérature déplacée' is also more particularly infused with her own favoured tropes of illegitimacy, betrayal, contamination, and vilification. Lê celebrates the disruptive nature of a writing that is difficult to situate, by writers who are themselves difficult to situate, as a productive, creative force which prompts the remapping of understandings of identification and belonging. When Lê describes 'une littérature qui se voudrait malvenue, voire inconvenante' [a literature which seeks to be unwelcome, even unsettling], she celebrates the illegitimacy of a writing which breaches the norms of a canon whose legitimacy Lê throws into doubt.⁵⁸ As a result, Lê locates identity and belonging neither in a nation, a culture, or a canon, but in writing itself, and in a writing that is to be invented and forged. For exiled women writers, for whom the pre-exile parameters of belonging are no longer in place, writing remains a domain sufficiently flexible and malleable as to afford a place of belonging, and a language in which to express that belonging. Lê advocates inventing a writing which is knowingly 'uncivilised', disrespectful of authority and which contaminates language from the outside, and above all which seeks to resolve the rupture of exile by remaining within, inhabiting, and appropriating the in-between: 'Une mauvaise parole qui ne serait donc pas une parole d'exil, une parole chassée de son refuge, mais une parole qui se moque de trouver un asile, une parole délivrée de toute tutelle, une parole qui se veut nomade' [An unsettling writing which is therefore not words of exile, words expelled from their refuge, but a writing which mocks the idea of finding a refuge, words delivered from any form of protection, a writing which considers itself nomadic].[59]

In the works of Cristina Peri Rossi and Linda Lê, and in *Solitario de amor* and *In memoriam* in particular, writing can be seen as a way, not of resolving exile, but of inhabiting exile. Such a literary project disrupts the usual discourse of the 'resolution' of exile in that these two authors appropriate the profound alienation of exile as a positive measure of identity rather than experiencing it as a state to be 'worked through', 'resolved', or 'overcome'. The act of writing is key to the appropriation of this space, and writing, then, can be said to be the new homeland which allows for the location and assertion of discursively constituted identity for the exiled female subject. Writing has been seen to play, initially, a fundamentally practical role for both authors in that it affords them a vehicle through which to come to terms with the immediate dislocation of displacement — both in terms of insertion into the adoptive society and a forum for the negotiation of the identity crisis that exile provokes — before subsequently affording them a space in which to relocate their identity. After more than half a lifetime in exile, writing has afforded both Lê and Peri Rossi the negotiation of displaced identity beyond fixed markers of identity, where a nomadic sense of identity that celebrates the transitory, contradictory and fluid space of exile can be expressed. The act of writing becomes the way in which they create for themselves the new homeland conceived within the displacement of exile, and the writerly project itself constitutes a sense of identity and site of belonging.

Notes to Chapter 5

1. Cristina Peri Rossi, *Solitario de amor*, 2nd edn (Barcelona: Lumen, 1998) [first edition: 1988] [*Solitaire of Love*, trans. by Robert S. Rudder and Gloria Arjona (Durham, NC: Duke University Press, 2000)]. All textual references and citations refer to the 1998 edition.
2. Linda Lê, *In memoriam* (Paris: Christian Bourgois, 2007).
3. Cristina Peri Rossi, *La nave de los locos* (Barcelona: Seix Barral, 1984) [*The Ship of Fools*, trans. by Psiche Hughes (London: Allison and Busby, 1989)].
4. Linda Lê, *Lettre morte* (Paris: Christian Bourgois, 1999).
5. Linda Lê, *Les aubes* (Paris: Christian Bourgois, 2000).
6. Consuelo Arias, 'Writing the Female Body in the Texts of Cristina Peri Rossi: Excess, Monumentality and Fluidity', in *Literature and Homosexuality*, ed. by Michael J. Meyer (Amsterdam: Rodopi, 2000), pp. 183–203, (p. 184).
7. Parizad Tamara Dejbord, 'Narciso enamorado y los paraísos irrecuperables en *Solitario de amor*', in *Cristina Peri Rossi*, pp. 171–208.
8. Arias, p. 189.
9. Dejbord, p. 71.
10. Arias, p. 193.
11. Araújo, *La Scherezada criolla*, p. 35.
12. Araújo, *La Scherezada criolla*, p. 63.
13. Kantaris, *Subversive Psyche*, p. 57.
14. Kantaris, *Subversive Psyche*, p. 19.
15. Taylor, *Disappearing Acts*, p. 27.

16. Hughes, p. 272.
17. In Cristina Peri Rossi, *El museo de los esfuerzos inútiles* (Barcelona: Seix Barral, 1983).
18. In Cristina Peri Rossi, *Una pasión prohibida* (Barcelona: Seix Barral, 1986).
19. In Cristina Peri Rossi, *Desastres íntimos* (Barcelona: Lumen, 1997).
20. Modified from the published translation, which reads: 'I speak a language no one knows, because my body is different from hers', p. 19.
21. Roy F. Baumeister, 'Basic Conceptual Issues', in *Identity*, pp. 11–28.
22. See Benedetti.
23. Roberts, p. 334.
24. Linda Lê, *Calomnies* (Paris: Christian Bourgois, 1993) [*Slander*, trans. by Esther Allen (Lincoln and London: University of Nebraska Press, 1996)].
25. Linda Lê, *Les Trois parques* (Paris: Christian Bourgois, 1997).
26. Argand, 'Entretien avec Linda Lê'.
27. Modified from the published translation, which reads, 'she has a slender waist' (p. 3), which somewhat dilutes the confounding of the masculine and the feminine in Peri Rossi's writing project, as 'having a slender waist' is arguably a conventional ideal of feminine beauty and desirability.
28. Butler, p. 10.
29. Butler, p. 12.
30. Lê, *Les aubes*, p. 27; p. 28.
31. Lê, *Les aubes*, pp. 28–29.
32. Linda Lê, *Les Évangiles du crime* (Paris: Julliard, 1992), p. 233.
33. Lê, *Les aubes*, p. 29.
34. See Linda Lê, *À l'enfant que je n'aurai pas* (Paris: Nil, 2011).
35. Argand, 'Entretien avec Linda Lê'.
36. See Vásquez and Araujo.
37. See Henke.
38. Mary Beth Tierney-Tello, *Allegories of Transgression and Transformation: Experimental Fiction by Women Writing under Dictatorship* (Albany: State University of New York Press, 1996), pp. 8–9.
39. Cixous, 'Le rire', p. 41.
40. Cixous, 'The Laugh', p. 878.
41. Modified from the published translation, 'my eternally present obsession', p. 32, which emphasises the 'obsession' over the narrator's sense of perpetually inhabiting the present.
42. Juan Carlos Onetti, *El pozo* (Montevideo: Signo, 1939) [*The Pit*, trans. by Peter Bush (London: Quartet, 1991)].
43. Luisa Valenzuela, *Cola de lagartija* (Buenos Aires: Bruguera, 1983) [*The Lizard's Tale*, trans. by Gregory Rabassa (New York: Farrar, Strauss and Giroux, 1983)].
44. Linda Craig, *Juan Carlos Onetti, Manuel Puig and Luisa Valenzuela: Marginality and Gender* (Woodbridge, Suffolk: Tamesis, 2005), p. 4.
45. Frederic Jameson, *Postmodernism, or The Cultural Logic of Late Capitalism* (London: Verso, 1991), p. 6.
46. Pérez Sánchez, p. 130.
47. Kaminsky, *Reading*, pp. 119–20.
48. See Jane Bradley Winston, 'Playing Hardball: Linda Lê's *Les Trois Parques*', in *France and 'Indochina': Cultural Representations*, ed. by Kathryn Robson and Jennifer Yee (Lanham, MD: Lexington, 2005), pp. 193–206 (p. 195), for an analysis of Lê's disruptive yet aspiring position within the French literary canon.
49. Lindsay, *Locating*, p. 30.
50. Lindsay, *Locating*, p. 31.
51. Linda Lê, *Un si tendre vampire* (Paris: Table ronde, 1987).
52. Linda Lê, *Fuir* (Paris: Table ronde, 1988).
53. Linda Lê, *Solo* (Paris: Table ronde, 1989).
54. Linda Lê, *Tu écriras sur le bonheur* (Paris: Presses universitaires de France, 1999). This publication compiles prefaces to works by a large number of displaced authors, such as (amongst others) Joseph Conrad, Ingeborg Bachmann, Thomas Mann, and Marina Tsvetaieva.

55. Lê, *Tu écriras*, p. 329; p. 330; p. 331.
56. Audrey Lasserre and Anne Simon, 'Introduction: Woman's Land', in *Nomadismes des romancières contemporaines de langue française*, ed. by Audrey Lasserre and Anne Simon (Paris: Sorbonne Nouvelle, 2008), pp. 9–14. (p. 14) (original italics).
57. Lê, *Tu écriras*, p. 330.
58. Lê, *Tu écriras*, p. 331.
59. Lê, *Tu écriras*, p. 335.

CONCLUSION

Through an analysis of the novels of Nancy Huston, Linda Lê, Malika Mokeddem, Laura Restrepo, Cristina Peri Rossi, and Cristina Siscar, this book has sought to delineate certain tendencies observed in the literary negotiation of women's identity following the experience of exile. It has argued that exile is a privileged site for the renegotiation of women's identity beyond the restrictive and alienating roles within which women are often confined in the birth country. Although in the past the term exile has evoked a solitary, male figure, I have argued that exile derives its privileged status for women from its common usage as a metaphor for women's historical positioning in society, as well as from being a phenomenon that is increasingly experienced by women, thus leading women to exploit the coincidence of femininity and exile in new and productive ways. Without wishing to reduce these writers to the monothematic designation of exiled women, exile has been shown to be a major and shared factor in the works of these six writers and one which raises the question of the defining markers of women's identity in particularly vivid ways. Firstly, we have seen that rupture with the birth society, and consequently with its roles and restrictions, reveals the otherwise invisible, or perhaps unnoticed ways in which identity is marked out and moored. This is particularly significant for women, for whom the granted roles in the birth society are not necessarily particularly beneficial or advantageous. Secondly, the rupture of 'given' identity markers or boundaries of belonging, which may be seen as 'natural', has been shown to reveal the constructed nature of identity, in turn raising the possibility of women's own self-determination and the expression of a sense of identity that was less readily available to them before exile.

The process of renegotiating and relocating women's identity in exile has been seen to raise the apparent aporia of the question of belonging. I have argued that women are banished by a 'forced choice' from a site that was never really 'theirs'. While the fact of displacement into exile and rupture with the given roles at 'home' are seen to disrupt the desire to return to the problematic site of belonging that was left behind, this does not entail a desire to altogether forgo any sense of belonging. Exiled women writers have been seen to reject the partial sense of belonging extended by the birth country where this has failed to offer them a full sense of belonging in favour of a space where the potential for subjective development is more readily available. The examination of the texts of these six writers has revealed that these exiled women, rather than abandoning any sense of belonging, do indeed seek out a space and sense of belonging. Yet rather than seeking to recover the partial belonging framed by alienation and marginalisation that was lost and left behind in exile, it is a new site of belonging they seek to define for themselves, modeled along new gender paradigms and roles. This new sense of belonging, located beyond static, given markers of identity has been demonstrated to be enacted in a nomadic mode, or through the development of nomadic subjectivity. Rather than the relinquishment of any sense of belonging — it is, after all, not a state of identarian freefall — nomadism is an assertive position in which exiled women may determine and define their own sense of belonging. Through the experience of exile, these authors reinterpret women's identity in ways that resist foreclosure into historical sexual and domestic roles, where displacement provides a space in which to seek out and articulate a new, less alienating sense of belonging, and a redefined site of home that pulls away from the political, sexual, familial, and cultural limitations that the birth country presented.

That these authors do indeed envisage and articulate new identities for themselves is illustrated in the ideal protagonists that are presented in their novels. If writing constitutes a way of relocating and redefining the self in the space of displacement where former identity markers and ties are disrupted, the narrative space of writing also becomes a site for which ideal identities can be envisaged in the representation of their protagonists. This can be seen in the works of Cristina Peri Rossi in her ambivalently gendered protagonists, who reject established paradigms of gender and gendered social hierarchies. The ideal self is presented in Laura Restrepo's works through protagonists who aim to bring about real social and political change in the home country through their journalistic efforts. Linda Lê's protagonists, for the most part writers who present themselves as unhindered by ties of any kind — including gender — suggest a personal ideal self that is characterised precisely by non-definition and whose only declared sense of allegiance is to writing. Cristina Siscar's sense of an ideal self in her works is one that seeks to achieve peace, and to restore the right to a sense of belonging that was damaged by exile, and Malika Mokeddem, as seen, outlines perhaps the most explicit ideal self in her self-referential protagonists who can be said to aim to offer an example of liberation to future generations of Algerian women constrained by the societal limitations by one who has to a large degree distanced herself from them.

The novels of the writers analysed here testify to a nonconformity with the roles and possibilities available to them in the birth country, roles which are re-envisaged and re-invented in the spatial displacement of exile, and in the alterity of writing. While it would be absurd to suggest that these women became exiles because of a certain 'predisposition' to the state of exile, it is clear that Lê, Huston, Mokeddem, Restrepo, Peri Rossi, and Siscar all experienced varying degrees of alienation from the birth society even before political upheaval, migration, or the pursuit of safety or freedom to undertake a certain lifestyle, activity, or profession prompted the departure from the homeland. Also of note is that of these six writers, only Restrepo and Peri Rossi were exiled, in part, for their writing, and it was their deviation from other norms that played a major role in all six writers' exile, their deviations from norms of femininity being a primary factor. This book has emphasised the need to take into consideration the fact that these women, intellectuals and for the most part privileged, had the means at their disposal to construct new lives and new identities for themselves abroad. The conclusions reached here are based on the thinking of a group of women intellectuals who express themselves in writing, and it is indeed writing that has been both a means and an end in their experience as exiled women. We have seen that writing has not only afforded them the medium in which to reflect on and negotiate the identarian processes of exile, but has also been the forum in which to express the newly defined nomadic self. That all of these writers, without exception, have described writing as a site of home and belonging points to its fundamental significance as a way of redefining a sense and space of belonging for women in exile.

Furthering existing research on the concept of nomadism as a tool for analysing contemporary women's writing, this study identifies the current trend of nomadism in exiled women's writing in French and Spanish and demonstrates the transcultural applicability of the notion across exiled women's writing. Hybridity — both generic and linguistic — has also been shown to be a fundamental aspect of these works which straddle genres and voices in their endeavour to represent the negotiations which exiles necessarily undergo in displacement, indicating the inadequacy of homogeneous narrative strategies and discrete genres in isolation to accurately represent women's experiences of exile. In my readings of these texts, I have shown ways in which each author blends the fictional with the non-fictional, the subjective with the objective, and the historical with the literary, to forge a new literary nomadism of the in-between that reflects the nomadic subjectivity of its exiled women authors.

While this book has revealed the discursive practices of exiled women, the particular sense of belonging that is articulated in exiled women's texts, and the hybrid textual strategies in which exiled women's nomadic subjectivity is expressed, it has raised a number of areas for further consideration which it has not been within its scope to fully address. A certain discomfort with self-referentiality can be noted in the texts of these writers despite a clear drive to discursively negotiate their own trajectories of exile. This is evident in protagonists that very nearly yet not entirely resemble their authors, and suggests an undertaking to distance themselves from the clichéd association of women's writing with autobiography, clichéd, not because this link does not exist, but because it is often denigrated or trivialised. Each author's propensity for generic hybridity across her corpus suggests a possible strategy for overcoming such anxiety, leading these authors to address the challenges and difficulties of their individual experiences of exile more explicitly in essays or theoretical works which complement the claims made in their fictional works. The, at times, problematic nature of some of these claims indicates another tension that might be further considered in terms of the highly controlled presentation of self that is evident in both fictional and non-fictional representations. I have already explored the problematic reliability of the narrative voice in some exiled women's writing, and its impact on a certain sense of authenticity with regard to the self-representation of the subject as she renegotiates her position in the setting of exile. A notably self-conscious discursive self-representation might be said to follow inevitably from a nomadic configuration of identity, which ponders and defines subjectivity within available parameters, and which is forcibly extremely aware of itself. We might equally explore how the highly controlled presentation of self in exiled women's writing relates to other ways in which women's writing more generally might be said to be highly controlled, as seen, for instance, in the recent trend in contemporary French-language women's writing for a pared-down, restrained, and precise writing style. And finally, more attention might be paid to the discrepancy between the strong sense of individuality expressed in exiled women's texts and the apparently contrasting position of collectivity and representativity to which some exiled women writers can be said to aspire. We have seen that while adopting a position of gendered collectivity in the home country, women exiles may concurrently assume a singular voice of leadership within that collectivity which consolidates the prevalent tendency for identification through differentiation which has been seen to characterise exiled women's identity. The reconciliation of individual realisation with collective action might be considered in light of recent feminist theory to reflect on the problems and possibilities elicited by such a negotiation between apparently incompatible motivations. A consideration of these questions would lead to a greater understanding of the issues at stake in exiled women's writing, and the ways in which they relate to concerns expressed in other areas of twentieth- and twenty-first-century women's writing.

This book equally seeks to open new avenues of research into a wider range of women's writing and displacement. Further investigation in this field might consider the representation of modes of women's mobility on a wider, comparative scale to further question the ways in which the tropes and terminology of displacement are used. Such research might explore what transcultural women writers — such as exiles, migrants, expatriates, travellers — can be said to share, and in what ways these categories of movement can be said to overlap. On another level, the writers here analysed, although contemporary, were displaced by circumstances which have now passed into recent history. Future research might also investigate the literary negotiations and nomadic subjectivities that will come out of current conflicts that continue to displace and impact on women in particular ways, such as the popular uprisings taking place in the Middle East at the time of writing, to contribute to a more profound understanding of a broader range of nomadic subjectivities. It would also be of value to extend the scope of investigation to include a transcultural analysis of contemporary visual arts in order to consider additional, non-discursive ways in which nomadic subjectivity might be expressed across women's cultural practices, since these forms too offer great scope for the exploration and representation of women's exile. If this study has emphasised the importance of language and writing as a vehicle of the negotiation of women's exile, we can ask how aesthetic practices that are not (solely or primarily) linguistic might manifest the particular difficulties of exile, such as those of language and the linguistic shift.

Above all, this book has sought to show that while marginalisation remains a lasting and defining feature of exiled women's lives, the alienating marginalisation preceding exile becomes a positive, creative, and chosen position of liminality in the sense that Rosi Braidotti evokes when she declares that while exile is to varying degrees a chosen condition, it remains for the exile to determine the manner in which exile is inhabited. The nomadic subjectivity that is expressed in the writing of Linda Lê, Nancy Huston, Malika Mokeddem, Cristina Peri Rossi,

Laura Restrepo, and Cristina Siscar signals not the end of women's alienation in dominant masculine culture, but an indication of how a radical change of the fixed surrounding structures that have shaped and sustained identity can provide an enabling space for the realisation and expression of a dynamic and productive femininity.

BIBLIOGRAPHY

ADORNO, THEODOR, *Minima Moralia: Reflections from Damaged Life*, trans. by E.F.N. Jephcott (London: Verso, 1978) [first edition: 1951].

AGUILAR, GONZALO, 'Prólogo para un ensayo sobre el exilio', in *Travesías de la escritura en la literatura latinoamericana: Actas de las X Jornadas de Investigación* (Buenos Aires: Instituto de Literatura Hispanoamericana, 1995), pp. 179–89.

AHMED, SARA, CLAUDIA CASTAÑEDA, ANNE-MARIE FORTIER, and MIMI SHELLER, *Uprootings/Regroundings: Questions of Home and Migration* (Oxford and New York: Berg, 2003).

AMRANE-MINNE, DANIÈLE DJAMILA, 'Women and Politics in Algeria from the War of Independence to Our Day', in *Research in African Literatures*, 30.3, Special Edition: 'Dissident Algeria' (1999), 62–77.

ARAÚJO, HELENA, *La Scherezada criolla: Ensayos sobre escritura femenina latinoamericana* (Bogotá: Universidad Nacional de Colombia, 1989).

—— 'Yo escribo, yo me escribo...', *Revista Iberoamericana*, 132–33.51, Special Edition: 'Escritoras de la América Hispánica' (1985), 457–60.

ARGAND, CATHERINE, 'Entretien avec Linda Lê', in *Lire* (April 1999), <http://www.lexpress.fr/culture/livre/linda-le_803102.html> [accessed 23 January 2014].

—— 'Entretien avec Nancy Huston', *Lire* (March 2001), <http://www.lexpress.fr/culture/livre/nancy-huston_804287.html> [accessed 23 January 2014].

ARIAS, CONSUELO, 'Writing the Female Body in the Texts of Cristina Peri Rossi: Excess, Monumentality and Fluidity', in *Literature and Homosexuality*, ed. by Michael J. Meyer (Amsterdam: Rodopi, 2000), pp. 183–203.

AUSTIN, J. L., *How to Do Things with Words*, ed. by J.O. Urmson (Oxford: Clarendon, 1962).

AVERIS, KATE, 'La casa de la escritura: Entrevista con Cristina Siscar' (Buenos Aires, March 2009), <http://www.igrs.sas.ac.uk/centre-study-contemporary-womens-writing/languages/catalan-galician-spanish/cristina-siscar> [accessed 23 January 2014].

—— 'The Formal Architecture of Identity in Nancy Huston's *L'Empreinte de l'ange*', *Francosphères*, 1.2 (2012), 171–84.

—— 'Neither Here nor There: Linda Lê and Kim Lefèvre's Literary Homecoming', *Women in French*, Special Issue: 'Women in the Middle' (2009), 74–84.

—— '*Le "vrai" moi*: Nancy Huston's Concern for Authenticity', *Essays in French Literature and Culture*, 45 (2008), 1–18.

BAUMEISTER, ROY F., *Identity: Cultural Change and the Struggle for Self* (Oxford: Oxford University Press, 1986).

BENEDETTI, MARIO, *El desexilio y otras conjeturas* (Madrid: El País, 1984).

BENSMAÏA, RÉDA, *Experimental Nations, or The Invention of the Maghreb*, trans. by Alyson Waters (Princeton: Princeton University Press, 2003).

BESEMERES, MARY, *Translating One's Self: Language and Selfhood in Cross-Cultural Autobiography* (Oxford: Peter Lang, 2002).

BEVERLEY, JOHN, 'Anatomía del testimonio', *Revista de crítica literaria latinoamericana*, 13.25 (1987), 7–16.

—— 'Introducción', *Revista de crítica literaria latinoamericana*, 18.36, Special Issue: 'La voz del otro: testimonio, subalternidad y verdad narrativa' (1992), 7–19.

BOA, ELIZABETH, and RACHEL PALTREYMAN, *Heimat — A German Dream: Regional Loyalties and National Identity in German Culture 1890–1990* (Oxford: Oxford University Press, 2000).
BOCCANERA, JORGE, '"Yo concocí los dos exilios": Entrevista con Cristina Siscar', in *Tierra que anda: Los escritores en el exilio* (Buenos Aires: Ameghino, 1999), pp. 51–61.
BONN, CHARLES, *La Littérature algérienne de langue française et ses lecteurs* (Ottawa: Naaman, 1974).
BOURAOUI, NINA, *La voyeuse interdite* (Paris: Gallimard, 1991) [*Forbidden Vision*, trans. by K. Melissa Marcus (Barrytown, NY: Station Hill Press, 1995)].
BRAIDOTTI, ROSI, *Nomadic Subjects: Embodiment and Sexual Difference in Contemporary Feminist Theory* (New York: Columbia University Press, 1994).
BUTLER, JUDITH, *Gender Trouble: Feminism and the Subversion of Identity*, 2nd edn (London and New York: Routledge, 1999) [first edition: 1990].
CHAULET-ACHOUR, CHRISTIANE and LALIA KERFA, 'Portrait de Malika Mokeddem', in *Malika Mokeddem: Envers et contre tout*, ed. by Yolande Aline Helm (Paris: L'Harmattan, 2000), pp. 21–34.
CIXOUS, HÉLÈNE, 'Le rire de la Méduse', *L'Arc* (1961), 39–52 ['The Laugh of the Medusa', trans. by Keith Cohen and Paula Cohen, *Signs*, 1.4 (1976), 875–93].
CLIFFORD, JAMES, 'Diasporas', in *The Ethnicity Reader*, ed. by Montserrat Guibernau and John Rex (Cambridge: Polity, 1997), pp. 283–90.
CRAIG, LINDA, *Juan Carlos Onetti, Manuel Puig and Luisa Valenzuela: Marginality and Gender* (Woodbridge, Suffolk: Tamesis, 2005).
CRUZ CALVO, MERY, 'La construcción del personaje femenino en *Dulce compañía*', in *El universo literario de Laura Restrepo*, ed. by Elvira Sánchez-Blake and Julie Lirot (Bogotá: Alfaguara, 2007), pp. 135–47.
DAVEY, FRANK, 'Big, Bad, and Little Known: The Anglophone-Canadian Nancy Huston', in *Vision/Division: l'œuvre de Nancy Huston*, ed. by Marta Dvorak and Jane Koustas (Ottawa: University of Ottawa Press, 2004), pp. 3–21.
DAY, LORAINE, 'Trauma and the Bi-lingual Subject in Nancy Huston's *L'Empreinte de l'ange*', *Dalhousie French Studies*, 81 (2007), 95–108.
DEJBORD, PARIZAD TAMARA, *Cristina Peri Rossi: Escritora del exilio* (Buenos Aires: Galerna, 1998).
DÉJEUX, JEAN, *La Littérature féminine de langue française au Maghreb* (Paris: Karthala, 1994).
DELEUZE, GILLES, and FÉLIX GUATTARI, *A Thousand Plateaus: Capitalism and Schizophrenia*, trans. by Brian Massumi (New York: Continuum, 1987) [first edition: 1980].
DÍAZ, GWENDOLYN, *Women and Power in Argentine Literature: Stories, Interviews and Critical Essays* (Austin: University of Texas Press, 2007).
EAGLETON, TERRY, *Exiles and Emigrés: Studies in Modern Literature* (London: Chatto and Windus, 1970).
EIDELBERG, NORA, 'Roma Mahieu y el desarraigo en el exilio', in *Extraños en dos patrias: Teatro latinoamericano del exilio*, ed. by Heidrun Adler, Adrián Herr, and Almuth Fricke (Frankfurt am Main: Vervuert, 2003), pp. 48–65.
EVANS, JANE E., 'Accommodating Arabic: A Look at Malika Mokeddem's Fiction', in *The Selected Works of Jane E. Evans* (2005), <http://works.bepress.com/jane_evans/22> [accessed 23 January 2014].
FOSTER, DAVID WILLIAM, 'Latin American Documentary Narrative', *PMLA*, 99.1 (1984), 41–55.
FRANCO, MARINA, *El exilio: Argentinos en Francia durante la dictadura* (Buenos Aires: Siglo Ventiuno, 2008).
GANDESHA, SAMIR, 'Leaving Home: On Adorno and Heidegger', in *The Cambridge Companion to Adorno*, ed. by Tom Huhn (Cambridge: Cambridge University Press, 2004), pp. 101–28.

GEDALOT, IRENE, 'Can Nomads Learn to Count to Four? Rosi Braidotti and the Space for Difference in Feminist Theory', *Women: A Cultural Review*, 7.2 (Autumn 1996), 189–201.

GEESEY, PATRICIA, 'Commitment and Critique: Francophone Intellectuals in the Maghreb', in *North Africa in Transition: State, Society, and Economic Transformation in the 1990s*, ed. by Yahia H. Zoubier (Gainesville: University Press of Florida, 1999), pp. 143–57.

GONZÁLEZ BERNALDO DE QUIROS, PILAR, 'Presentación: Emigrar en tiempos de crisis', *Anuario de Estudios Americanos*, 64.1 (2007), 7–17.

GORDON, DAVID C., *The French Language and National Identity (1930–1975)* (The Hague: Mouton, 1978).

GREEN, MARY JEAN, 'Reworking Autobiography: Malika Mokeddem's Double Life', *French Review*, 81.3 (2008), 530–41.

GROS, ISABELLE, 'Malika Mokeddem: Une enfance détruite et une écriture de l'espoir', in *Malika Mokeddem: Envers et contre tout*, ed. by Yolande Aline Helm (Paris: L'Harmattan, 2000) pp. 175–83.

GURR, ANDREW, *Writers in Exile: The Identity of Home in Modern Literature* (Brighton: Harvester, 1981).

HAGE, MADELEINE, 'Introduction to Linda Lê', 'A New Generation of French Women Novelists' Colloquium, New York University, New York (3–4 November 1995), quoted in Jack A. Yeager, 'Culture, Citizenship, Nation: The Narrative Texts of Linda Lê', in *Post-Colonial Cultures in France*, ed. by Alec G. Hargreaves and Mark McKinney (London and New York: Routledge, 1997), pp. 255–67.

HARRINGTON, KATHARINE, *Writing the Nomadic Experience in Contemporary Francophone Literature* (New York: Lexington, 2012).

HELM, YOLANDE ALINE, 'Entretien avec Malika Mokeddem', in *Malika Mokeddem: Envers et contre tout*, ed. by Yolande Aline Helm (Paris: L'Harmattan, 2000), pp. 39–51.

HENKE, SUZETTE, *Shattered Subjects: Trauma and Testimony in Women's Life-Writing* (New York: St Martin's Press, 1998).

HOLMES, DIANA, 'Écrire est un verbe transitif: Les voix narratives de Nancy Huston', in *Nomadismes des romancières contemporaines de langue française*, ed. by Audrey Lasserre and Anne Simon (Paris: Sorbonne Nouvelle, 2008), pp. 83–91.

HUGHES, PSICHE, 'Interview with Cristina Peri Rossi', in *Unheard Words: Women and Literature in Africa, the Arab World, Asia, the Caribbean and Latin America*, ed. by Mineke Schipper, trans. by Barbara Potter Fasting (London: Allison and Busby, 1985), pp. 255–74.

HUSTON, NANCY, *Âmes et corps: Textes choisis 1981–2003* (Paris: Babel, 2004).

—— *Les Braconniers d'histoires* (Paris: Thierry Magnier, 2004).

—— *Cantique des plaines* (Arles: Actes Sud; Montreal: Leméac, 1993).

—— *Désirs et réalités: Textes choisis 1978–1994* (Paris: Babel, 1995).

—— *Dire et interdire: éléments de jurologie* (Paris: Payot, 1980).

—— *Dolce agonia* (Arles: Actes Sud; Montreal: Leméac, 2001).

—— *Dora demande des détails* (Paris: École des loisirs, 1993).

—— *L'Empreinte de l'ange* (Arles: Actes Sud; Montreal: Leméac, 1998) [*The Mark of the Angel*, trans. by Nancy Huston (New York: Random House, 1989)].

—— *L'espèce fabulatrice* (Arles: Actes Sud; Montreal: Leméac, 2008).

—— *Histoire d'Omaya* (Paris: Seuil, 1985).

—— *Instruments des ténèbres* (Arles: Actes Sud; Montreal: Leméac, 1996).

—— *Jocaste reine* (Arles: Actes Sud; Montreal: Leméac, 2009).

—— *Jouer au papa et à l'amant: de l'amour des petites filles* (Paris: Ramsay, 1979).

—— *Journal de la création* (Paris: Seuil, 1990).

—— *Lignes de faille* (Arles: Actes Sud; Montreal: Leméac, 2006).

—— *Limbes/Limbo: un hommage à Samuel Beckett* (Arles: Actes Sud; Montreal: Leméac, 2000).

———*Mascarade* (Arles: Actes Sud Junior, 2008).
———*Mosaïque de la pornographie* (Paris: Denoël, 1982).
———*Nord perdu: suivi de Douze France* (Arles: Actes Sud; Montreal: Leméac, 1999).
———*Passions d'Annie Leclerc* (Arles: Actes Sud; Montreal: Leméac, 2007).
———*Pour un patriotisme de l'ambiguïté: notes autour d'un voyage aux sources* (Montreal: Fides, 1995).
———*Prodige: polyphonie* (Arles: Actes Sud; Montreal: Leméac, 1999).
———*Professeurs de désespoir* (Arles: Actes Sud; Montreal: Leméac, 2004).
———*Reflets dans un œil d'homme* (Arles: Actes Sud; Montreal: Leméac, 2012).
———*Les Souliers d'or* (Paris: Gallimard, 1998).
———*Tombeau de Romain Gary* (Arles: Actes Sud; Montreal: Leméac, 1995).
———*Trois fois septembre* (Paris: Seuil, 1989).
———*Une adoration* (Arles: Actes Sud; Montreal: Leméac, 2003).
———*Les Variations Goldberg: romance* (Paris: Seuil, 1981).
———*Véra veut la vérité* (Paris: École des loisirs, 1992).
———*La Virevolte* (Arles: Actes Sud; Montreal: Leméac, 1994).
HUSTON, NANCY, and VALÉRIE GRAIL, *Angéla et Marina* (Arles: Actes Sud-Papiers; Montreal: Leméac, 2002).
HUSTON, NANCY, and SAMUEL KINSER, *À l'amour comme à la guerre: correspondance* (Paris: Seuil, 1984).
HUSTON, NANCY, and RACHID KORAÏCHI, *Tu es mon amour depuis tant d'années* (Paris: Thierry Magnier, 2001).
HUSTON, NANCY, and MIHAI MANGIULEA, *Lisières* (Paris: Biro, 2008).
HUSTON, NANCY, and GUY OBERSON, *Poser nue* (Paris: Biro, 2011).
HUSTON, NANCY, and RALPH PETTY, *Démons quotidiens* (Paris: L'Iconoclaste, 2011).
HUSTON, NANCY, and LEÏLA SEBBAR, *Lettres parisiennes: Histoires d'exil*, 2nd edn (Paris: J'ai lu, 1999) [first edition: 1986].
HUSTON, NANCY, and TZVETAN TODOROV, *Le Chant du bocage* (Arles: Actes Sud; Montreal: Leméac, 2005).
HUSTON, NANCY, and VALÉRIE WINCKLER, *Visages de l'aube* (Arles: Actes Sud; Montreal: Leméac, 2001).
JAMESON, FREDERIC, *Postmodernism, or The Cultural Logic of Late Capitalism* (London: Verso, 1991).
JARAMILLO GONZÁLEZ, SAMUEL, 'Segmentación social e imaginación', in *El universo literario de Laura Restrepo*, ed. by Elvira Sánchez-Blake and Julie Lirot (Bogotá: Alfaguara, 2007), pp. 149–56.
JOSEPH, MAY, *Nomadic Identities: The Performance of Citizenship* (Minneapolis: University of Minnesota Press, 1999).
KAMINSKY, AMY K., *After Exile: Writing the Latin American Diaspora* (Minneapolis and London: University of Minnesota Press, 1999).
——— 'Gender and Exile in Cristina Peri Rossi', in *Continental, Latin American and Francophone Writers: Selected Papers from the Wichita State University Conference on Foreign Literature 1984–1985*, ed. by Eunice Myers and Ginette Adamson (Lanham, MD: University Press of America, 1987), pp. 149–59.
———*Reading the Body Politic: Feminist Criticism and Latin American Women Writers* (Minneapolis and London: University of Minnesota Press, 1993).
JEREMIAH, EMILY, *Nomadic Ethics in Contemporary Women's Writing in German: Strange Subjects* (Rochester, NY: Camden House, 2012).
KANTARIS, ELIA GEOFFREY, 'The Politics of Desire: Alienation and Identity in the Work of Marta Traba and Cristina Peri Rossi', in *Forum for Modern Language Studies*, 25 (1989), 248–64.

—— *The Subversive Psyche: Contemporary Women's Narrative from Argentina and Uruguay* (Oxford: Clarendon, 1995).
KAPLAN, CAREN, 'Deterritorializations: The Rewriting of Home and Exile in Western Feminist Discourse', *Cultural Critique*, 6 (1987), 187–98.
—— *Questions of Travel: Postmodern Discourses of Displacement* (Durham, NC, and London: Duke University Press, 1996).
KELLMAN, STEVEN G., *The Translingual Imagination* (Lincoln: University of Nebraska Press, 2000).
KHORDOC, CATHERINE, 'Variations littéraires dans *Les Variations Goldberg*', in *Vision/Division: l'œuvre de Nancy Huston*, ed. by Marta Dvorak and Jane Koustas (Ottawa: University of Ottawa Press, 2004), pp. 95–111.
KRAMSCH, CLAIRE, 'The Privilege of the Nonnative Speaker', *PMLA*, 112.3 (1997), 359–69.
LÊ, LINDA, *À l'enfant que je n'aurai pas* (Paris: Nil, 2011).
—— *Les aubes* (Paris: Christian Bourgois, 2000).
—— *Au fond de l'inconnu pour trouver du nouveau* (Paris: Christian Bourgois, 2009).
—— *Autres jeux avec le feu* (Paris: Christian Bourgois, 2002).
—— *Calomnies* (Paris: Christian Bourgois, 1993) [*Slander*, trans. by Esther Allen (Lincoln and London: University of Nebraska Press, 1996)].
—— *Le Complexe de Caliban* (Paris: Christian Bourgois, 2005).
—— *Conte de l'amour bifrons* (Paris: Christian Bourgois, 2005).
—— *Cronos* (Paris: Christian Bourgois, 2010).
—— *Les Dits d'un idiot* (Paris: Christian Bourgois, 1995).
—— *Les Évangiles du crime* (Paris: Julliard, 1992).
—— *Fuir* (Paris: Table ronde, 1988).
—— *In memoriam* (Paris: Christian Bourgois, 2007).
—— *Kriss: suivi de L'Homme de Porlock* (Paris: Christian Bourgois, 2004).
—— *Lame de fond* (Paris: Christian Bourgois, 2012).
—— *Lettre morte* (Paris: Christian Bourgois, 1999).
—— *Marina Tsvétaïéva: comment ça va la vie?* (Paris: Jean-Michel Place, 2002).
—— *Personne* (Paris: Christian Bourgois, 2003).
—— *Solo* (Paris: Table ronde, 1989).
—— *Les Trois parques* (Paris: Christian Bourgois, 1997).
—— *Tu écriras sur le bonheur* (Paris: Presses universitaires de France, 1999).
—— *Un si tendre vampire* (Paris: Table ronde, 1987).
—— *Voix: une crise* (Paris: Christian Bourgois, 1998).
LINDSAY, CLAIRE, '"Clear and Present Danger": Trauma, Memory and Laura Restrepo's *La novia oscura*', *Hispanic Research Journal*, 4.1 (2003), 41–58.
—— *Locating Latin American Women Writers* (New York: Peter Lang, 2003).
LIONNET, FRANÇOISE, *Autobiographical Voices: Race, Gender, Self-Portraiture* (Ithaca, NY: Cornell University Press, 1989).
LIROT, JULIE, 'Laura Restrepo por si misma', in *El universo literario de Laura Restrepo*, ed. by Elvira Sánchez-Blake and Julie Lirot (Bogotá: Alfaguara, 2007), pp. 341–51.
Malika Mokeddem: Envers et contre tout, ed. by Yolande Aline Helm (Paris: L'Harmattan, 2000).
MANERA, MATTHEW, 'Plainsong and Counterpoint', *Canadian Forum*, 73 (1994), 36–38.
MANRIQUE, JAIME, 'Entrevista con Laura Restrepo', in *El universo literario de Laura Restrepo*, ed. by Elvira Sánchez-Blake and Julie Lirot (Bogotá: Alfaguara, 2007), pp. 353–67.
MCCLENNEN, SOPHIA, *The Dialectics of Exile: Nation, Time, Language and Space in Hispanic Literatures* (West Lafayette, IN: Purdue University Press, 2004).
MCILVANNEY, SIOBHÁN, '"Les mo(r)ts ne nous lâchent pas": Death and the Paternal/Amorous Body in Linda Lê's *Lettre morte*', *Romanic Review*, 100.3 (2009), 373–88.

MILLER, CHRISTOPHER L., *Nationalists and Nomads: Essays on Francophone African Literature and Culture* (Chicago and London: University of Chicago Press, 1998).
MOKEDDEM, MALIKA, *La désirante* (Paris: Grasset, 2011).
—— *Des rêves et des assassins* (Paris: Grasset, 1995) [*Of Dreams and Assassins*, trans. by K. Melissa Marcus (Charlottesville: University of Virginia Press, 2000)].
—— *Les Hommes qui marchent* (Paris: Ramsay, 1990).
—— *L'Interdite* (Paris: Grasset, 1993) [*The Forbidden Woman*, trans. by K. Melissa Marcus (Lincoln and London: University of Nebraska Press, 1998)].
—— *Je dois tout à ton oubli* (Paris: Grasset, 2008).
—— *Mes hommes* (Paris: Grasset, 2005) [*My Men*, trans. by Laura Rice and Karim Hamdy (Lincoln and London: University of Nebraska Press, 2009)].
—— *La Nuit de la lézarde* ((Paris: Grasset, 1998).
—— *N'zid* (Paris: Seuil, 2001).
—— *Le Siècle des sauterelles* (Paris: Ramsay, 1992) [*Century of Locusts*, trans. by Laura Rice and Karim Hamdy (Lincoln and London: University of Nebraska Press, 2006].
—— *La Transe des insoumis* (Paris: Grasset, 2003).
MOLLOY, SYLVIA, 'Sentido de ausencias', *Revista Iberoamericana*, 132–33.51, Special Edition: 'Escritoras de la América Hispánica' (1985), 483–88.
MOTTE, WARREN, *Fables of the Novel: French Fiction since 1990* (Normal, IL: Dalkey Archive Press, 2003).
MOUNT, FERDINAND, 'The Power of Now: The Tricks and Traps of Political Fiction', *The Guardian*, Review Supplement (4 July 2009), pp. 2–4.
NAVIA, CARMIÑA, 'El universo literario de Laura Restrepo', in *El universo literario de Laura Restrepo*, ed. by Elvira Sánchez-Blake and Julie Lirot (Bogotá: Alfaguara, 2007), pp. 19–37.
Nomadismes des romancières contemporaines de langue française, ed. by Audrey Lasserre and Anne Simon (Paris: Sorbonne Nouvelle, 2008).
ONETTI, JUAN CARLOS, *El pozo* (Montevideo: Signo, 1939) [*The Pit*, trans. by Peter Bush (London: Quartet, 1991)].
ORLANDO, VALÉRIE, 'Écriture d'un autre lieu: la déterritorialisation des nouveaux rôles féminins dans *L'Interdite*', in *Malika Mokeddem: Envers et contre tout*, ed. by Yolande Aline Helm (Paris: L'Harmattan, 2000), pp. 105–15.
—— *Nomadic Voices of Exile: Feminine Identity in Francophone Literature of the Maghreb* (Athens: Ohio University Press, 1999).
—— 'To Be Singularly Nomadic or a Territorialized National: At the Crossroads of Francophone Women's Writing of the Maghreb', *Meridians: Feminism, Race, Transnationalism*, 6.2 (2006), 33–53.
ORTIZ, FERNANDO, *Cuban Counterpoint: Tobacco and Sugar*, trans. by Harriet de Onís (Durham, NC: Duke University Press, 1995 [first edition: 1947].
PÉREZ SÁNCHEZ, GEMA, *Queer Transitions in Contemporary Spanish Culture: From Franco to 'la Movida'* (Albany: State University of New York Press, 2007).
PERI ROSSI, CRISTINA, *Acerca de la escritura* (Zaragoza: Prensas Universitarias de Zaragoza, 1991).
—— *El amor es una droga dura* (Barcelona: Seix Barral, 1999).
—— *Aquella noche* (Barcelona: Lumen, 1996).
—— *Babel bárbara* (Caracas: Angria, 1990).
—— *La ciudad de Luzbel y otros relatos* (Montevideo: Trilce, 1993).
—— *Cosmoagonías* (Barcelona: Laia, 1988).
—— *Cuando fumar era un placer* (Barcelona: Lumen, 2002).
—— *Cuentos reunidos* (Barcelona: Lumen, 2007).
—— *Desastres íntimos* (Barcelona: Lumen, 1997).

—— *Descripción de un naufragio* (Barcelona: Lumen, 1974).
—— *Diáspora* (Barcelona: Lumen, 1976).
—— *Estado de exilio* (Madrid: Visor, 2003).
—— *Estrategias del deseo* (Barcelona: Lumen, 2004).
—— *Europa después de la lluvia* (Madrid: Fundación Banco Exterior, 1987).
—— *Evohé: poemas eróticos* (Montevideo: Girón, 1971).
—— *Fantasías eróticas* (Madrid: Temas de Hoy, 1991).
—— *Indicios pánicos* (Montevideo: Nuestra América, 1970).
—— *Julio Cortázar* (Barcelona: Omega, 2000).
—— *El libro de mis primos* (Montevideo: Biblioteca de Marcha, 1969).
—— *Lingüística general* (Valencia: Prometeo, 1979).
—— *Mi casa es la escritura: antología poética* (Montevideo: Linardi y Risso, 2006).
—— *El museo de los esfuerzos inútiles* (Barcelona: Seix Barral, 1983).
—— *Los museos abandonados* (Montevideo: Arca, 1969).
—— *La nave de los locos* (Barcelona: Seix Barral, 1984) [*The Ship of Fools*, trans. by Psiche Hughes (London: Allison and Busby, 1989)].
—— *Otra vez Eros* (Barcelona: Lumen, 1994).
—— *Poesía reunida* (Barcelona: Lumen, 2005).
—— *Por fin solos* (Barcelona: Lumen, 1994).
—— *El pulso del mundo: artículos periodísticos 1978–2002* (Montevideo: Trilce, 2003).
—— *La rebelión de los niños* (Barcelona: Seix Barral, 1980).
—— *Solitario de amor*, 2nd edn (Barcelona: Lumen, 1998) [first edition: 1988] [*Solitaire of Love*, trans. by Robert S. Rudder and Gloria Arjona (Durham, NC: Duke University Press, 2000)].
—— *La tarde del dinosaurio* (Barcelona: Planeta, 1976).
—— *Te adoro y otros relatos* (Barcelona: Plaza y Janés, 1999).
—— *La última noche de Dovstoïevski* (Madrid: Mondadori, 1992).
—— *Una pasión prohibida* (Barcelona: Seix Barral, 1986).
—— *Viviendo* (Montevideo: Alfa, 1963).
PETERS, JOHN DURHAM, 'Exile, Nomadism and Diaspora: The Stakes of Mobility in the Western Canon', in *Home, Exile, Homeland: Film, Media, and the Politics of Place*, ed. by Hamid Naficy (London and New York: Routledge, 1999), pp. 17–41.
POLIT DUEÑAS, GABRIELA, 'Sicarios, delirantes y los efectos del narcotráfico en la literatura colombiana', *Hispanic Review*, 74.2 (2006), 119–42.
POWELL, DAVID, 'Dimensions narratives et temporelles du jeu musical dans trois romans de Nancy Huston', *Francophonies d'Amérique*, 11 (2001), 49–64.
PRATT, MARY LOUISE, *Imperial Eyes: Travel Writing and Transculturation* (London: Routledge, 1992).
RAFFO, JULIO C., *Meditación del exilio* (Buenos Aires: Nueva América, 1985).
RESTREPO, LAURA, *Delirio* (Bogotá: Alfaguara, 2004) [*Delirium*, trans. by Natasha Wimmer (London: Harvill Secker, 2007)].
—— *Demasiados héroes* (Bogotá: Alfaguara, 2009) [*No Place for Heroes*, trans. by Ernest Mestre-Reed (New York: Nan A. Talese and Doubleday, 2010)].
—— *Dulce compañía*, 2nd edn (Bogotá: Alfaguara, 2005) [first edition: 1995] [*The Angel of Galilea*, trans. by Dolores M. Koch (New York: Crown, 1998)].
—— *Historia de un entusiasmo*, 2nd edn (Bogotá: Aguilar, 1999) [first edition: 1986].
—— *Hot sur* (Mexico: Planeta, 2013).
—— *La isla de la pasión* (Bogotá: Planeta, 1989).
—— *Leopardo al sol* (Bogotá: Alfaguara, 1993).
—— *La multitud errante* (Bogotá: Planeta, 2001).
—— *La novia oscura* (Bogotá: Alfaguara, 1999).

—— *Olor a rosas invisibles* (Buenos Aires: Sudamericana, 2002).
—— *Otros niños* (Bogotá: El Ancora, 1993).
—— *Las vacas comen espaguetis* (Bogotá: Carlos Valencia, 1989).
RESTREPO, LAURA, ROBERTO BARDINI, and MIGUEL BONASSO, *Operación príncipe* (Mexico: Planeta, 1988).
RESTREPO, LAURA, and ROBERTO BURGOS CANTOR, *Del amor y del fuego* (Bogotá: Tercer Mundo, 1991).
ROBERTS, EMILY VAUGHAN, 'A Vietnamese Voice in the Dark: Three Stages in the Corpus of Linda Lê', in *Francophone Post-Colonial Cultures*, ed. by Kamal Salhi (New York: Lexington, 2003), pp. 331–42.
SAID, EDWARD, *Reflections on Exile and Other Essays* (Cambridge, MA: Harvard University Press, 2000).
SEIDEL, MICHAEL, *Exile and the Narrative Imagination* (New Haven and London: Yale University Press, 1986).
SISCAR, CRISTINA, *Los efectos personales* (Buenos Aires: De la Flor, 1994).
—— *Las lineas de la mano* (Buenos Aires: Colihue, 1993).
—— *Lugar de todos los nombres* (Buenos Aires and Montevideo: Puntosur, 1988).
—— *Reescrito en la bruma* (Buenos Aires: Per Abbat, 1987).
—— *La Siberia* (Buenos Aires: Mondadori, 2007).
—— *La sombra del jardín* (Buenos Aires: Simurg, 1999).
—— *Tatuajes/Tatouages* (Paris: Correcaminos, 1985).
—— *El viaje: Itinerarios de la lectura* (Córdoba: Alción, 2003).
SPENCER, CLAIRE, 'The Maghreb in the 1990s: Approaches to an Understanding of Change', in *North Africa in Transition: State, Society, and Economic Transformation in the 1990s*, ed. by Yahia H. Zoubier (Gainesville: University Press of Florida, 1999), pp. 93–108.
STORA, BENJAMIN, *Algeria 1830–2000: A Short History*, trans. by Jane Marie Todd (Ithaca, NY, and London: Cornell University Press, 2001).
SUÁREZ, JUANA, *Sitios de contienda: producción cultural colombiana y el discurso de la violencia* (Madrid: Iberoamericana, 2010).
TAYLOR, DIANA, *Disappearing Acts: Spectacles of Gender and Nationalism in Argentina's 'Dirty War'* (Durham, NC, and London: Duke University Press, 1997).
TAYLOR, SUE, 'Hans Bellmer in the Art Institute of Chicago: The Wandering Libido and the Hysterical Body', <http://www.artic.edu/reynolds/essays/taylor.php> [accessed 23 January 2014].
TIERNEY-TELLO, MARY BETH, *Allegories of Transgression and Transformation: Experimental Fiction by Women Writing under Dictatorship* (Albany: State University of New York Press, 1996).
TODOROV, TZVETAN, *L'Homme dépaysé* (Paris: Seuil, 1996).
TORRES, LUIS, 'Exile and Community', in *Relocating Identities in Latin American Cultures*, ed. by Elizabeth Montes Garcés (Calgary: University of Calgary Press, 2007), pp. 55–83.
Une enfance d'ailleurs: 17 écrivains racontent, ed. by Nancy Huston and Leïla Sebbar (Paris: Belfond, 1993).
El universo literario de Laura Restrepo, ed. by Elvira Sánchez-Blake and Julie Lirot (Bogotá: Alfaguara, 2007).
VALENZUELA, LUISA, *Cola de lagartija* (Buenos Aires: Bruguera, 1983) [*The Lizard's Tale*, trans. by Gregory Rabassa (New York: Farrar, Strauss and Giroux, 1983)].
VÁSQUEZ, ANA, and ANA MARÍA ARAUJO, *Exils latino-américains: La malediction d'Ulysse* (Paris: L'Harmattan, 1988).
WINSTON, JANE BRADLEY, 'Playing Hardball: Linda Lê's *Les Trois Parques*', in *France and 'Indochina': Cultural Representations*, ed. by Kathryn Robson and Jennifer Yee (Lanham, MD: Lexington, 2005), pp. 193–206.

WOLFF, JANET, *Resident Alien: Feminist Cultural Criticism* (New Haven: Yale University Press; Cambridge: Polity, 1995).
WOODHULL, WINIFRED, *Transfigurations of the Maghreb: Feminism, Decolonization, and Literatures* (Minneapolis and London: University of Minnesota Press, 1993).
Writing New Identities: Gender, Nation and Immigration in Contemporary Europe, ed. by Gisela Brinker-Gabler and Sidonie Smith (Minneapolis and London: University of Minnesota Press, 1997).
YEAGER, JACK A., 'Compte rendu: Linda Lê, *Slander*', *Études francophones*, 13.1 (1998), 259–62.
——'Culture, Citizenship, Nation: The Narrative Texts of Linda Lê', in *Post-Colonial Cultures in France*, ed. by Alec G. Hargreaves and Mark McKinney (London and New York: Routledge, 1997), pp. 255–67.

INDEX

Adorno, Theodor 59
Aguilar, Gonzalo 16
Ahmed Sara et al. 30
alienation 2, 19, 20, 26, 27, 46, 60, 126, 130–31, 138, 140–41, 160, 163–64, 167
Amzallag, Michèle 27
Araújo, Helena 50–51, 55–56, 135–36
Arias, Consuelo 133–35

Baumeister, Roy F. 20, 111–12, 138
Bellmer, Hans 92
belonging 18, 19, 20, 23, 28, 30, 58–59, 67, 95, 130, 150, 152, 158–60, 163–65
Benedetti, Mario 17, 53, 138
Bensmaïa, Réda 123
Besemeres, Mary 40–41, 76–77
Beverley, John 120
Bonn, Charles 102
Braidotti, Rosi 28–34, 40, 48, 57–59, 126, 159, 166
Butler, Judith 147–48

Cixous, Hélène 155–56
Clifford, James 10, 14
corporeality 110, 112, 145–57
Craig, Linda 156–57
Cruz Calvo, Mery 125

Davey, Frank 94
Day, Loraine 90
Dejbord, Parizad Tamara 25, 134
Déjeux, Jean 15–16, 99, 101
Deleuze, Gilles and Félix Guattari 27–29, 32, 58, 159
Díaz, Gwendolyn 68
displacement:
    a collective experience 24
    comparative experiences 68, 98–103
    conceptualisation of 9–10, 11, 166
    gendered, spatial displacement 109
    psychological displacement 105
    social mobility 112–18
Djebar, Assia 56

Eagleton, Terry 23
education 112–14, 116–17, 131
Eidelberg, Nora 120
Evans, Jane E. 123
exile 1, 10
    desexilio 17, 138
    economic exile 32
    as an embodied experience 24, 145–46
    enforced vs voluntary 11–17
    el exilio dorado 15
    forced choice 17, 58, 163
    the masculine model of exile 18, 23–24, 71, 163
    as metaphor for women's relation to dominant culture 20, 163
    particularity of women's experiences 23, 163
    political 12
    political vs cultural 16
    post-exile 17
    the processes of 18, 24, 82
    the resolution of 71–72, 77, 78, 154, 160
    the return from 103, 108–09
    in Spanish 10
    women's 'double exile' 20

femininity:
    alternative models of 110, 115, 130–38, 142–43, 146–57
    and the experience of exile 2, 23
    the expression of 58
feminism 156–58
    écriture féminine 156
    feminist reading strategies 38, 133
    writing as a feminist act 51
Foster, David William 102, 125
Franco, Marina 12, 13, 26, 75

Gandesha, Samir 60
Gedalot, Irene 30
Geesey, Patricia 45
gender:
    gender solidarity 118, 121–22, 124
    gendered spaces 109–10, 111
    gendered writing strategies 99, 121, 133–38
    as identity marker 31, 130, 141
    patriarchal ideals 24
Gombrowicz, Witold 86
González Bernaldo de Quiros, Pilar 90
Gordon, David C. 21
guilt 14, 87
Gurr, Andrew 24, 98

Heker, Liliana 68
Helm, Yolande Aline 122
Henke, Suzette 100

178 INDEX

home 1, 10, 17–20, 29–30, 59, 103
  associated roles 19, 26–27, 49–50, 110, 130, 135, 142, 163–64
  discontinuation of the association of women with home 19–20
  in French and Spanish 10–11
  as site of familiarity and belonging 18
  writing as site of 95, 165
homeland 1
  maternal and paternal associations 18
  the nation 21
  re-encounter with 98, 118
  writing/literature as homeland 22, 160
Hughes, Psiche 27
Huston, Nancy:
  Âmes et corps 39, 59
  autobiographical nonfiction 39–40
  biography 41–42
  Cantique des plaines 94
  Désirs et réalités 13, 31, 69, 77–78
  disruption of the association of the maternal and the homeland 18
  experience of exile 67–70
  Journal de la création 77
  L'Empreinte de l'ange 70–95
  Lettres parisiennes 13–14, 21, 68, 76, 112
  on nomadism 59
  politicisation of texts 55, 87–89
  on privilege 31
  self-identification by differentiation 21
  as 'voluntary' exile 13

identity:
  by continuity 20
  by differentiation 20
  fragmentation/multiplicity 77, 93, 144–45
  'home-based' identity 24, 98
  national identity 21–22
  negotiation of identity following exile 1, 118
  nomadic identity, *see* nomadic subjectivity
  political vs personal markers of identity 47
  a socially driven phenomenon 21

Jameson, Frederic 157
Jaramillo González, Samuel 106–07, 118
Jeremiah, Emily 29
Joseph, May 93–94

Kaminsky, Amy K. 11, 15, 18, 19, 20, 21, 38, 41, 43, 44, 46, 49, 53–54, 68
Kantaris, Elia Geoffrey 24–25, 32, 70, 136
Kaplan, Alice 33
Kaplan, Caren 9, 10, 14, 32, 60
Kellman, Steven G. 79, 123
Kramsch, Claire 46

language:
  acquisition of 73–75, 76–80, 89
  Arabic 44, 123; French 1, 70, 77–79; German 77–78; Spanish 1, 79
  language, gender and power 155–57
  linguistic hybridity 40–41
  linguistic nomadism 44, 79
  linguistic shift 40, 41–44, 47, 77, 80
  multilingualism 78–79
  non-linguistic communication 90–91
Lasserre, Audrey and Anne Simon 159
Lê, Linda:
  association of the paternal and the homeland 19
  autofiction 39
  biography 46
  Calomnies 144
  exile as metaphor 47
  Fuir 158
  In memoriam 131–32, 140–45, 148–54
  insider-outsider status 47, 150
  Les aubes 131, 139, 144, 148
  Les Trois parques 144
  Lettre morte 131, 139, 144, 153
  linguistic outsider 46
  literature as site of identification 22, 152–54, 158–59
  politicisation of texts 55
  Solo 158
  stereotype of the tortured, solitary writer 24, 157–58
  Tu écriras sur le bonheur 158
  Un si tendre vampire 158
  'Vinh L.' 149
Lindsay, Claire 21, 51, 101, 157–58
Lionnet, Françoise 33
locatedness 1, 68, 72, 87

Manera, Matthew 94
Manrique, Jaime 116
maternity 110–11, 146–47, 150–52
McClennen, Sophia 12
memory 83–85
migration:
  cultural migration 12
  family migration 12
  linguistic migration 67, 70
  professional migration 12
Miller, Christopher L. 33
Mokeddem, Malika:
  association of the paternal and the homeland 19
  autofictional protagonists 39, 115, 122, 124
  biography 45
  Des rêves et des assassins 110, 113, 122
  exile, hybridity and bodily grafting 25
  La Transe des insoumis 100, 110, 111
  Le Siècle des sauterelles 122
  Les Hommes qui marchent 122
  linguistic mobility 44–45

L'Interdite 25, 103–27
  Mes hommes 100, 111, 112
  politicisation of texts 24, 57, 102, 115, 124–26
  rejection of designation of 'exile' 20
  rejection of identification with the nation 22
  the symbolic return home 18
Molloy, Sylvia 56
Motte, Warren 47

narrative strategies 80–90, 132–56
  textual hybridity 102, 126, 165
Navia, Carmiña 119
nomad, figure of 29
  nomadic subject 30
nomadism 2, 29–30, 32, 59, 70, 78, 165
  nomadic citizenship 93–94
  nomadic consciousness 27–30, 33, 34
  nomadic ethics 31
  nomadic narratives 57–60, 158–60, 165–67
  nomadic style 34, 39, 126
  nomadic subjectivity 30–31, 58, 131, 159–60, 164–67
  nomadology 32, 33

Onetti, Juan Carlos:
  El pozo 156
Orlando, Valérie 33, 38, 49–50, 56–58, 99, 121–24

Peri Rossi, Cristina:
  biography 52–53
  exile and the gendered body 25, 145–48
  feminism 27, 158
  'Historia de amor' 137
  'La destrucción del amor' 137
  'La naturaleza del amor' 137
  La nave de los locos 131, 136, 142
  liminality 49–52, 53, 58–59, 139
  politicisation of texts 55
  renunciation of national identity 22
  Solitario de amor 25, 131–40, 145–48, 154–56
  stereotype of the tortured, solitary writer 24, 157–58
  writing as site of belonging 22
Peters, John Durham 30
Polit Dueñas, Gabriela 124

Raffo, Julio C. 23
readership 103, 119–27
representation 103–04, 118–27

Restrepo, Laura:
  biography 54–55
  Delirio 119
  Demasiados héroes 100
  Dulce compañía 103–27
  exile as process 18
  politicisation of texts 24, 55, 57, 102, 121, 126
  the return 'home' from exile 17
  textual hybridity 55–57
Roberts, Emily Vaughan 141

Said, Edward 40, 69, 98
Sánchez-Blake, Elvira 125
Sebbar, Leïla 13
  Lettres parisiennes, see Huston, Nancy
Seidel, Michael 59–60
Siscar, Cristina:
  biography 42–43
  denial of guilt 14–15
  experience of exile 67–70
  generic hybridity 40
  identification with the nation 22
  La Siberia 92
  La sombra del jardín 70–95, 132–33
  Los efectos personales 86
  politicisation of texts 87
  Reescrito en la bruma 72–73
Suárez, Juana 119
subjectivity:
  exiled subjectivity 17
  female subjectivity 19

Taylor, Diana 42
Todorov, Tzvetan 19–20
Torres, Luis 60

Valenzuela, Luisa:
  Cola de lagartija 156
Vásquez, Ana and Ana María Araujo 20, 26, 33, 69, 80

will 13–14, 16–17, 32
Wolff, Janet 19, 23, 30, 32, 33, 106
Woodhull, Winifred 10, 29
writing 24, 26, 47, 48–51, 56, 58–60, 92, 94–95, 99–101, 122–27, 131–32, 151–60, 164–67
  testimonio 120